It was a photograph in a *Time* magazine article about The University of Alaska that sparked the imagination of a young Joel Rudinger and led to a life-changing, four-year adventure in the newly-added 49th state.

Lost and Found in Alaska is packed as full as a camp duffel bag on a forty-day hunting trek through the Alaskan Range, as challenging, yet satisfying, as a graduate instructor's first day of class. The real-life characters in this tale could have sprung from the imagination of Jack London: Fairbanks Annie, Hal (who wept when he heard "Danny Boy"), the beautiful half–native Bobbi, who stole this young man's heart, or the odd women who would lock a fellow in their basement. Even an appearance by a ghostly canine.

And what North wilderness saga would be complete without hot apple pie and coffee, disorienting twenty-four-hour nights, minus eighty-degree winds, gigantic mosquitoes attacking hardy gandy dancers, and a disastrous earthquake? Like most of life's difficult times, however, the author learns that even the most mundane acts, such as sorting mail or shoveling manure at a dairy farm can present a worthwhile lecture. If a college degree takes four years, Joel Rudinger's four years in Alaska advanced his education exponentially in hard-knock lessons and moments of spirituality: "What was that brilliant micro-second visible flicker of light? I was never religious, but I felt that this was a profound spiritual moment. I now and forever would be a part of this wild land."

—Christina Lovin, author of *A Stirring in the Dark,* and *What We Burned for Warmth.*

OTHER BOOKS BY JOEL D. RUDINGER

Symphonia Judaica: Jewish Symphony and Other Poems
(Bottom Dog Press/Bird Dog Publishing, 2015)

*BGSU Firelands: The Stories of Our College: 50ᵗʰ Anniversary
Publication.* (Bowling Green State University, 2015)

Sedna: Goddess of the Sea Cambric Press, 2006)

I Am the Hero of my Story and Other Pieces for Performance
(Cambric Press, 2006)

Lovers and Celebrations (Dearborn Press, 1984)

First Edition: 40 Poems (Gull Press, 1975)

BIRD DOG PUBLISHING

LOST AND FOUND
IN ALASKA

JOEL D. RUDINGER

BIRD DOG PUBLISHING
HURON, OHIO

ISBN: 978-1-974504-25-7
Bird Dog Publishing
An Imprint of Bottom Dog Press, Inc.
PO Box 425, Huron, OH 44839
Lsmithdog@aol.com
http://smithdocs.net

Credits:
Consulting Editor: Larry Smith
Layout Design and Cover Design: Susanna Sharp-Schwacke
Interior Photographs: Joel D. Rudinger's personal archive

ACKNOWLEDGEMENTS

I would like to thank Larry Smith, a colleague and friend, for his sustaining energy behind the Firelands Writing Center and Bottom Dog Press and for his continual support of this project since it began in 2015. I would also like to thank the members of the Firelands Writing Center: Richard Norgard, Nancy Dunham, and Patrick O'Keefe for their help at our monthly meetings. Thanks also to Kurt Landefeld for his encouragement and support.

Contents

Part One

Part Two

Dedication

To my loving wife Susan Pocotte for her
long-standing patience with my obsession
with this memoir.

PART ONE

"I learn by going where I have to go."

— Theodore Roethke

1: THE CALL

April, 1960

The third-floor classroom of University Hall was sweat lodge hot. At the back of the room, a black metal pedestal floor fan blasted the hot air around, but it didn't help. While we were waiting for the professor to walk in, a few of us gathered in front of a couple large, crank-open windows hoping for a breeze of fresh air.

The windows had deep, bottom sills. I hopped up on one and looked out. Below, students were dragging themselves along the steaming sidewalks. One had just crashed his bike into a concrete post and had fallen off. Books from his handlebar basket lay scattered along the curb and onto the grass. I was leaning out to see what else was happening when Ned, a classmate, tapped me on the arm with an open magazine.

"Hey, Joel, take a look at this! This is really something!" He handed me an issue of *Time* magazine opened to an article on the University of Alaska near Fairbanks. Alaska had become the 49th state in January of 1959, just sixteen months earlier. In the middle of the page was a small black and white photograph of several bearded students standing on either side of a skinned-out moose cape hanging from the window of a girl's dormitory on the campus. The size of its rack dwarfed the men next to it.

"How about that?" Ned laughed as he tickled at the photo with his finger. "Can you imagine something like that here at Bowling Green?"

I had never seen anything like it. It was funny and weird. The article said the University of Alaska only had five hundred students, many from the "Lower 48" and foreign countries from around the world.

Alaska. I had read a few of Jack London's stories about this faraway place, its cold, the deadly brutality of nature: *Call of the Wild*, *White Fang*, "To Build a Fire."

I stared at the picture. A moose hanging from a dormitory window ledge. I was sitting on a window ledge. "How strange is this?" I thought.

"Dr. Brogan's coming," a girl in the front row called. I handed the magazine back to Ned, hopped down and got to my seat just as the prof walked in. He apologized for being late and spent the rest of the hour talking about William Blake's poem "The Tyger." The first two stanzas of the poem were like a light switching on in my brain.

> Tyger Tyger, burning bright,
> In the forests of the night;
> What immortal hand or eye,
> Could frame thy fearful symmetry?
>
> In what distant deeps or skies.
> Burnt the fire of thine eyes?
> On what wings dare he aspire?
> What the hand, dare seize the fire?

The image of those bearded students up in Alaska standing next to the huge dangling moose was the only thing in my mind while Brogan went on to discuss Blake's poem.

After class, I walked through the afternoon heat back to my room off-campus and thought about Blake's poem. "What the hand, dare seize the fire?" It was a disturbing line. What exactly did it mean? Why did it resonate with me so deeply? For some reason it got me thinking about my present life and where a degree in biology from Bowling Green State University might lead me.

My thoughts, like Blake's tiger, were swirling. "What the hand, dare seize the fire?" My mind was racing like a burning horse.

When I saw that Alaska article, something in me changed. I felt different. I felt excited. It was all coming into focus. Yes! I needed to get away from Ohio and all things familiar. Yes, seize the fire; go north, go to Alaska! Start fresh. Start over. "What the hand, dare seize the fire?" The poem had spoken to me. My hand dared!

I couldn't find anything written about the University of Alaska in the library and the magazine profile was brief. I knew only that the school was small. I wondered if they had a graduate program in English. I seized "the fire" and the next day wrote a letter to find out:

May 3, 1960
Dean of Students
University of Alaska College, Alaska

Dear Sir:

I am a graduating senior at Bowling Green State University in Ohio.

My first two years of college were at Ohio University where I was in pre-medicine. I transferred to

12

Bowling Green in 1958 and will graduate this June with a major in biology. However, it is in English and American Literature, my minor areas of study, that I have found my voice and my new life focus.

I am interested in attending the University of Alaska if you have a graduate program in English. Please let me know if you have such a program and if I would qualify. I would also like to know if you offer graduate teaching assistantships.

Thank you.

Sincerely,
Joel Rudinger

Just after I mailed my letter, I saw a copy of the new May 2nd issue of *Time*. On page 42 was an article called "Upgrading in Alaska," with a comment by Dr. Ernest Patty, the outgoing president of the University of Alaska, bashing the earlier *Time* article. Patty said, "If students still use car trunks as deep-freezers, they seldom skin moose in the dormitories and hang the carcasses outside the windows."

Now I really wanted to go. He didn't say "never." He said "seldom."

Ten days later, I got a large airmail envelope with an application for admission to the University of Alaska Graduate School, a course catalog, and a signed personal letter from Dr. Edward Voldseth, the Dean of Students. To top it off, they offered me a graduate teaching assistantship. The fact that I didn't have a major in English didn't matter.

The university motto at the top of the letterhead was *Ad Sumum*, Latin for "To the Top." How perfect was that?! If they would take me, I would go. "To the top" it said. To the top of the world. That's where Alaska was.

I hadn't told my parents about my interest in going to Alaska in case the university responded with a negative. The next day I drove home to Toledo with a load of laundry. Mom wasn't there when I arrived, so I sat at the piano in the living room and doodled around with a jazzy version of "Moonlight Sonata." Jon, my younger brother, was out playing with his friends, but my sister Susan was home and came thumping down the stairs with a book in her hand. When she heard the piano, she knew it was me.

"Where's Mom?" I asked.

"At Dad's store working," Susan said. "I think she'll be home around 5:30. Anyway, I'm going out for burgers with Angie." She pivoted around on the bottom step and thumped back upstairs.

I played the piano for a while and then wandered into the kitchen to see if there was any tapioca pudding in the fridge. There wasn't. I got my sack of laundry from my car and took it to the basement to start a wash. When I came up, Mom was pulling in the drive.

"Hi," I said. "Need any help?" She was standing in the doorway cradling two large brown paper bags from the grocery.

"Susan phoned me and said you were home," she said as she put milk and eggs in the fridge.

I went over to the breakfast nook and sat down. Outside, a car horn beeped, and Susan clumped down the stairs, poked her head into the kitchen, said "goodbye" and left.

"Sorry I don't have any pudding," Mom said, "but I can fry you up a slice of ham and boil a couple ears of corn. I have to go back to the store and pick up Irv in an hour."

"I can wait," I said. "I have a laundry going anyway."

"Good," she said. "How about a beer?"

"Sure," I nodded. She was not your usual 1950s mom.

At first, I thought it was funny drinking beer with my mother. I had gone through two years at Ohio University, even pledged a fraternity, but had resisted beer until I was a junior at Bowling Green.

When I transferred to Bowling Green, I had moved into the third floor of Rogers Hall. I had two roommates, Bill and Ed. Bill was an ex-marine paratrooper on a veteran's scholarship. Ed was a six-foot-two, lanky, fifth-year physical education major on academic probation.

One Friday evening, Bill and Ed each playfully grabbed one of my arms, guided me down the hall and three flights of stairs, out of the dorm, and over to my car in the parking lot.

"Hey, Joel, we want you to take us to Unie's."

Unie's was a popular college hangout, a stand-alone bar a couple miles east of town. When we got there, Bill pointed to a small table near the dance floor.

As we sat down, a cute, smiling waitress came over.

"Three bottles of Budweiser and three bags of beer nuts," Bill said. The waitress looked at me and grinned.

A minute later the girl brought the beer and snacks. Bill and Ed leaned back, started to drink, and stared at me. Waiting. The only alcohol I had ever consumed was a few sips of sweet concord wine at our family's annual Seder dinners, but there I was, a beer bottle in front of me, with my two roommates, surrounded by students I knew from my classes.

I didn't want to look stupid, and I knew I wasn't going to escape it, so I lifted the bottle and sipped it one slow swallow at a time until ten minutes later it was empty. The beer was cold and bitter. It tasted tingly and sharp on my tongue, but it was okay. When I finally finished, Bill ordered a second round. This one tasted better. I drank it. I ate my beer nuts. I slammed my empty beer bottle down on the table with a bang. I felt giddy. It was a new feeling. A little ping went off in my head. I watched students slow dancing in and out of a small dark room on the far side of the room. A juke box was playing Norrie Paramore's "Theme from a Summer Place." I was happy to be there. Where had this been all my life?

"Hey, okay," I grinned. "How about another?" Bill laughed and shook his head and put money on the table for the beer, then they pulled me up from my seat and led me back to my car. I was wobbly, but I drove the three miles back to Rogers Hall without going off the road. That was all I remembered.

The next day they told me that when they got me back up to the third floor, I was laughing and hooting and pounding on every door until we got to our room at the end of the hall.

Two days later, I drove home to do a laundry and, as usual, went to the piano. Mom was home and came in from the kitchen and sat next to me on the piano bench.

"I have some news," I said. She leaned towards me waiting. "I had two beers at a bar with my roommates."

Her eyes got big. She jumped up, grabbed her purse, ran out the front door to the car without a word, and drove away. I had no idea why.

Ten minutes later, she burst through the front door with a six-pack of beer and went into the kitchen, I heard her pop open two bottles, then she came back to the piano and handed one to me.

"Now you're a man," she grinned. We clinked our bottles together in a toast and laughed. It had taken me twenty-one years.

Susan heard us from upstairs and came down the steps to check out the noise.

"What's going on?" she asked.

"Your brother had his first beer," Mom said, raising her bottle.

"It's about time," Susan said, and turned to go back up the steps.

2: The Announcement

Back to the present. Mom got two beers from the fridge and sat down across from me at the kitchen table.

"Okay, Joel, what's up? I know that look."

"Well, here it is." I sat up straight to look serious. I took a long sip of beer to add drama and looked deep into her blue wondering eyes. "I'm going to go to graduate school in Alaska."

So there it was. You just can't pussyfoot around that kind of news. No games. I told her everything. About the *Time* magazine article, my query to the university, Dean Voldseth's welcoming response, and the assistantship offer.

She sat in silence. I described the photo in the magazine with the bearded students and the moose hanging from the dorm window and that the image was like a door opening in a wall I had never even been aware of before, and that there I was, twenty-one years old and had done absolutely nothing in my life worth remembering.

I told her that I saw no future for myself in Toledo. I didn't belong to any group, I had no serious girlfriend, had no job prospects. The few neighborhood friends I had had in high school had joined the Army, married, or moved away. I was hungry for adventure and not the predictable kind that would control and define my every movement. "Who knows what's waiting for me up north?" I said.

I could tell she was shocked but intrigued. She herself was bright and creative but had never been able to go to college. She had married young, had three kids, and never had much money. Her outside joys consisted of volunteer work for the Toledo Art Museum, teaching religious history for Sunday school, acting in a local theatre company, and presenting a volunteer educational program called Dolls for Democracy for local church groups. None of these things paid any money. She knew I was aware that things were not going well financially for our family.

"You've always gone your own way, always lived in your own world," Mom said softly. She was struggling to understand. "Alaska? Where in Alaska?" Her voice was quiet.

"The university is in College, Alaska, a few miles north of Fairbanks," I said.

She'd heard of Seward's Folly and the Land of the Midnight Sun. She had read some Jack London novels, too.

"What's really exciting," I said, "is that Alaska has been a state for only a year and a half. There's not a lot of people up there. Probably mostly Eskimos living in igloos hunting whales and seals, and there's bears and moose and eagles everywhere." I laughed. I knew it was a dumb response. I had done a little research after getting the application and found out some basic things, like the State's population was only about 250,000 people, mostly men, and that the capital was a land-locked seaport named Juneau. The largest city was Anchorage, and there was a large U.S. military presence throughout the state because of the threatening Cold War with the Soviet Union.

Mom got up, got a bag of pretzels from the cupboard, and brought it back to the table.

"The university is small," I continued. "Only five hundred students, many who come from countries from all over the world." I saw a sparkle in her eye. "Of course, I still have to send back the application and my college transcripts, and I need to take the Graduate Record Exam. According to the Dean of Students, their graduate program in English is only a few years old and even though I don't have an English major, they're open to my coming." Mom bit into a pretzel. "And," I continued, "I asked about a graduate teaching assistantship. They said they could use a few more GA's. If I get accepted with an assistantship, my academic year's salary would be $3,000. That should be enough for me to live on. Tuition and university housing would be paid for too."

Mom was beginning to share my excitement. I think she wanted to go herself. The phone rang. It was my brother Jon asking if he could have supper at a friend's house. Mom said yes. The phone rang again. It was Dad. He was ready to come home. Mom left to pick him up at the store, and I wondered if she would tell him my news on the drive home.

Half an hour later, the front door opened. Mom came in followed by my father.

"Hi, Dad. How are things at the store?" I never knew if this was a good question.

Ever since the day two crooks in phony delivery uniforms had walked out the back door of his store with an entire rack of business suits in the middle of the day, he'd been depressed and angry. Even so, he hardly ever talked about business, at least with me.

"Okay," he said. "How's Bowling Green? When's graduation?"

"Graduation is June 5th," I said. This was only the second week in May. "Did Mom say anything to you about why I drove in today?"

"No."

He went over to his easy chair and picked up his newspaper, the *Toledo Blade*. We seldom talked about what went on in my classes.

When I'd start to tell him about a field trip, a research project, or something I was writing, after a minute or two he'd drift off into his paper.

"Well, I have exciting news." I swung around on the piano bench to face him.

"You're getting married? You got a job?" He looked over the top of his glasses with a smile.

"No. More exciting than that." I wasn't sure how he would take this. "I'm thinking of going to graduate school in Alaska." The newspaper dropped to his lap. He looked at me stunned. The next five seconds seemed like an hour.

"RUTH?" Mom was in the living room in a second. I think she'd been behind the door waiting for the call.

Dad pushed back in his chair in silence. He knew I had applied to graduate schools at Ohio State University and Toledo University which was just at the end of our street. But Alaska? I told him what I had told Mom. He listened. When I was done, he went silent. It was too radical an idea. But he saw my excitement and I repeated why I wanted to go: I was twenty-one and had done nothing in my life worth remembering.

I saw tears in his eyes. After a minute he said, "If that's what you want to do...."

Dad wasn't prepared to talk about it, and I didn't have any more to add, so he retreated into his newspaper. Mom went back into the kitchen to make supper. I waited a few seconds then went upstairs to see what was in my closet that I could use in the freezing north.

After supper, I drove back to Bowling Green to fill out the paperwork. The next morning, I mailed requests for transcripts to the collages I had attended. Ten days later, the University of Alaska sent me a letter stating that my application had been received, transcripts were arriving, and I would need to send a final BGSU transcript following graduation.

The week after graduation, I was formally accepted into the University of Alaska graduate college, was offered the teaching assistantship, and received, signed, and returned the contract. The graduate school wrote back that they would have someone meet me at Fairbanks International Airport when I arrived in September.

Now I had to figure out how to pay for my plane ticket. What did I have that I could sell? I made a list: my green 1954 two-door Buick; my Slingerland drum set; my Webcor reel-to-reel tape recorder; my 8mm movie camera and projector; my bicycle.

I also needed money to ship up my books, clothes, and supplies. I bought a large steamer trunk for $60. It was expensive, but it was sturdy, had a good lock, and was big enough to pack my typewriter, books, camera, tripod, and most of my clothes. I figured I would fly up with one or two suitcases and ship the trunk by train to Seattle early and then get it trucked up from there to Fairbanks and have it waiting for me when I landed. I knew my Buick would sell quickly to a high school student, so I didn't put it up for sale until August.

August came. I hadn't sold anything on my list. A guy in a band called me about my drum set but never showed up. I had a buyer for my car for $600. He was willing to wait until I left in September if I knocked $50 off. I did and he gave a small down payment. Basically, my trip costs were covered.

My sister Susan had overheard Mom and Dad talking. She told me before I left that Mom was excited that I was taking on this new adventure and Dad had become proud of me and was telling all his friends in his bowling league.

In the second week of August, Dad and I crammed my heavy steamer trunk into the back of his car and drove it down to the train station.

I was nervous about shipping all my things this way, taping the destination address on the top. I used the University of Alaska post office as Dean Voldseth had suggested. I hoped it would get to Seattle all right and make the connection with a trucking company that would drive up the coast into Canada, over to Dawson Creek, and the 1,500 miles up the ALCAN Highway. I hoped I had allotted enough time. I hoped that no one would steal it or try to break into it. I hoped I wasn't making a stupid decision. But then what choice did I have? I paid for the shipping and crossed my fingers. It was now out of my control. Things would be as they would be, and I'd find out everything when I got to Fairbanks.

On the Wednesday before Labor Day, Mom and Dad drove me to the Toledo airport.

"Mom, would you save all the letters I send home?" I asked.

"Of course, I will," she said. "I'll save them all. They'll be great reading when you come back home."

Dad slipped me a $20 bill and gave me a hug. My cheek was wet with his tears when he pulled away. My flight was called, and I got in line to follow the other passengers into the plane.

My flight out of Toledo was booked to Chicago Midway. From there, I was transported via helicopter to O'Hare. The wait at O'Hare was short and soon I was on a plane to Seattle's Sea-Tac airport where I would board an Alaska Airlines flight nonstop to Fairbanks.

3: TOUCHDOWN — SEPTEMBER 7, 1960

The Alaska Airlines flight took off from Seattle's Sea-Tac airport. One of the passengers on the flight from Chicago to Seattle was a teenager named Tommy going to Fairbanks. "I'm going up to the University of Alaska to study wildlife management," he told me. Tommy was interested in hunting big things, like caribou, moose, and rogue bears. I wasn't sure if he wanted to be a wildlife manager or a wildlife killer. Then he started to talk excitedly about his rifle collection back in Michigan and his new Browning 30.6 with a 10-power scope. "I have it disassembled in my suitcase," he said. "I'm gonna go hunting as soon as I get settled in the dorm." He grinned with anticipation. "I'm going to join the rifle team first thing," he grinned. "They compete and travel around the State, even down in the Lower 48."

"Good for you," I said. "Sounds like fun. Fun with a gun."

"Yeah! Yeah! Fun with a gun," he laughed.

Back at BGSU, on the first day of duck season, half the male students, and some of the young women as well, cut class to go hunting. It was a tradition. I had never had an interest in guns or hunting, but now that I would be living in Alaska, I could see that things were going to change. It was time to think about moving forward. I had to change if I was going to grow. I would buy a gun.

The Canadian mountains below us were tall and sharp and barren. The air over them was crystal clear. It was all beautiful and new. I only looked away when the young dark-haired stewardess came down the aisle passing out ham and cheese sandwiches, peanuts and crackers in cellophane bags, and sweet cold Cokes.

The captain's voice pierced the drone of the engines to announce that we had entered the Alaska Time Zone and that the Rockies had given way to the Alaska Range. The pilot announced it was 11:00 a.m. Alaska Standard Time. My watch, which I hadn't changed since I left Ohio, read 3:00 p.m., a time difference of four hours. I reset my watch. The act of moving the hour hand back four hours made stepping into a new life a reality. Not only was there a spatial distance between me and my family, now there was a distance of both space and time. I was really here, about to drop out of the sky into a land of unpredictable, unimaginable adventure.

"I'll point out Mount McKinley when we get close," the captain said. "If the North Peak is clear, we'll alter our course a bit so we can get a look. If the peaks are shrouded in clouds, as they usually are, we won't change course. Mount McKinley at 20,230 feet is the highest mountain in North America. It's about a 120 miles south of Fairbanks," he added.

I could feel the excitement around me. Half the people on this flight were, like me, probably flying this route for the first time. The captain made one more comment.

"The Alaska natives call Mount McKinley *Denali*, the native word for 'Great One.' Most Alaskans call it that."

The plane droned on through the clear blue sky. I leaned over and, from the window, watched the earth pass under us as we arrowed onward. Hours later, I felt a slight shift and the plane banked gently to the left.

"We're in luck," announced Captain Loudspeaker over the intercom. "Mount McKinley is out today. A beautiful view." There was a brief pause. "Look on the left. We'll be passing close to the north rim in five minutes." I was in seat D on the right side of the plane. The passengers across the aisle on the left saw us straining to see and leaned back to give us a second or two to view it. And I did see it, sharp and clear and covered in brilliant shining snow.

"Please prepare for our descent," the stewardess announced. "We'll be landing in thirty minutes. Make sure your seat belts are fastened and tray tables are up in their upright position." She started down the aisle with a large plastic bag, gathering the last bits of trash. Her hand touched my shoulder as I handed her my sandwich wrapper and empty Coke can. In thirty minutes, I would touch Alaskan soil for the first time.

When I got to baggage claim, I saw my suitcases among a pile of others being unloaded from a flatbed cart. At the rear of the baggage area, a man wearing a dark suit and tie was holding up a sign with my name printed in large black letters. I went over and identified myself. The man holding the sign was Dr. Voldseth, the Dean of Students. He'd come personally to take me back to campus.

"Welcome to Alaska," he said and stuck out his hand. He had a welcoming smile and I felt tension and nervousness I hadn't been aware of melt away. When I had my suitcases, we left the terminal and walked to his car and headed for the university in College, Alaska, a township zoned separately from the city of Fairbanks. It had its own post office.

I cranked down the window. It was a sunny 55 degrees. Bright purple and red flowers drooped over the edge of hanging baskets

21

along a freshly blacktopped road out of the airport. It was a good start, a beautiful start.

We pulled onto Airport Highway and headed towards down-town Fairbanks. A river bordered the highway on our left.

"That's the Chena River," said Dr. Voldseth. "It's used mostly to move cargo and coal to and from the Interior."

I didn't see any large transport boats, but I did see a lot of small ones tied up along the shore.

"What are those small boats for?" I asked.

"Those are mainly for fishing," Dr. Voldseth said. "Most are owned by locals who fish for a living. If you follow the current west, the Chena runs into the Tanana River, which is larger. The Tanana flows into the Yukon River and that empties into the Bering Sea."
This was interesting stuff. I'd check it out on a map when I had time.

Up ahead, I could see the city of Fairbanks. A tall, silver, shiny metallic building stood out as the sun reflected off it. It was at least eight stories high. It wasn't a skyscraper, but it dominated the skyline. As we approached, from our angle it looked like a vertical blaze of fire rising above the roofs of the low darker buildings surrounding it. I put up a hand in front of my eyes to shield them from the blinding glare.

"That's the Northward Building," Dr. Voldseth said, nodding in its direction. "It's the tallest city building in Alaska north of Anchorage. It's the major apartment building in Fairbanks as well as an office building with street-level shopping. There's a nice restaurant and bar at street level my wife and I go to."

I didn't expect to see this kind of modern structure in Alaska. We didn't have anything that tall in Toledo.

We crossed a two-lane bridge over the Chena. Immediately to our right was an old stone-steepled Catholic church. On the other side of the road I saw a sign that read "International Bar". It was a stand-alone white wood-shingled building only a little smaller than the church. I thought our exit from the city was ironic and funny, driving to the university by passing between a church and a bar. It felt wild and untamed. It felt like . . . Alaska!

As we left the river and city behind and turned onto College Road, the landscape opened up. We passed a few businesses, a small grocery, a laundry, and a trailer park. At Mile One on College Road, we came to a sign that said Creamers Dairy, a large farm with long set-back cow barns. It was huge, with grazing pastures a half mile long. In the distance beyond it, I could see a mountain range.

Further down the road on the left, we drove past a small chaotic plot of land full of mangy dogs chained to filthy pee-stained shelter boxes, which were anchored in place about fifteen feet apart. The dogs looked scrawny and dirty. Some were sitting on top of their little muddy houses, some lay sprawled in the dirt, but most were pacing back and forth like anxious prisoners trapped in their cells. I guess the look of shock on my face broadcast my surprise and horror.

"I know what you must be thinking, Joel," Dr. Voldseth said. "But it's not as bad as it looks. Those are racing dogs. When there's snow, their trainers hook them up to their sleds and race them. The mushers think of them as athletes and you don't want fat athletes. They may look ragged, but they are fed plenty of fresh meat and kept in good shape. Right now, it's off season and they're bored, but later in the day they'll get unhooked and exercised. There's a saying I heard when I moved here. 'If you're rusty, love your husky. An unloved dog doesn't win.' There are a few dog mushers who work on campus. I'm sure you'll meet them. They can tell you more. Racing dogs are a part of life up here."

Past the College township post office, the road curved hard left up a hill. The campus was perched at the top. We made a right turn up a drive, passed a "University of Alaska—Founded in 1935" sign, and headed for a parking lot by a long, two-story red-paneled building.

"That's Bunnell Hall," Dr. Voldseth said. "It houses the College of Arts and Sciences, classrooms, and the library." We walked into the building to meet Dr. Magee, the chairman of the English Department. He wasn't in, but Dean Voldseth showed me the room which would be my office.

"Now that you've seen where you'll work, let me drive you over to your housing."

"Great," I thought. "Now I can see the dorm window the moose was hanging out of." I was excited. I saw two buildings near the student union. One looked like the dorm in the photo as we walked back to the car. But instead of opening the trunk where my suitcases were, he got into the driver's seat and waited for me to get in.

"I can carry my bags," I said, looking at the dorms across the way.

"Oh, you're not living on campus," he said. "The dorms are full. We've arranged for you and a few other graduate students to stay at Fort Wainwright on the other side of Fairbanks. Some are already there. Oh, yes, I forgot to tell you," said Dr. Voldseth. "Ladd Air Base was just transferred over to the Army and has been renamed Fort Wainwright. You may hear it called by either name."

When I was told my housing would be taken care of, I assumed it would be on campus, a short walk to my office. If it got down to thirty below, I'd be in trouble. However, the university had an arrangement with the military base. At least for the first semester, most new single male grad students were to stay in the Fort Wainwright CBQ, the Civilian Bachelor's Quarters. The shuttle busses back and forth were free.

We drove back through Fairbanks and on to the security gate at Fort Wainwright. The dean had made this trip dozens of times and the guard at the gate waved us through. A small formation of soldiers was marching in silent lockstep across a field to our left. Other than them and a few government cars parked along the road, the base looked empty. Ahead, I saw a plain-looking sign with black block letters on a gray background spelling "CBQ #2." The stark building looked to be made of poured concrete, two long floors of windows, and no exterior decoration. We parked the car, I got my bags out of the trunk, and we walked to a wide-open double-door front entrance.

A skinny middle-aged soldier in an immaculately pressed uniform sat at a metal desk behind a metal desk lamp, a metal pencil holder, and a black telephone. Other than that, the desk was bare, and I wondered what the heck he did all day to keep from going nuts. He saw us come in and reached into a drawer. He pulled out a folded map of the base and handed it to me, along with a room key numbered 17. An identical map was on the wall and Dr. V pointed out the locations of the mess hall, the Civilian Club, the Post Exchange (the PX), and the bus stop. He also handed me a stamped official security pass which would allow me to get on and off the base when riding the bus or walking to and from town.

"Joel, any questions?" Dr. V asked.

"No, at least not yet."

"Good. I'll tell Dr. Magee we stopped by. When you come to campus tomorrow, he'll explain your teaching assignment and get you registered. If you have any questions later, stop by my office."

We shook hands and he left. Through the large window, I watched his car drive away.

So here I was, on Fort Wainwright somewhere outside Fairbanks, Alaska. What was next?

"Which way to room 17?" I asked the soldier at the desk. Not that it was hard to figure out, but I was curious if he could talk. So far, he hadn't said a word.

"Up that hall," he motioned with his head. Then he turned away and stared down at his empty desk.

"I just got here from Ohio," I said. "Where are you from?" Now he had to talk.

"Alabama," he growled. "Only three more months and I'm out of here." He kept focusing on the telephone. He didn't look up.

Room 17 was halfway down the corridor and I unlocked the door and went in. It was small but was designed for two. There were two desks, two cots, two chairs, two dressers, and one closet. Rooms 17 and 18 formed a joint suite with a common bathroom with one sink, shower, and toilet. The two guys in room 18 and my roommate hadn't shown up yet. I unpacked my bags, put the map in my jacket pocket, and walked to the Civilian Club which was only two hundred yards away. I hadn't eaten since my plane landed and I was hungry. It was 1:30 in the afternoon, Alaska Time. The last meal I'd had was on the flight out of Seattle, around 9:00 a.m. Pacific Time, five and a half hours earlier.

Even though it was after the usual lunch time, there were quite a few people sitting around at tables. It was cafeteria style. I picked up a tray and checked out the menu posted on the wall behind the hot food trays. I ordered sirloin tips, hot rolls and butter, a tossed salad, a baked potato, and coffee, all for $1.15. A can of beer was 35 cents. I saved that thought for later that evening. "Ahh," I thought, "the Army life for me."

After lunch, I went to the Post Exchange, the PX. It looked a lot like any grocery store back home except not only was there a food section but an area with hunting supplies, including knives, handguns, rifles, and ammunition. Most of the shoppers were women, military wives, some with kids. I didn't buy anything. I just checked it out and then went to find the bus stop. My map showed it between the CBQ and the Civilian Club. A schedule was posted inside the sheltered waiting area. Bus transportation to the university was eight times a day, with stops in Fairbanks. I could ride straight through to the U of A or get off in town. The bus was free. Military wives and personnel took classes at the university and it was part of their benefits.

The afternoon was nice, still in the upper fifties, and I walked around the grounds. Off in the distance, two squads of soldiers were marching in formation. On the plane from Seattle, a couple of men in uniform with combat patches on their shirts were talking about Russia and the Cold War. They mentioned the DEW line. I had no idea that the Cold War would be connected to Fort Wainwright, but it was.

At 5:30 p.m., Dean Voldseth arrived back at the CBQ with two graduate students, John, from California, who was going into geophysics, and Tom, from Montana, a second-year graduate student in geology and mining. They had been assigned to room 18. Tom had lived on base the year before and had friends in Fairbanks and around the area.

Tom was a big guy, tall and wide, kind of like a brown bear before it goes into hibernation. He was growing a beard. While I was wearing a wrinkled cotton oxford cloth dress shirt, cuffed cotton trousers, ribbed black socks and black leather shoes, he was wearing a plaid wool hunting shirt, tan canvas pants, wool socks, and cleated boots. He was even wearing suspenders. I didn't know anyone who actually wore suspenders, but they looked comfortable. Tom said he wasn't teaching this semester. He was just taking classes and working on his thesis, so he could dress any way he wanted. I envied his wardrobe. But I did have that new pair of Red Wing hiking boots in my trunk, which had not yet arrived.

"Hey, Joel. What are you doing tomorrow?" Tom asked.

"I'm going to campus and see what I need to get ready for classes," I said.

25

"I have a better idea," he said. "How about coming moose hunting with me and my buddy Leo? Leo just drove his pick-up up the ALCAN highway from Tacoma and wants to do some hunting."

"I'd like to," I said, "but I'll have to take a rain check. I don't have a gun and my outdoor clothes haven't arrived yet. I sent them ahead by train weeks ago but who knows where they are."

"Okay, another time," Tom said. Then the three of us went to dinner. "Best steaks in town," Tom said. I knew the price was right and so I ordered one medium rare even though I had had sirloin tips for lunch. This time I had a beer. The background music over the loudspeakers was country western star Ferlin Husky singing his "On the Wings of a Snow-White Dove." I was on beer number two and it was a fine evening.

> On the wings of a snow-white dove
> He sends His pure sweet love
> A sign from above (a sign from above)
> On the wings of a dove (on the wings of a dove)

The next morning, when I woke up, John and Tom were gone. I put on my wrinkled clothes and a light jacket and walked over to the mess hall for breakfast. The air was chilly. Afterward I waited for the bus to campus. Six other guys were waiting for the bus as well. We drove out through the base security gate and headed towards Fairbanks. Three got off at the downtown bus station, and two native girls wearing colorful gingham parkas appeared from nowhere and climbed on. The bus turned right on Cushman and drove over the Chena, past the Catholic church and the International Bar. We passed Creamers Dairy and the yard full of pacing racing dogs. Things were starting to feel familiar. A new American flag with fifty stars was hanging in front of the College post office (Hawaii had just become a state as well) and we drove up the hill, around the bend, and soon turned right onto campus.

In Bunnell Hall, the graduate assistants' office had three desks, two near the door and one against the back wall, facing into the open room. I took that one. One wall of the room had floor-to-ceiling shelves crammed with leather-bound books. The collection was impressive. I remembered how my mother had had a little library in our basement filling two built-in bookcases full of hard bound volumes given to her by my grandmother. There had been maybe a hundred books on those shelves. This office collection might have had a thousand. I thought if I ever had time, just for fun I might make a count.

I walked across campus to the student union. The bookstore, barbershop, and recreation room were in the basement. I checked the list of textbooks my students had to buy and picked up a set for myself.

I also bought a new dictionary, some pencils, red and black grading pens, and a grade book.

After I brought the supplies back to my office, I wandered around the campus. I saw the dorm that looked like the one in the magazine photo. The name over the entrance read Wickersham Hall. I was sure this was the one.

Behind the dorms was an outdoor hockey rink. The university had a hockey team and, as there was no other rink around, I thought this is where they probably played their matches. There were no bleachers or seats for fans, so I really wasn't sure. If it got down to 20 below zero, it would be pretty damn cold.

I went back to the Bunnell building and climbed the stairs to check out the library. It was small, but their literature collection seemed good. I knew I probably would be spending a lot of time up there. When I returned to my office, an elderly woman with gray hair tied up in a bun walked in.

"Hello," she said. "You must be Joel, our new graduate teaching assistant. Welcome to the University of Alaska. I'm Dr. Minnie Wells." She said she had been teaching at the university for years and that she and her husband had a small gold mine west of Fairbanks at Manley Hot Springs on the Tanana River. "In the summers that's what we do," she said with a smile, "look for gold." She never said how much gold they dug out. Dr. Wells was everyone's favorite professor I found out, because, as the students would say, "Minnie Wells has a heart of gold, even if she can't take it to the bank." When I told her that most of my gear and clothes were somewhere in limbo, she brought me a warm blanket. Dr. Wells said the books covering the office wall were her personal collection.

Two days later after meeting with an English teaching committee, I took the shuttle bus back to Fort Wainwright. My trunk from Ohio had finally arrived and Dean Voldseth had had someone drive it out to the CBQ. It was waiting for me at the front desk. Now I had my warm clothes and my new Red Wing boots.

I went to dinner and sat at a table off to the side. The song, "On the Wings of a Snow-White Dove," was playing again over the loudspeaker. Whenever it played, people in the dining hall lifted their beers and loudly sang along. Tonight, at supper, forty or more tenor voices filled the room. It was wonderful, mindless happiness. The room was warm and full of music and song, and my hamburger's onions were grilled to perfection. What could be better than this?

4: ALASKAN BREAKFAST

September 6, 1960

The next morning after breakfast I was going to take the bus into Fairbanks and walk the five miles to the university in my new boots. But someone knocked on the door as I was brushing my teeth. Who would that be 8:00 a.m., 0800? (I was trying to learn military time since I lived on an army base.) I opened the door to Tom from room 18.

"Glad you're still in," he said. "John and I are going to the university and thought you'd like to join us."

I was hungry and would have liked to have gotten my breakfast at the Civilian Club, but I didn't have any friends up here yet, so I thought I'd go and buy breakfast later in the Student Union.

"Sure," I said. "Let me finish up." I put on my pants and shirt, put on my glasses, and started to pull on my boots.

"Got a warm coat and a hat?" he asked.

"Yes. Why?"

I looked over. John was standing in the open doorway. "We're going to take a short cut," he said. I was confused. What did he mean take a short cut?

"Yeah," said Tom. "We're going to walk it." What did they mean walk it? I didn't have to ask. My face must have done it for me. "We're going to hike over to Leo's place halfway to Fairbanks from here. We thought you'd like to come along."

I had thought the five miles between the Fairbanks bus station to the university would be a good workout, but the idea of an extra mile or two didn't seem to faze Tom or John. I thought, "What the hell. It's an adventure."

"Sure," I said and laced up my boots, pulled on my coat, put my wool cap in my pocket and we left.

We were supposed to show our security passes to walk off the base, but the two MPs at the gate waved us through.

About half a mile up the road, a wide dirt path angled off to the right and disappeared around a clump of thick bushes. It looked like a primitive private drive. I noticed deep tire tracks in the dirt. The guys started to follow the road. My new boots were stiff and needed

28

breaking in and it was a challenge to keep up. I thought it strange that someone could build an access road so close, within actual sight of a military checkpoint. I had a lot to learn about Alaska. A convoy of five jeeps passed by on the main road behind us on their way to the checkpoint. Some of the drivers glanced over at us as we stepped off onto the angled path, but they didn't stop or slow down.

When we went around the first bend, we lost sight of the main road and continued our hike for about fifteen minutes. I glanced at my watch. It was just turning 9:00 o'clock, 0900.

"There it is," pointed Tom. Ahead was a dented, gray aluminum twenty-two-foot house trailer. A red Ford pick-up with a slash of rust was parked beside it.

"Hey, Franks!" John shouted. The trailer door popped open and a huge shaggy orange dog burst out barking followed by Leo Franks, who stepped out onto the ground with bare feet. Franks was wearing a long sleeve thermal undershirt tucked into the waist of mud-stained blue jeans. Leo grinned.

"Come on in," he called. "I'll get us some breakfast. You Joel?"

"Yes," I said. "Glad to meet you. How'd your hunt go yesterday?"

"Good, heh Tom? Take a look." He pointed to the back of his pick-up. I walked over to the truck. In the flat bed behind the cab was a large dead stiff gray wolf. I didn't see any blood. "He'll skin out nice," smiled Franks. "A clean pelt like that will buy beans for a month. Come on in. Killer, come!" The big dog turned and ran back to the trailer and disappeared through the open door.

It was cramped inside the metal box, but we all found a place to sit. Franks went over to his tiny refrigerator and pulled out a six-pack. He had a church key laying on the counter and popped open a bottle for each of us. Tom and John raised their beers in salute and drank deeply. I did the same.

Cold beer in the morning isn't as tasty as it is at night. This was cold, that was okay, but it was bitter. Anyway, the four of us sat there in the chilly morning air, wedged into the tiny trailer, sucking beer, while Leo detailed his hunt, where he spotted the wolf and how he had only fired one shot to bring him down.

I was listening carefully. This was the life I was about to enter. I could feel Leo's pride since for him it meant money to buy food. It was more than a trophy. And I thought there was so much I needed to do. Get ready for my classes, buy a rifle, learn how to shoot, write up lesson plans, meet the English faculty, find out about ski classes, do a laundry, climb a mountain. So much to do.

Before we left the trailer, we each had had four beers. It was now past 10:30 and we left for the rest of our hike to the university. We said goodbye to Leo and stumbled out of the trailer and peed on the first tree we could find. Tom led the way and guided us to a winding dirt path that he said would take us into Fairbanks, so we followed it in silence until we hit the south end of Cushman Street. The effect of the beer had worn off and I was tired. But my feet were breaking-in my stiff new boots as step followed step. They were getting more comfortable.

John turned around smiling. "Well, Joel, what did you think of your Alaskan breakfast?"

"Well," I smiled, "I can honestly say that it's a breakfast I'll never forget." Tom laughed and raised his right hand to the sky in a mock salute and we turned up Cushman and headed north towards the Chena River and College Road.

The next morning, I had coffee, bacon, toast, and scrambled eggs for breakfast at the Civilian Club and then took the bus into Fairbanks. I walked the five miles from town to the university alone. On the hike on College Road, I got familiar with every crack and pothole. I studied every store front along the way. I even discovered the small government office where I had to go to get my Alaska driver's license.

When I passed the dog yard that had looked so wild from Dean Voldseth's car, it now looked empty and pathetic. The dogs were gone. The dog houses had all been painted white, but each one now had raw wood showing through peeling paint and the door frames were shredded by the constant rubbing of the dogs' metal chains. The gross yellow stain and stink of dog urine was everywhere. Each little sleeping box had a flat tarpaper roof that the dogs could rest on, but the edges were torn and ragged. Only by walking the road could such details be seen. I felt sorry for the dogs even though everyone at the university said they were like finely tuned athletes and were happy with their lives. They lived to run, they said. Training was in their blood. They had healthy food and clean water. And if the shelters looked ragged, they were still warm havens from the cold. I thought of all the wild animals I had seen behind bars in city zoos. I realized that these racing dogs were freer and joyful in their teamwork. And, yes, they were loved and cared for by their owners. Already I was learning to think like an Alaskan.

Past Creamer's Dairy on the other side of the road, the vast tundra was flat and barren. It rose and fell like rolling waves on a silent sea.

Even though the university was five miles from town, I covered the distance in an hour using a technique called Indian Walking which I learned in grade school. Every day, I Indian walked from my home to my school, eight city blocks away. Indian walking was running fifty paces, walking fifty paces, running fifty, walking fifty, and so on. Since you used different muscles to walk and run, the body didn't get tired and you could keep up a good steady pace for a long time.

5: My First Class

Classes started on September 7, the Wednesday after Labor Day. Starting midweek gave everyone a chance to get into rhythm. Returning students could settle in, new students could meet their roommates and buy their books from the bookstore. There were tryouts for the hockey and rifle teams, and ROTC students signed up for a tour of Fort Wainwright. The midweek start also gave faculty time to have department meetings and finetune their lecture notes.

This was my first time as a college instructor. I was nervous and anxious about walking into my first class. Standing in front of a roomful of strangers, young college students in this far-off land to teach them how to think and express themselves in writing would be a challenge.

I had always been shy and hated to speak in public. I was so shy that when professors in my classes called out names alphabetically to take attendance, my heart would pound. When my name was called, I'd raise a hand and with a trembling, cracking, almost inaudible voice mumble, "Here." I understood why so many people said that speaking in public was scarier than death. Now I had to stand in front of a room full of judgmental strangers as a teacher in order to earn money to stay in Alaska.

I knew that there were only five hundred students on campus and that only forty or fifty of them would be in my classes, but I had no idea of what kind of cultural mix would be sitting in front of me when I walked through the door. Would the class be mostly native Alaskans? Would it be mostly guys? Articles I had read about the university said that students came here from all over the world, some just to train for a climb up the north slope of Mount McKinley. Would they all know how to speak English? Would they even want to learn?

It was time. I put on the new green plaid sport coat my father had given me, straightened my tie, gathered my books and lecture notes, and walked nervously down the hall.

When I entered the classroom, I looked around. It looked like any freshman college class in the Lower 48 except these students were better dressed. The girls wore dresses, lipstick, and barrettes in their well-brushed hair. The guys were neat with ironed shirts, pressed trousers, some with polished shoes. There was an energy of anticipation in

31

the air. I'd seen sloppy first-day freshman classes in Ohio, but these kids sat up tall and straight and looked eager to learn. For many native Alaskans, going to college was a life-altering event. Most were the first in their families to graduate from high school. These students didn't take a college education for granted.

As my eyes scanned the room, I realized that this was a life-altering day for me as well. It was my first time in front of a class. I would be teaching them, but they would also be teaching me.

Some of the students were born in Alaska, but they could have been from anywhere in the world. As I looked around, it occurred to me that most of them were only a year or two younger than me. I wouldn't turn twenty-two until December.

At that moment I realized that I could do this. I walked to the front of the room, stood tall, introduced myself, and handed out the syllabus listing the goals of the course, what we would read, how many essays we would write, and my office hours. I said that I hoped everyone would feel open enough to have individual meetings with me even if they just wanted to talk. The next thing I knew a buzzer went off in the hall announcing class was over and everyone disappeared out the door.

Well, almost everyone. Two students came up as I was gathering my notes. One was a young man with a warm but nervous smile. He introduced himself as Stephen. He said he was twenty-six and had recently escaped from the bloody communist take-over in Budapest, Hungary. He didn't go into details except to say that he had escaped to Alaska in 1959, just last year.

"I'm not very good in English," he said, "but I will work hard for you and do my best." He smiled hopefully and reached out to shake my hand.

"I'm glad to meet you, Stephen. I'll do my best to help you. Please feel free to stop by my office anytime if you need help."

"Thank you, Mr. Rudinger," he said. "I'm living in the student trailer court at the bottom of the hill behind campus. I cut hair to pay for my heat and food. If you ever need a haircut, I only charge a dollar."

I nodded. "Thanks, Stephen. I'll remember that." We shook hands again. He smiled and left the room.

The other student waiting for me was a girl, tall and blonde and dressed as if she were going to a business meeting. Fresh pink lipstick, the sweet scent of pumpkin spice, polished black leather shoes, a white blouse, black slacks with a matching black knitted vest. I thought she was beautiful.

"Hello," she said. "I'm Magdel. It's very nice to meet you." She reached out to shake my hand. "My father is also a professor in Giessen, Germany." She had a German accent but spoke perfect English. Her soft firm grip didn't pull away as I looked into her blue eyes. I told her what I had said to Stephen, that my offer to help was an open invitation should she need it or want it.

"Yes. Okay," she said. She lowered her chin a little and left the room with a backward smiling glance.

Alaska was full of surprises.

In the third week of September, the world turned golden. The hills around campus were rich with autumn birch. Walking the trails through the woods to and from the university's ski hills and all the way to Chena Ridge, a nearby area where some faculty lived, was like walking through tunnels of glowing sulfur, a world of bright yellow with splashes of red and orange wherever I turned. The five-mile hike from College to Fairbanks was also beautiful but different, as the smaller taiga-based trees across the flatter landscape looked like a Van Gogh painting, like he had taken his brush and madly flung red and yellow and hot orange paint across a twenty-mile canvas.

Colder air had also arrived and began to eddy through the fiery trees so that breathing became fresh and deep. I knew the cold air signaled a turnaround from a short beautiful fall. I thought of some the soldiers' young wives taking my classes who had told me how they feared the oncoming winter and the darkness. As for me, the unknown and unpredictability of the Alaskan winter was part of my adventure. "Bring it on," I thought. "Bring it on."

I was teaching two three-hour sections of freshman composition while taking three three-hour graduate courses of my own. Between grading essays, preparing lectures, scheduling conferences, and keeping up in my own course work, I didn't have much time to play. But Dr. Arthur Wills and a few of the English faculty had a Shakespeare club which met once a week. Half a dozen faculty and invited visitors gathered in a circle for coffee and doughnuts to read aloud a Shakespearean play chosen by Dr. Wills. It was something I looked forward to. The back and forth reading from a script, taking on the voice of Hamlet or Romeo or King Lear was a chance to bond with other faculty and gave me break from my office and coursework and all the cares therein. It was also a way to forget the long dark days as winter came on. The Fairbanks area was losing six minutes of sunlight a day.

The Shakespeare get-togethers were a welcomed break, but I wanted to do new things, Alaskan things. So, the third week in October, I bought a rifle from the Fort Wainwright Post Exchange and downhill skis from a pawnshop in Fairbanks. I also bought an eight-inch hunting knife in a leather sheath. True, the rifle was only a Remington single shot .22 and the skis were used and scratched, but for me they symbolized the great outdoors.

6: Fairbanks Annie

The first time I see Fairbanks Annie is early in October. She is large and wide, a big woman about fifty with ragged gray-white hair that hangs below her ears. She is wearing black faded shapeless clothes that cover her broad body like tents draped over tents. Over these is a patched, man's extra-large, knee-length, black, unbuttoned wool coat even though it is above 40 degrees. A large burlap sack hangs heavily over her left shoulder, bulging with unidentifiable lumps.

Pulled down over her wild hair, she wears a drooping wide brimmed man's felt hat. When she passes me, I notice pencil-wide holes punched into the hat's brim just above her ears. From each hole dangles a piece of twisted gray twine eight inches long that swings from side to side as she walks. She wobbles from side to side as she moves from store front to store front, but there is something about her that seems strong, defiant, and independent.

A shoe store owner is sweeping the sidewalk in front of his shop with a long-handled broom. The old woman passes by him, eyes down. No eye contact. Nor does he look up at her. She passes us both without a sign that she even knows we're standing almost in her path.

"Who is that?" I ask the store owner. He glances over at the woman moving away.

"Annie. Fairbanks Annie," he says and continues sweeping. Obviously, he isn't giving her a lot of thought. But I am curious.

"Does she live around here?" I ask.

"Don't really know," he says. "I'm told she's homeless and that everything she owns is in that sack. She doesn't cause any trouble though. Just walks around town all day." He brushes a small pile of dirt into the street, then goes into his shop and closes the door behind him. End of discussion.

As I watch, Fairbanks Annie reaches the end of the block, turns left at the corner, and disappears from sight.

That next Friday after class, Fred Hankinson, a geology student I had met in the bookstore, invited me to join him and a couple of his friends for a beer at Tommy's Elbow Room on Second Avenue. Tommy's is the main college hangout in Fairbanks. The students go there because it's always warm and friendly. A large stone fireplace is built

34

into the back wall and a log fire is always popping and blazing. Part of the fun of Tommy's is when you go up to the bar to buy a beer, you can roll dice with the bartender for double or nothing. Each gets one die. If you roll and win or tie, you both roll again. High number wins, but you have to win two out of three. If the bartender wins on the first roll, game over. It's the house advantage.

This day, rather than wait for the bus on campus, I have caught a ride into town with a student who lives in Fairbanks with his family. He is a local and knows about Annie but has never been curious about her and really has nothing to say about her other than he has seen her. He said he hardly ever hangs around the town except to go to the movies or help buy groceries. He is more into hunting and fishing. As far as he is concerned, this Ragbag Annie, as he calls her, is just some crazy old townie walking around Fairbanks.

"Why do you call her Ragbag Annie?" I ask. "Someone else I talked to called her Fairbanks Annie."

"That big rag bag she always carries around. That's what all the kids call her. She's been walking around Fairbanks with that old bag since before I was born."

"What do your mom and dad call her?" I ask. He is silent a moment.

"I don't know," he says looking over at me. "I don't remember them calling her anything." Then he laughs. "But my uncle, he calls her a crazy old clootch."

The tall spire of the Catholic church looms up ahead. When we cross the bridge over the Chena, he pulls over and lets me out.

"Thanks for the ride," I say.

"Yeah, see you in class." He smiles and drives off. I head for Tommy's.

Even though it is only 5:00 p.m., it's dark as night, but Second Street is lit up. In addition to the streetlamps along the curb, the time and temperature sign of the First National Bank on the corner is welcoming sight as are the neon lights of the bars and stores open for business. A block down the street, I notice the movie theatre's marquee advertising *The Lost World*. That's where I feel I am.

As I stand at the corner, I'm surprised to see Annie coming out of Tommy's Elbow Room. Tommy's is a college hangout, but there is no doubt it's her, wearing the same black droopy clothes, bent forward under her heavy sack. When she leaves the Elbow Room, she turns left. Two doors down is the Chena Bar where the natives go to drink. Two men are coming out of the Chena Bar. A juke box from inside is blasting loud country music into the street. One of the natives sees Annie, stands back and holds the door open. She walks in and the door closes behind her. The street goes silent.

I walk into Tommy's and find a seat near the fireplace. My favorite jazz tune, Dave Brubeck's "Take Five," is playing over a loudspeaker.

There are only about ten people in the bar. Fred isn't there, so I go over, pay for a beer and fill a large paper cup with free popcorn and take it back to a table to watch the fire.

I can't stop thinking about Annie. So many questions. Where did she live? Where did she eat? Did she have money for food? Who were her friends? Did she even have friends? Was she accepted everywhere she went? What did she do all day? She was so different from anyone I had ever known.

When I check my watch, it's 6:00 p.m. Fred isn't going to show. I finish my beer, put on my coat, and leave. The bus terminal is several blocks south on Cushman. I want to catch the next ride to Fort Wainwright, but before I start for the station, I want to peek in the Chena Bar and see if Annie is still in there.

I can't see through the front window which is covered on the inside with old newspapers, so I open the door and step in. The room is packed with local natives drinking beer and whisky. The juke box is blasting "Mack the Knife." Every stool at the bar is filled and the air is thick with cigarette smoke. A group in the back is throwing darts and near them is a busy pool table. I check out the crowd at the bar, but I don't see Annie. A dozen men and a very short woman in a red parka turn around and stare at me standing in the open door. Everyone stops talking. The only sound for a few seconds is the juke box. I am a white college guy in the Chena Bar. There is no sign on the door that says, "Natives Only," but it's clear that this is their home space. It occurs to me that Tommy's in its way is the same, a culture-specific space of a different kind. Who did I always see in there? College kids and their dates, young professionals. Natives never.

I look around, but I don't see Annie. I don't know why I'm so curious, but I am.

The bus is on time and I am back on the base by 8:00 p m.

The following week, one of my students told me that Big Ray's Army surplus store on Second Avenue had gotten a shipment of Army white felt bunny boots. The army was phasing out the felt boots for rubber ones. I wanted to get a felt pair for snow shoeing before the permanent snow came even though they were large and bulky.

I cut across the road to the railroad tracks near campus to walk the line into town and to see if any animals would pop up along the way. I saw plenty of large black birds but not one moose or bear or fox or rabbit. Maybe not seeing a moose or bear was a good thing, because they could kill me. I hadn't considered that until I was halfway to town. The innocent mindset of a cheechako. I had a Boy Scout knife in my pocket, but it wasn't much of a weapon. I laughed as I remembered how grown-up all us boys thought we were walking to grade school with a knife in our pockets. I saw a couple grease-stained workers crossing the tracks ahead of me as I neared the railroad station, but that was the only other animal life I saw.

Big Ray's was exciting. There was Army surplus stuff all over the place: bins of heavy arctic wool pants, olive khaki outdoor work shirts, long johns and coats, gray heavy ribbed socks for skiing or hiking, short-handled folding G-I shovels used to dig fox holes, cases of hunting knives and rifles and handguns, cubby holes filled with ammunition, packboards and backpacks, sleeping bags, and even a bin of old WWII arm patches.

I checked out used downhill and cross-country skis and gut-laced snowshoes. Towards the back of the store were hunting boots, ski boots, and, yes, what I had come for, the white, ankle-high, bunny boots. The army had used them for Alaska deep-winter training. I bought a pair and headed to Tommy's.

A block ahead, a man wearing a long black wool overcoat stepped out of the Hide-A-Way bar and stood on the sidewalk holding the door open. A young native woman wearing knee-high mukluks and an open fur parka came out. Following right behind her was Fairbanks Annie. She turned right. Although I was half a block behind her, I could still see those two raggedy strings hanging from the brim of her hat swinging back and forth as she passed under the streetlights.

If she walked these streets over and over every day, she had to know every inch of this town, every crack in every sidewalk, every pair of shoes or parka displayed in every storefront window. She was a silent untapped encyclopedia of Fairbanks' living history.

Annie was close to the Fairbanks Bar. She hesitated in front of the door. She waited. Seconds later, the door swung open, someone was holding it for her, and she walked in.

I wondered, did she have some kind of honor or prestige among the local people? She was an enigma.

As I passed the window of the bar, I glanced in. The bartender was pouring whiskey into a glass. Three or four men were sitting mid-bar, but I didn't see Annie. I continued on to Tommy's Elbow Room to get a beer and think about other things.

7: INVITE TO THE HUNT

November 11, 1960

"Rudy!" Dr. Charles (Chuck) Keim came out of his office. "Rudy," he called down the hall. "Got a minute?" Dr. Keim taught journalism and was the Dean of the College of Arts and Letters. I had met him when he came to an English Department meeting at the beginning of the semester and once at a Shakespeare reading. I knew he was talking to me because he was looking at me and walking in my direction. And there was no one else in the hall. But "Rudy"? Me? I had never been called that before.

Being a quick study, I said, "Hi, Dr. Keim," and walked over.

Chuck Keim was a powerful looking man, six-foot two, broad across the chest and shoulders, with reddish-brown combed back hair. I had heard that sometimes after work he would strap on a pair of snowshoes and take off with a backpack and a rifle. He looked like a hunter even when he wore a suit and tie.

"Do you own a gun?" he asked out of the blue. The question didn't surprise me. This was Alaska.

"Yes," I said. "I just bought a rifle at the Post Exchange on Fort Wainwright."

"What kind did you buy?" he asked, smiling.

"It's a .22 single shot Remington." It was the first gun I had ever owned, and I bought this one only because I thought maybe I could hunt rabbits with it. Shooting bigger game wasn't on my mind.

"A Remington .22 is a nice rifle, Rudy," he said. "Are you interested in hunting?"

I had never shot a pistol or a rifle. Growing up in a suburban neighborhood in West Toledo, squirt guns were the only guns I had ever had. The only thing I had ever shot was a round of golf. I wasn't sure where this was leading, but, yes, as long as I was going to live in Alaska, I was interested in doing a lot of new things. Hunting was one of them. I wanted to learn how to slalom downhill on my new skis, snowshoe across the tundra, fish for salmon, hike, kayak, climb mountains, and hunt. All of it.

"Yes," I said. "I would like to learn how to hunt." It was the truth. Dr. Keim smiled and patted my shoulder.

Well," he said. "I don't know what your plans are for next summer, but in August I work as a guide for Hal Waugh. Hal is a big game outfitter. One of the best. I talked to him yesterday about our annual Rainey Pass hunt at Post Lake and your name came up. He said if you're interested in working for him as a packer to let me know and I'll pass on the word."

"What's a packer?" I asked.

"A packer is a pack-bearer, Rudy. You go out on the hunt with the guide and the hunter and if someone shoots an animal, your job is to help pack out the meat and bring it back to base camp. If it's a good size moose or caribou, usually the hunter brings out the rack, his trophy for the kill. You look like you're in pretty good shape. It would be something you'd never forget."

That comment cinched it. I had come up to Alaska to make memories, to do things I could never do back home. To live, to have adventure. I said, "Yes." No hesitation.

"Come with me, Rudy," Dr. Keim beckoned. "I'll show you where Post Lake is."

I followed him back to his office. In his bookcase was a thick folder of maps. He pulled out a National Geographic map of Alaska, unfolded it on his desk and put his finger on a tiny lake in the middle of nowhere. "This is Post Lake," he said. "Hal Waugh owns the sole rights to hunt there." He pointed. "Just east of it is the south fork of the Kuskokwim River. Up here." He slid his finger north and east to a mountain. "This is Mount McKinley. Post Lake is about seventy-five miles southwest of McKinley National Park." He slid his finger down the map to Anchorage. "We fly out of Anchorage on a float plane and land on Post Lake next to camp." His finger landed on a blank spot by the lake. "It's about 120 miles from Anchorage so it's right in the middle of nothing. The closest village we could walk to in case the planes couldn't get in is McGrath, up here." Dr. Keim pointed to a dot north-northwest and halfway between Mount McKinley (Denali) and Post Lake.

"How far a walk is that?" I asked.

"About four days," he said smiling. I looked at him in disbelief. "But don't worry. I've been working for Hal for years and we've never had to walk out." He laughed.

"Dr. Keim," I asked, "how long is this hunt usually?"

"Call me Chuck, Rudy." He opened a desk drawer and pulled out his corncob pipe, pinched some tobacco out of a pouch, tapped some into the bowl, and lit it with a wooden match. I watched and smelled a whiff of white pungent smoke rise to the ceiling. "The hunt usually is two to three weeks for clients, but you'll need to fly in a few days early to help set up camp. Hal will be there already with some of the regulars and you'll work with them. The pay is twenty dollars a day. Would you like me to tell Hal you're interested?" He stood up still looking down at the large map spread out on his desk. I felt that in his mind he was already there. "I usually fly in the day before the clients," he said. "This year Fred Boyle is going to be a guide, too. He'll fly in with me." Boyle was the ski coach at the university.

"Yes. Thank you. I would like the job," I said. "It sounds fantastic. Maybe I can write a story about it afterwards."

Chuck looked up with a grin. As a professor of journalism, that caught his attention. "I'm a writer myself," he said. "Right now I'm working on a biography of the Alaskan archeologist Dr. Otto Geist." Otto Geist, he explained, had worked and studied in the far north for years studying Inuit culture.

Just then his phone rang, he nodded that it was official business, and I left. I walked down the hall in a happy daze to my office. I couldn't believe what had just happened.

The Post Lake hunt wasn't until mid-August. This was only November. That gave me time to get in shape. No problem, I thought. Plenty of time.

I told Jack Davis about the job offer. Jack was a second-year grad student from New Zealand living down the hall from me. He had heard of Hal Waugh.

Waugh was known as one of the biggest names in Alaskan big game hunting. Hunters from all over the world booked expeditions with him. He was known as a guy who delivered. I kidded Jack about me having nine months to get in shape. We laughed.

"Are you up for a deep-knee bend contest? To see if you really need to get in shape?" Jack wasn't much taller or heavier than me and I felt I was in good shape, but I hesitated. "For a beer," he said.

"You can do it," said one of his friends who was also in the room.

"Okay," I said. "Yes."

Jack went first. He took a spot in front of the window. I watched his body flexing and bobbing up and down, up and down. "Holy shit," I blurted out when he hit eighty knee bends. He laughed and kept going, counting out loud as his body went up and down, up and down, like a steam-driven piston.

I counted aloud "90, 100, 110!" He looked at me and grinned.

"I don't believe it!" I said. I was impressed. I was worried.

He fixed his eyes on me and kept on going. Up and down. Up and down. He paused for a few seconds, then continued. I stopped counting at 150. Jack grinned and walked over to a chair by the door. He didn't look at all tired. There was even a bounce to his step.

"Okay," he said. "Your turn."

"Okay," I said. "My turn." I couldn't believe it. A 150 squats.

He made it look easy. But if it was easy for him, god damn it, it would be easy for me. I went to the middle of the room, a little worried but confident. I focused my eyes on a bush just outside the window. Slow and easy, I thought. Keep it slow and easy. And breathe.

The first twenty knee bends weren't bad. After that, I started to slow down. But I couldn't stop. It was a matter of pride. "Don't over-think this," I thought.

In my mind I counted. At thirty squats, my right knee was getting twingy. At forty-five, my left knee was in pain. But I couldn't stop. It was a matter of pride.

I couldn't stop, but I could slow down, draw it out.

"63, ow, ow, ow, 68, ow, ow, ow, 74." (Holy cow. This is crazy). My knees were rubber, my butt was aching. "81," I groaned and dropped to the floor. I tried, I really tried, but I had lost the beer. When I tried to stand up, I couldn't.

Jack applauded. "Great job, Joel," he said. "Eight-one deep knee bends is quite a feat."

The other guy in the room gave a little cheer. "Yay for Joel," he grinned.

"You did 150," I moaned, grimacing at Jack.

"Oh, didn't I tell you? I'm a mountain climber. I've done 300."

I hurt from the ribs down. My knees felt like pumpkin mush. My legs were unmovable, dead. But it was a fair contest.

I learned something. Being in shape for climbing over and around mountains would be no small task and Post Lake was in the middle of the Alaska Range. Okay, I had lost the bet and I learned I didn't have a clue about extreme challenges needed for life in the great outdoors. If ignorance was bliss. I was one happy guy.

8: Learning to Ski and Survive

First Ski

A week after the squatting contest, a foot of snow fell in the higher elevations. Since I could finally walk without grimacing, I thought I'd go out to a ski hill to loosen my legs. After class on Friday, I caught a ride with Marie Munson who was going up to Ester Dome. Marie was from Minnesota and had grown up on the slopes. This was my chance to try out my new skis.

My first attempt at downhill skiing was a success, a great success! Without a hitch, the rope tow pulled me smoothly to the top of what experienced skiers called the "bunny hill." It was the lowest hill at the resort, but it looked high enough for me. I stood at the top undaunted by the late-day darkness since there were floodlights on poles scattered down the slope. I looked around, pulled my ski cap down over my ears, made sure my bindings were tight, that my skis were parallel, then I tucked my poles under my armpits, crouched, and pushed off.

It was beginner's luck. In seconds, I picked up speed and flew down the slope skimming over the tracks of those who had gone before me. I blasted through a series of small snowdrifts and aimed myself towards the lodge at the bottom of the hill. Everything was new and wonderful, exhilarating, fun. But as my skis carried me downward and forward at breakneck speed, I saw I was headed for a group of young women waiting in line for the lift. It was at that moment that I realized I didn't know how to turn, pivot, slow down, or stop. So I did what any new skier would do.

"Fore!" I yelled. "FORE! FORE!" (It always worked on the golf course.) One of the girls saw me coming, realized I didn't know what the hell I was doing, and yanked her friend aside as I shot past like a ball out of a cannon.

The ground flattened out near the bottom of the hill and I began to lose momentum. I had seen other beginners simply fall sideways to stop when they got slow enough. I decided to try it when I felt myself safe from breaking any bones. I force-dragged my ski poles behind me, pressed down and jammed them into a snowbank. I took a full header — two cartwheels and a somersault — on this my first trip down a hill.

I twisted my knee and sat the rest of the day in the lodge in front of the blazing fireplace with my feet up and got warm and happy with a couple rum and cokes. Marie came into the lodge two hours later.

Why was this first ski trip a great success? I lived to tell about it.

Second Attempt

I learned things as I talked about my first skiing attempt with others. You have to maneuver around the moguls, flex loose when you dip, squat down across the transverse slopes. You have to constantly bend and flex your knees. Above all, keep loose.

The next Saturday, I went back to Ester Dome with Marie. When we got there, she took the big lift to the top of Suicide, the advanced hill. Again, I headed to the rope tow up the bunny hill. As I pushed off from the top and jammed my poles into the icy crust to begin my descent, I tried to remember and use the some of the techniques I had been told about. But, even so, I was skiing down the slope a little too fast and not in total control.

Actually, that's an overstatement; I had almost no control. Now I knew why worn-down edges on downhill skis were not a good idea. Sharp edges give you a sharp cut when you want to change direction. Dull edges just slip-slide away. My secondhand skis from the Army surplus store had well-worn edges.

It must have been evident that I was a train wreck about to happen. Skiers on the hill below in line for the Suicide lift saw me coming and sidestepped quickly out of the way. This time the space between the lift and the lodge did not flatten. That's when I noticed that the parking lot below the lodge was cut into the hill. The slope I was on headed directly towards it. I was careening nearer and nearer to the parking lot drop-off and couldn't bend my knees to lift up or hop sideways to dig in the edges of my skis to change direction or slow down.

I stared at the nearing edge of the parking lot rushing towards me and the roofs of cars glistening visibly in the lodge's floodlights just beyond the upper rim of the lot. My poles skipped and skidded along the packed snow as I hit a stretch of ice. I tried to bend my knees one more time, but they locked up and I went airborne.

My feet landed on a narrow snow-packed strip between a rusty pick-up truck and a black Volvo and I slid to a painful stop, my butt on frozen tire ruts and my spine coming to an abrupt hard stop against the driver's door of a Land Rover. I looked up into the night sky. I was still alive see it.

Nobody back by the lifts bothered to check to see if I was alive or dead. Nobody looked in my direction. The skiers waiting for their chairlifts were on their way up and others coming down the hills behind me had their own problems.

To be honest, where I landed was completely out of sight. I was flat on the ground between three cars somewhere beyond the second row. All I could see was door panels and steel bumpers and a rear-view mirror laying by my leg in the snow. My left boot had popped out of its binding, but nothing was broken bone-wise, so I unhooked my right foot from the twisted ski and tried to stand. How do you get on your hands and knees when you can't bend your knees? I grabbed the front bumper of the Land Rover and pulled myself up. I saw where that rear-view mirror had come from.

I had only been at the ski hill for half an hour. The day was young, but I knew I wasn't going up again. The good news was that there was a lodge entrance at the end of the parking lot. So with both ski poles gripped in my right hand, using them for support, and my battered skis resting bravely on my left shoulder, I hobbled to the lodge, set my gear in the rack outside the door, and went in to find a seat near the fire. I bought a beer and a hotdog and waited.

Being late November, the daylight filtered away early. Marie came in an hour later red-cheeked and happy, sat down next to me, had a hot tea and a grilled cheese sandwich, and then we drove back to campus. I carried my skis to my office in the Bunnell building and caught the next bus to Fort Wainwright so I could stretch out with a heating pad and take a nap. When I got back on campus on Monday, I signed up for ski lessons.

The following Thursday was Thanksgiving. I went to dinner with friends at Professor Lee Salisbury's log cabin back in the woods. I sat by the fire most of the time and the heat did me some good, as did the rum-and-Cokes. But heading back to campus, I had to fold myself up in the back seat of a VW Beetle with two other guys and sing "Ninety-nine Bottles of Beer on the Wall" with them at the top of my lungs to keep from groaning.

On Friday, the world around Fairbanks came to a halt. Outside, the ice fog was so thick I couldn't see the edge of the road I was standing on. When I walked to the bus stop to catch the bus to the university, the frost coated my glasses inside and out. They were useless and I had to put them in my pocket. Inside the bus, it was sweltering; the defrosters were blasting, and the bus had to crawl forward at ten miles an hour until we got to the city limits. Other traffic on the road was slowed almost to a stop. It was hard driving between Fairbanks and the university since we had to pass through five miles of tundra and open farmland. The ice fog thickened and swirled over the highway and I could see a smoke-like wake of suspended crystals behind us as we chugged slowly forward.

*   *   *

Ski Lessons

The ski class met twice a week. Now that we were into December, the snow was around most of the time, although there didn't seem to be very much of it. It wasn't heavy snow or deep, but the air was frigid and wherever it fell it didn't melt. The aging snow became gray, ash-crusted and slick, but it was what it was, and it was all we had.

The ski class wasn't being taught by the ski coach Fred Boyle. The university had a tradition of hiring Father Mouché, a French missionary who taught survival skiing to Canadian Eskimos.

"Why would Eskimos need to ski?" I asked Father Mouché.

"Skiing is faster than snowshoeing and there are places dog sleds can't go," he said. It made sense, but it still seemed strange. So much for stereotypes. He had been teaching skiing for years and came to the university every fall to pick up a little money for supplies and visit friends before going back into the Canadian Yukon wilderness to tend his flock. "Skis are a European invention," he explained. "The Canadian and Alaskan natives always used dog sleds and snowshoes to go after game. It's a lot like the North American Indians who never invented the wheel. They traveled only on foot or by canoe. They didn't have horses until the Spanish brought them to the Americas in the sixteenth century."

Our class routine was to meet at the bottom of the shallowest slope for beginners, then side step up to the top, get in a crouch position, tuck poles under the armpits, baskets behind us, aim our wooden skis downhill, teeter on the edge, and then push off. If we pushed our heels outward, let the inner edges dig into the crust, crouched down, and kept the front of the skis in a closed V position, we could control our speed. I still had my same skis, but I had filed the edges down a bit to get a better bite.

When we got to the bottom of the hill, we would sidestep to the top again. After five or six runs, the class session would be over, although a bunch of us often stayed on to practice until it got too cold. I thought I was catching on well and felt ready for the intermediate hill where I could widen my V, go a little faster, control my speed, and end up where I actually wanted to be.

Chuck Keim came into my office while I was grading papers to invite me over to his place for dinner. I got my coat and we walked across campus to his home in the faculty housing area.

After supper with his gracious wife, we climbed up an open stairwell to a storage room above his garage he had converted into a writing studio. The room was warm. Two walls were lined with bookcases filled with stacks of manuscripts and books. A kitchen-size wooden table and a manual Smith Corona typewriter sat in front of a double-pane window that had a wide view of the campus.

"This is a great place to write," I said. It wasn't a large room, but it was perfect for thinking and writing.

"Yes," Chuck said. "I come up here every day."

I knew being a dean was demanding and time-consuming, even in such a small university, but under the fresh leadership of the new president, Dr. William Wood, the university was trying to grow, attract new students, create new programs as well as establish branches in outlying communities.

"When do you find time to write?" I asked.

"I make time," he said. "I'm up here every morning at 6:00 and work until 9:00, then go to my office." He showed me a two-inch-thick manuscript-in-progress of his biography of Otto Geist.

9: Dark Times — Over the Edge

After a week or two, it became comfortable and natural moving into the role of teacher. It was exciting being a presenter of new ideas and meeting students from other countries with their foreign values and perspectives. Some of their views challenged everything I had taken for granted growing up in Ohio. The stories and poems we read in class often brought out these differences.

I knew students who had escaped Soviet domination, the threat of ethnic extermination, of political and religious suffering. Students from educated European families who spoke German, Hungarian, Polish, Spanish, Norwegian, and Italian, English being their second language. Students from Nigeria, South Africa, Canada, young adventurers from Japan, Australia, and New Zealand. And among them dozens of beliefs from around the globe: Christian, Jewish, Mormon, Buddhist, Baha'i, Muslim, Hindu, and atheism.

Some UA students were from small Eskimo and Alaskan Indian villages — Haida, Tlingit, Tsimshian, and Aleut from the southwest; Yup'ik from the edge of the Bering Sea; Athabaskan from the Interior; Inuit and Inupiat from above the Arctic Circle. Some came from subsistence villages hunting and living off whales and seals, bears and caribou, moose and deer. Some lived off fish and crabs in the oceans. Alaskan students who were raised in more modern towns and cities had regular jobs.

There were students on campus from every corner of the United States: from the Northwest, the deep South, the Midwest, the East coast, from "California to the New York Island." It was Woodie Guthrie's "This Land is Your Land" come to life. Some of my students were young southern wives who had followed their soldier husbands up to Alaska, and transient college-age kids of military professionals who had never lived in one place for more than two years at a time.

Young men and women came to study and begin a career, or sometimes just to prepare to climb Denali, or simply to reject the boring routine of their lives, to embrace the beautiful flickering shadows of possibility and adventure, of unpredictable life in the last great frontier. Like me. All this variety in a student body of five hundred. The University of Alaska in Fairbanks was a unique place at a unique time. I embraced it.

There were occasional ski dates and evenings at Tommy's Elbow Room or the International Bar and the regular mellowing out from hot whiskey and cold beer at the CBQ on base. Sometimes a bunch of us graduate students would gather at Hess Hall in the dorm apartment of house parents Bucky and Judy Wilson, who would give us tea and cookies, comfort, catharsis, and company. They were welcoming loving friends to all of us when we got lonely or when the long black nights got depressing. They never turned anyone away.

The long dreary days of preparing lectures and grading essays for my two freshman writing classes were slowly taking a toll: office hours to keep, students coming in to talk about their writing, about the meaning of stories, about the meaning of life, about the darkening weather, about their loneliness, their sadness, their thoughts of suicide. Bucky and Judy Wilson had shown me how to respond. I tried to keep my promise to be a listener whenever a student needed me.

On a Saturday early in January 1961, the graduate students living on Fort Wainwright were transferred to Hess Hall, the Wilson's dorm on campus. I would miss the dollar beers, the constantly available food, and listening to happy choruses of "On the Wings of a Snow-White Dove," but I wouldn't miss the daily bus rides in the dark between the military base and campus. And now I'd be close to my office in Bunnell.

The Alaskan winter was cold and dark. In Fairbanks, for weeks the sun never rose above the horizon. If I were in my windowless inner office preparing for class or studying, I could go for days and miss the few minutes of light that might appear. Twenty-two-hour nights. Darkness. A lot of it. I knew this would happen. I thought I was mentally prepared for it.

What I wasn't mentally prepared for was the harsh and angry criticism of my writing by Dr. Bolgone, a newly hired assistant professor who argued that because I had not had an undergraduate major in literature, my ability to interpret and verbalize the literary merit of a main author in her course was flawed. She complained to the department chair that he never should have let me into the program as a teaching assistant with only a minor in English, that I was unversed in the use of academic language expected in a graduate level paper. She might have been correct, but for all the papers in literature classes I had written at Bowling Green State University, my writing was praised. One senior professor even told me that one of my research papers was publishable.

Time passed. By the third week of February, the days were getting longer with nearly nine hours of light. Temperatures had risen to a minus 20 degrees. Compared to the negative 40s and 50s, it was almost shirtsleeve weather.

But Dr. Bolgone's course was a mental challenge. It was futile to write for the angry bitch I knew was going to condemn my work, who was against me even being here. I enjoyed teaching. My own classroom was a place to explore ideas and where I had respect, but Bolgone's irrational anger was taking its toll. In March, I dropped her class. I was fed up with being beaten up.

Spring campus watermelon party. A sweet way to say goodbye to the bitter cold of Old Man Winter.

Spring break gave me time to think and reassess. When classes resumed, I made an appointment with Dr. Magee, the chair of the English Department. I had made a radical decision.

"I've decided not to come back to the university," I said. "Maybe I'm getting homesick. Maybe the darkness is getting to me. Maybe I'm just sick of Dr. Bolgone. She rejects everything I write even before I write it. After this semester, I'll be gone."

"I'm sorry to hear that," said Dr. Magee. "You have excellent potential as a graduate student, but now that you know the process, I think a little time off might make a difference. I hope you will come back and finish."

The week after spring break, a visiting Harvard professor who was teaching a course I was taking in the classical epic walked into class. "Ladies and gentlemen," he announced, "your assignment for next week is to read John Milton's *Paradise Lost*." I laughed at the irony of the assignment. *Paradise Lost*. If only he knew. After class, I ran up the steps to the library and found John Milton's book. Next to it was its sequel, *Paradise Regained*. I checked out both books.

The world works in strange ways. The next day, Chuck Keim left a note on my office desk. "Rudy, Hal Waugh wants to hire you as a packer. Let's get together to talk about it."

Yes! The job as a packer in the Alaska Range would be a life changer. It would be a memory forever!

10: Gandy Dancing on the Alaska Railroad

Summer was just a few weeks away. Since I would not be returning to continue my graduate work, I would lose my dorm room when the semester was over.

I needed to keep busy until mid-August when I would join Chuck and Hal Waugh for the hunt at Rainy Pass. Ken Reed, a fellow student at UA, mentioned that the Alaska Railroad was hiring laborers to level track. It wasn't something he was interested in, but I wanted to check it out. The ARR ran between Fairbanks in the north and Seward in the south. I thought maybe if I worked on the railroad, I could get down to see Seward. I'd heard it was a big fishing town on Resurrection Bay.

When I got into Fairbanks, I crossed the tracks to the railroad station. The passenger waiting area was small. Old wooden benches stained black with grease and tar lined the walls. The plank floor was clean but also stained from workers' boots. Built into the wall was a ticket window flanked by two bulletin boards with notices for State and Federal jobs as well as boarding instructions. I walked over to the bulletin board to check out the arrival and departure schedule.

The door behind me opened, and I turned to see a native man of about fifty holding a mop and bucket. He saw me looking at the schedule. "No more trains till tomorrow," he said. "We only get two a day. You need help?" he asked.

"Yes," I said. "I came to apply for a job."

He gave me a quick once-over. "Oh, you got to go to the employment office. Just go out that door behind you and turn right." He pointed. "It's at the other end of the station. What kind of job you lookin' for?"

"I heard the railroad is hiring laborers to work on the track."

His eyebrows raised. "Tough job," he said. "I worked the track when I was young. Like you," he added. "Good luck." He looked at me for a second and then started to mop the floor.

"Thanks," I said.

The employment office was at the end of the station platform. A young guy in polished work shoes, black wool pants, and a flannel shirt was sitting at a desk in front of the window looking out onto the tracks. He turned around and took off his glasses when I walked in.

"Hi," I said. "A friend of mine at the university said the railroad is hiring track workers for spring."

It was hot in the room, almost too hot to breathe. A wood burning stove in the corner was going full blast. The floor had the same black stains as the waiting room, but the painted walls were cleaner. A framed print of Governor William Eagan hung on the wall as well as several large black and white photos of trains dating from the opening of the Fairbanks depot. Next to the governor was a framed autographed photo of President Harding holding a long-handled sledge ready to come down on a nine inch spike to officially dedicate the station. The picture was dated July 15, 1923.

"Great photos," I said.

"I guess," he responded. "I never really looked at 'em." He got up out of his chair and came over to the counter. "You want work? We have openings for extra gang laborers," he said. "The pay is $3.16 an hour for a forty-hour week, less $32 a week for food. You'd leave here on a Sunday afternoon and start work Monday morning. The shift ends on Friday. Okay?"

"What about sleeping arrangements?" I asked. "Are tents set up for the workers?"

"You wouldn't want to sleep in a tent out there," he said. "It's open tundra." I knew it was the tundra, but I didn't see that as a bad thing. "No," he continued. "We have employee sleeping cars on a sidetrack. The cars are broken up into sleeping rooms. You'd sleep in there with a roommate. The beds are bunk beds. But it's free. No charge for the crew car."

"Will I need a sleeping bag?"

"That's up to you. The railroad provides sheets and a blanket if you want them," he said. "There's a change of sheets every Sunday. No charge."

"Okay," I said. "That sounds good. But what about weekends? Can I get down to Seward or Anchorage?"

"Well, you could," he said. "Employees can ride the train free, but the train you'd have access to is a commuter. It stops for everyone waiting by the track, anywhere, not just in the towns along the way. It could take ten hours to get to Seward and just as long coming back. If it was me, I wouldn't do it. You've be better off just coming back here to Fairbanks. It's a lot closer."

"So the work crew doesn't move up and down the tracks from day to day?" I asked.

"No," he said. "You'd be working mostly on a section of track about sixty miles out in the bush near Clear Air Force Station. But there's a lot to be done. When the crew gets done with that, they'll move down the track. It'll depend on need. So, you want an application?"

"Sure," I said.

He went over to a file cabinet and pulled out a form.

"Here you go," he said. "When you bring it back, you'll need to take a physical with our staff doctor here in town."

I hadn't thought about that, but I wasn't worried. I was in good shape, what with my skiing over the winter and all my long walks between town and the university. I took the application, said thanks, and left.

The following day I brought it back. The clerk took it, put it in a file, picked up his telephone, and set up a physical exam for me the following Monday, May first.

I went for my physical, got my temperature and blood pressure taken, ears, nose and throat checked, was told to drop my pants bend over and touch my toes. I got a long finger up my ass. I jumped. I hated that prostate finger check.

"This is like trying to rape a mouse," the doctor said with a laugh. He felt around, pulled his finger out, made a little popping sound with his tongue, and handed me a wad of toilet paper.

"Okay, wipe with this," the doctor said with a chuckle. "You check out. I'll send the railroad my report. Consider yourself hired."

He was quietly laughing as he peeled off his rubber glove. Then he noticed me staring at him. Maybe I was frowning. What did I do that so funny?

"Sorry for laughing," he said. "It's just that whenever I check a prostate, I think of a joke I heard in med school." He grinned. "Want to hear it?"

I could tell he wanted to tell it to me. It was weird but why not, I thought.

"Sure," I said.

"Well," he started, "this queer has a crush on his doctor and he wants to impress him, so he makes an appointment for a physical exam. He stops by a florist on the way. When the doctor tells the guy to bend over, he sticks his finger up his ass and gets jabbed by something sharp. 'Ouch,' he yells and then he slowly pulls a long thorny-stem yellow rose out of the patient's butt. 'What the hell is this?' the doctor says holding it up perplexed. The queer looks back at the doctor over his shoulder, smiles and says, 'Read the card, thilly.'"

Doctor Funnybones laughed again. I had to admit it was funny, especially watching his joy in telling it. I laughed, too. Then I went back to the ARR employment office.

"I took the physical," I told the clerk. "When will I know if I'm hired?"

"In about two weeks," he said. "We'll send you a notice if the results are good."

*   *   *

53

When the semester was over, Dr. Magee told me the university garden crew was short on help. I went to the employment office and they hired me on the spot. I would work on the university's garden crew until such time as the railroad would call me up. I told Bill, the head of the crew, and he was okay with it. I felt I was lucky to have the gardening job which started the day after I turned in my grades. One job ends; another begins.

The next morning on the garden crew, I dug holes and moved the dirt to plant trees. There were six other guys on the garden crew. A week passed. I noticed that every time Bill drove off to check on another job site, they would slow down or stop working. When there was a mid-morning or mid-afternoon fifteen-minute break, they would take twenty or thirty. It pissed me off that they were getting paid for doing nothing. I didn't stop my work during the breaks and, while they lay back on the grass drinking coffee or smoking cigarettes, I dug my holes and shoveled my dirt with a focused intensity. I was earning my pay, building up my physical body, and honoring my contract. But I was an outsider to this crew and they just hung back in the shade of a tree and watched me work. Or pretend I wasn't there. I wanted to shame them into doing their jobs, but it wasn't happening. I had to respect myself, live with myself. The only thing to do was work and tune them out.

Bill knew that I was a good worker and that the others in the crew were not. When I mentioned that I had to move out of the dorm, he invited me to share his cabin in the woods a couple miles from campus. But I had baggage. Physical baggage. The steamer trunk I had shipped up when I left Ohio was too large to take with me if I moved around. I had no choice but to send it back to Toledo.

In the trunk, I packed all my unused clothing, books, plus a couple of Alaska native-carved good-luck soapstone billikens for my brother and sister. They were the perfect Alaskan souvenir. The trunk was heavy. Bill and I lugged it to his station wagon and drove it to the train station in Fairbanks where I paid to have it shipped by rail back to Ohio. All that useless stuff had been weighing me down both physically and mentally. Now I felt free to pick up and go anywhere.

I sold a winter coat for twenty bucks to a student moving back to the Midwest and used the cash to buy a "kidney buster," a World War II field-tested carry-frame that strapped on your back and wrapped around and rested on your hip bones for hiking and hunting. I was going to use it at Post Lake.

Bill lived in a two-room log cabin he had built himself. It had solid wood plank floors but no electricity, plumbing, or running water. For light he used an oil lamp and candles. There was a small outhouse in the back about fifty yards away. He had built that, too.

A clear stream ran near the cabin and that's where I went to collect water in a bucket for washing up and making coffee on his wood burning Franklin stove. When we washed dishes in the kitchen, the gray water drained into a bucket under the sink. Bill didn't charge me rent since I helped him get water and chop wood for the stove.

I thought about the upcoming work on the railroad and the August hunt, which was supposed to last until September. After that, I had no idea what I would do. I had no plans to finish my graduate degree, I might be drafted, but I didn't want to go back to Ohio to a life of mediocrity. Roger Landrum, a friend from Bowling Green State University, had written me that he had signed up for the Peace Corps just started by President Kennedy. He wanted me to join him. I wrote him back to wish him luck.

One evening, I met a guy at Tommy's Elbow Room who was on his way back to California after working on the DEW line near Point Barrow. He said the Distance Early Warning system was on an isolated military base and was America's best defensive response to the Cold War with the Soviet Union and their nuclear bombs.

"If the DEW line radar ever picks up Soviet bombers coming in over the Arctic Ocean or the Bering Sea, we'll have our jets in the air in minutes and blow those bastards out of the sky," he said. He was passionate about the DEW line's importance to our country's defense.

"What's it like up there?" I asked.

"Well, it colder than shit up there," he said. "But the food is good, there's plenty of booze, and there are new movies at the base club every night." I remembered the cheap food and good music on Fort Wainwright. Such easy times. "Civilian jobs run for eighteen months and are good for occupational deferments from the army," he said. "And I can't complain about the pay. A thousand dollars a month, after taxes." He'd been up there since late 1959 and had just finished his eighteen months.

"The military pays that kind of salary because it's considered isolation pay," he said. "The money was good, but the place was driving me nuts and I didn't want to sign on for a second stint. Plus, I gotta tell ya', buddy, I'm really horny." His girlfriend in California had sent him a Dear John letter and he wanted to get back to reconnect. He was taking a plane out in the morning. He finished his beer, bought each of us another, and we sat back and stared into the flaming logs crackling in the fireplace.

I thought about applying for a job at Point Barrow. It was a new idea. The money would be great. Twelve thousand dollars would be a good stake to keep me going for quite a while, but the thought of being stuck 325 miles north of the Arctic Circle freezing my butt off with a company of paranoid soldiers and bored civilians in a constant state of high alert was not the kind of adventure that would move me forward. I kissed the imaginary 12,000 bucks goodbye and bought us both another beer.

A couple days later I got word that I'd been hired for the railroad job and I would start on Sunday. I told Bill I was leaving.

"Sorry to see you go, Joel," he said. "But I knew the garden crew was temporary." We drove into Fairbanks to the Elbow Room. "One for the road," he said. "The railroad."

On Sunday morning, June 4th, Bill drove me into Fairbanks to catch the 8:00 a.m. train to the job site about thirty miles down the tracks. Other than my typewriter, rifle, snowshoes, kidney buster and backpack, which I left with Bucky and Judy Wilson to store for me back at the dorm, everything else I owned I stuffed into my Army duffle bag.

When I walked into the depot, the train was refueling. A line of about ten other workers began to form on the platform waiting to board. It took me only a second to realize that I was the only white guy there. All the others were Eskimo or Athabaskan Indian. I was six feet tall and weighed a buff 145 pounds. Without exception, they were shorter and thinner.

The engineer gave a single short whistle blast and the line of workers climbed on board and paired off. They went to the back, leaving a front row seat for me and my duffle. Five minutes later another toot and the train began to move. I sat back and leaned against the window and watched the landscape passing by.

The train moved slowly out of town and into the tundra, miles of flatland on either side covered with knee-high tan craggy grass and glistening bogs. We passed by the slopes of Chena Ridge, then chugged back into flat land and more muskeg, then over a steel bridge crossing the Tanana River. Fifteen minutes later the train stopped in the small village of Nenana to let a few local passengers board. Then back to the flat areas again. The train chugged on slowly as if to prolong the ride. I turned around. All the natives behind me were sleeping.

We arrived at the job site at 10 o'clock. The section gang foreman, Don LeMay, had been notified that I, an inexperienced newbie, had signed on and came over and stood in front of me. He was a short, dirty-haired blond guy maybe in his mid-thirties. He already had been sent my paperwork.

"Hey, Rudinger," he said. "I need you to sign some forms. Over there."

He pointed to an outdoor wooden table made from weathered two-by-fours. When we got to the table, he pulled a sheet of paper out of a tin box for me to sign and date my arrival. When I had signed it, he dropped it back in the box and pointed out the dining car and a line of sleeper cars. They sat off to the side on a short length of rails parallel to the main tracks.

"Supper at 4:00 pm. Breakfast tomorrow at 5:00 a.m. I put you in sleeper car number three, room two. Your roommate is Horace Smoke."

"Thanks," I said. "Do I get a key to room two?"

"What for?" LeMay snorted. "You got money in that duffel? You one of those rich college kids?" He spat into the dirt by his foot. "We don't need no keys here."

I had no idea how he knew I had been at UA. His reaction surprised me, but I didn't think it would lead to trouble. Just then another worker stepped out of the dining car and got LeMay's attention and he walked off. I hoisted my duffle to my shoulder, went over to the sleeping car, climbed up the steel steps and found the narrow door to sleeping area number 2. The room was tight, just space enough for the double bunk bed, two folding chairs, a built-in dresser, and a four-foot wide free-standing closet bolted to the wall.

As I shifted my duffle to the floor, in walked my roommate, Horace Smoke. Horace was a native, older than the young crew on the morning train from Fairbanks. He was friendly and seemed curious about who I was. At least he wanted to talk. He told me he was the old man of the section gang, forty going on forty-one.

"Not many men like me doing this kind of hard labor," he said, "but the money is good. I need the money." I liked him. He was a storyteller. He told me that ten years earlier, back in 1951, he had won a big dogsled race. He said he'd tell me about it later.

A bell sounded outside. "Lunch time," he said and turned and walked out the door. I tossed my duffle on the open bunk, the top one, and followed him to the dining car. He sure walked fast.

After lunch, I walked around the work area and checked out the tracks. I was curious what my job would be. The native workers sat around the ground in groups of five or six, just sitting, smoking cigarettes, drinking Cokes. I didn't see Horace or LeMay or the other white guys I had seen at lunch.

I looked at my watch. It was 3:15 p.m. I heard a soft buzzing whine in the air and suddenly I was under attack by an undulating cloud of Arctic mosquitoes, hundreds of thousands of them, rising out of the tundra around the work site. Holy crap. Now I understood why sleeping in a tent out here was a bad idea. I had no choice but to escape to my sleeping room. The dining car was closed. Back in my room, I took off my boots and lay down on the bunk. Horace Smoke was somewhere else.

Ten weeks till the Post Lake hunt.

I closed my eyes and fell asleep.

11: ARR Journal

June 5 (Monday)
    First day on the job. We worked today from 7:30 a.m. to 4:30 p.m. dressing track and stacking ties. Physically exhausted. Went to bed around 10:00 p.m. Hot sweats all night—sleeping bag soaked. Even the mosquitoes couldn't keep me from sleeping. Tomorrow we begin work at 6:00 a.m. and work until 3:00 to beat the clouds of afternoon mosquitoes.

June 6 (Tuesday)
    Today we pulled ties and tamped. I was a nipper, tamping loose gravel under the tracks with a long-handled shovel. I wondered all day what the hell I was doing here. I thought maybe I hate my own guts. This is lousy torture. Had a great conversation with Horace in the sleeping car before we hit the sack. He told me about his winning a big dog sled race in the Yukon. The Yukon Quest. He said the prize was ten thousand dollars. I wondered why he was here if he had earned that kind of money. He said that was ten years ago and the money was long gone.

June 7 (Wednesday)
    Easier day. Trying to work out a rhythm and keep body movement efficient. I don't know how to do that yet but I'm watching the others who have been here awhile and hope to figure it out. How do you jam your shovel into the stones, lift, turn, and throw your load a hundred times an hour? If they can do it, I can do it. And they're smaller than me.

June 8 (Thursday)
    Today was the hardest day yet. I lost all power in my arm and back. I am seriously thinking of making tomorrow my last day here. The experience is not worth the pain. The foreman isn't making it any easier. I can hardly bend over and he's calling me lazy.

*   *   *

June 9 (Friday)

Worked regular hours. Caught train to Fairbanks at 8:04 p.m. and arrived at 9:00 p.m. Stopped at Northward Building to see Leda Juul, but she wasn't home. Walked to campus and saw Judy and Bucky Wilson and Marie Munsen. Got to Bill's cabin to sack out at 12:30. It was good to see him.

While I was in Fairbanks the next day, I sent a letter home.

June 10, 1961

Dear Folks,

I have completed one full week of work on the Alaska railroad. It has been the bloodiest, hardest week I've ever spent. Don LeMay, the foreman, says that the hard work will build me up, make me strong.

When I say bloody, take me literally. Hordes of mosquitos half an inch long suddenly rise up and burst forth out of the tundra surrounding us in thick, shifting, hungry, rapacious clouds two or three times a day. The world around us hums and whines with the crescendo of their buzzing and they get in my eyes and ears and nose and mouth with every breath I take. I stand there choking and spitting crushed bugs. The natives on the crew get a kick out of it because the mosquitoes don't land on them. Maybe it's something in their blood or something they eat. I feel like a target, a feeding ground, a magnet.

Yesterday one the native guys came over to me while I was leveling track and ran his cupped hand down the back of my shirt from my neck to my waist and scooped off a handful of mosquito pulp as large as a snowball. I kid you not. It was so gross I had to laugh. Minutes later, on some cosmic signal, the mosquitoes vanished back into the tundra. Gone in a second. This happens several times a day. I can't judge the time when exactly they come and go since it's nearing the summer solstice and there's sunlight here almost all the time.

The crew consists of seventeen men plus Don LeMay, the foreman, and his sidekick. Beside me, there are three men from Minnesota, three white Alaskans, and ten Alaskan native Eskimos and Indians, mostly Athabaskan.

The natives avoid the white guys when they're off the job. They're friendly and helpful while we're working, because we work in teams, but after supper, they have their own powwows around their own campfires before turning in. And the foreman and his buddy don't talk to anyone. I think it's because they have mosquito repellent they don't want to share. I've hinted for some, but they ignore me. There's no booze here at all for socializing, mainly because the natives can't handle it without getting crazy. They wait till they can get to town.

Because of the mosquitoes, our daily schedule now starts at 4:45 a.m., breakfast at 5:00 a.m.; on the job at 6:00 a.m.; lunch at 10:00 a.m.; stop work at 3:00 p.m.; dinner at 4:00 p.m.; to bed at 9:00 pm. The schedule is good because we avoid most of the mosquitoes which come out and attack us around 3:00, although recently they have been less predictable, sometimes coming at us at 3:10.

The work itself consists of (1) digging out rotten ties, (2) pulling spikes, (3) lifting the track with long crowbars, (4) pulling the rail plates off the ties, (5) pulling the ties out, (6) digging fresh holes in rock and gravel, (7) sliding new ties into the holes, (8) replacing the rail plate, (9) spiking down the rail on the new tie, (10) filling in the holes with our long-handled shovels, (11) smoothing over the gravel, (12) stacking the ties, and (13) rebuilding the embankments. It's all done by hand. We have no power tools or heavy-duty railroad equipment. It's a never-ending, back-breaking job for a lousy $3.62 an hour. My gross income a week is $126.40. Board is $32 a week, about forty percent of my gross, and federal and state deductions account for another twenty to twenty-five percent so, my total take-home pay is about $70. This is for a forty-hour week, rain, wind, and mosquitoes.

We're working only about thirty miles from Fairbanks and I get a pass each week which can take me anywhere the ARR goes, from Seward to Fairbanks. But as the clerk at the employment desk told me, I could get down to Seward, but I'd be spending ninety percent of my time riding the train.

The crew as a whole is hard working and there is no gambling or fighting. At least not in camp. I hear otherwise when they get into Fairbanks.

In the meantime, I'm sitting in a coffeehouse in Fairbanks letting my hands rest. I came in on the 9:00 p.m. train last night (Friday) to use my weekend here to take a shower and clear up business on campus. I was supposed to go to a wedding tonight on Fort Wainwright, but I'm not dressed for it, so I'll just sit here and watch people.

Tomorrow is Sunday and I go back to gandy dancing on the railroad. I'll buy some bug repellent before I leave.

Hope all is well at home,
Take care,
Joel

The next day on the job, the army of mosquitoes predictably rose up out of the tundra droning their whining hum of bloodsucking death. But this time I was prepared. On Saturday, I had gone to the army surplus store in Fairbanks and bought a khaki cap with attached mosquito netting. I put it on, pulled the netting down so it covered my face and throat, and jammed my sweat stained hat down over it. I felt at least I could keep the bugs out of my mouth and ears. I also started to wrap the leg bottoms of my wool pants tightly around my ankles and tuck them into the tops of my boots. That way the bugs couldn't fly up my pant legs. I had bought leather work gloves to protect my hands, but the constant shoveling ripped out the seams the first day and they were useless. I also bought two cans of mosquito repellent, but Monday night after supper they went missing.

LeMay, as usual, assigned me to move gravel with the natives. The other white guys he moved to the rear and gave them the job of pounding spikes into the iron track plates on the rails.

In May when I had worked on the university garden crew, I knew I might be working on the railroad in June, so I pushed myself to take the heavier jobs to build myself up. I thought I was in good shape. But despite my preparation, my staying power was nothing compared to the young natives working around me. They were good workers, tireless and strong, constantly shoveling gravel or prying up the heavy creosoted ties, and they never complained. They worked in silence, each with his own task, each one quiet and efficient. They worked as a team, heads down, focused, automatic.

No one wore a watch but, like the predictable rising of the mosquitoes, they responded to some internal clock, knowing exactly when to start, when to look up and go to lunch or stop at the end of the shift. It was as if some external power were pulling their strings. Like a band of marionettes, when it was time, all their heads popped up at once. I saw this every day, and every day I was impressed. Maybe this was the instinct that helped them survive for 10,000 years above the Arctic Circle: not to question but to do. Not to wonder, just to be.

Horace Smoke, the old man on the crew, was about five-foot ten and filled out and solid. He had the strong body of a man who worked with his hands. Sometimes before we turned in, we would talk.

"I'm Athabaskan," he said, "from Yukon Territory."

"What are you doing working on the Alaska Railroad?" I asked. "Do you have family back in Canada?" I was interested in his background.

"Yes," he said. "I have a wife and two kids back home. But the money working here is better than what I can make there, so I come here. I've worked on the Alaska Railroad four summers. This is my fifth."

The working season for the railroad was long. For the veteran workers, it went from April into September when the snows and freezing air came.

"Don't you miss them?" I asked.

"Oh, sure," he said. He didn't elaborate.

One evening before turning in, Horace told me again that when he was younger, he raced dogs. "Two years I won the big Yukon Quest race. Made a lot of money. Ten thousand dollars." His eyes crinkled when he talked about it. He was proud of his wins. He told me about training his dogs, choosing the best one to be leader, the supplies he needed. One thing was clear: he was a natural storyteller and filled his adventures with excitement and details. He had graduated from high school but had never had an interest in school beyond that.

Horace was fun to talk to and was, in his own way, a role model for the younger natives on the crew. I could understand that. He was almost twice their age and his acceptance of everyone's quirks made him a fatherly friend to everyone, perhaps even to the asshole foreman.

Horace worked within twenty feet of me wherever I was. I was amazed at his stamina, his constant movement, his efficiency with his shovel. I also noticed that he used the same shovel every day. At the end of a day's work, we turned our shovels into Pete, the second in command. Pete would put them in a locker built into the end of the mess car. He counted each piece of equipment, put it in its place, and padlocked them in at night. Every spade, shovel, sledge, pickax, and pry bar had its place, and in the morning, when they were reissued to us, everyone checked out his favorite tool. I saw extra shovels and other tools in there, but I didn't see any difference between one and another. Being the last one hired onto this gang, I always got last choice. When I held a different shovel in each hand, I did feel a slight difference in balance but nothing I thought that would make one better.

I had been working on the Alaska railroad almost two weeks. I had gone up to campus the previous Saturday and had sneaked into my old dorm for a shower. There was drinking water at the worksite, and a couple gravity sinks to wash your hands and face, but there were no showers and only one metal tub to rinse clothes. The temperatures since Sunday had risen into the mid-80s and all the sweat and dirt on my clothes began to add up. My two long-sleeved, heavy work shirts and my wool work pants were stiff with mosquito pulp.

The work, the hours, the mosquitoes, the pace, my sore and bleeding hands, the pain of trying to jam a shovel into rock and gravel finally got the best of me when the foreman Don decided to call me out.

"Hey, Rudinger," LeMay yelled. "Get that shovel movin'! Come on! Dig! Dig! Dig! Get your ass in gear. Pick it up!" Then he turned his back, turned around to his buddy Pete and laughed. I exploded.

"Hey, LeMay," I yelled back, "you son of a bitch. I don't see you doing any work." And I pulled my shovel back over my shoulder and whipped it at him. I could feel it peel raw skin off my raw blisters as I let go. "Goddammit!" I hissed. The shovel flew low and fell far short of its target. Which was probably a good thing. I never realized that I could have that level of rage. A new layer was peeled away from the onion. What had just happened?

The natives around me looked over and grinned. I saw their teeth. Their eyes crinkled up and brightened for a second and then they turned back to their digging, heads down, smiling. One of them chuckled. Damn it! I wasn't being funny. I was pissed.

Don LeMay laughed, shook his head, and walked up the tracks to the white crew sitting around on a stack of ties. I looked at my hands. Every finger was torn and bleeding. Then I clambered down the gravel embankment I'd been working on, retrieved my shovel, and tried to go back to work. The trouble was my hands hurt so badly and were so swollen that I could hardly grip the handle. Then I got my foot caught between two dug-out ties, twisted my ankle, and could hardly walk.

So that was it. I cradled the shovel in my bent elbows and hobbled back to the mess car, leaned the shovel against the equipment locker and went to my sleeping room to lay down until the shift was over. But it was sweltering in there, so I got up, went to the bathroom in the mess car, rinsed off my hands and face, and waited behind the mess car in the shade.

There were dozens of birds hopping around in the tundra. I watched them catching bugs until the shift was over and everyone came back.

Pete returned at 3 o'clock and pulled a box up by the equipment locker and sat down. LeMay came up a minute later. I went over.

"Don," I said. "I want to let you know that I hereby submit my resignation."

"You do what?" he asked. "You submit your fucking what?" He leaned into me, inches from my face, his fists doubled up on his hips. He was four inches shorter than me and I wanted to bust him in the nose. I just looked him in the eye.

"I quit," I said. Maybe he could understand that.

"Okay, you quit," he repeated. "So?"

"So nothing. I'll take the train back to Fairbanks on Thursday when it comes through."

"Okay. So?"

"So you can fill out my time sheet, do whatever paperwork you need to drop me from the crew."

"Oh, yeah. Well, I'm going in this weekend and I'll drop it off at payroll." He walked off.

That was it.

When the crew went back to work the next day, I stayed in camp with my camera to take pictures and write in my journal. All day I watched Horace and the others dig out and pry up and ram new ties into place. I admired their stamina, their focus, their patience. I knew they weren't making a lot of money, but they were making some, and I wondered what they did in the winter when they had to go back to their homes and villages.

I also wondered what I would be doing for the next six weeks when I got back to town. I didn't have a clue. Post Lake seemed far away.

I wrote a letter to Rhody, my grandfather back in Cleveland.

June 19, 1961
Dear Rhody,

A lot has happened since I last wrote. As you know, school is over, and I have been working at various jobs picking up odd pennies. When school was officially out, May 22, I was jobless, but three days later the university hired me on the buildings and grounds crew. For about ten days, I dug holes and planted trees. Then the job I had applied for on the Alaska Railroad came through. I left my gardening job and took up with the railroad, but after two weeks of leveling track manually with shovels and a crowbar, I decided that that kind of work was not for me. I handed in my resignation on Thursday morning and spent the rest of the day resting and taking pictures for the future. That evening, I took the train back into Fairbanks.

With phenomenal luck, I walked to campus the next morning and got my job back on the buildings and grounds crew. I went to work at ten that morning, so I was out of work for less than a day. Now I hose down flowers and trees for eight hours a day, five days a week, for $2.50 an hour. It is the easiest $100 a week I've ever earned   .

Working the railroad, I learned a great deal about myself. For one, I'm not the superman I had thought. I was thoroughly and painfully exhausted by the time each day was over   .

The meals were good but expensive. The standard rate was $1.60 a meal for three meals a day. But I believe I ate my share, plus. Despite all the food though, I lost eight pounds. However, I do feel better and my muscles are more solid across my chest and in my back and arms. They should be after lifting 150-pound ties and swinging heavy spike mauls and heaving shovels of gravel and stones all day. I'm glad that I quit but not at all sorry that I tried it. It was a good experience. At least I can say that I was once a gandy dancer on the Alaska Railroad.

I hope you had a good Father's Day. I did. I spent the day in my cabin resting and writing, cooking my meals and drinking cold beer with a friend. This was the first lazy day I've spent in a month, but I would rather be doing something.

Hope you are well,
Joel

12: Target Shoot

Back on campus, I found a note in my mail slot from Chuck Keim inviting me to join him at the university's rifle range. Chuck told me that he sighted in his rifle there several times a year. Since he had gotten me the job working with Hal Waugh and I'd be on the Post Lake hunt for at least two weeks, he wanted to see me shoot. "Your life might depend on it, Rudy," he said.

I only had a single shot .22 rifle, but even though it was small for the wilderness, he could at least check out what I could or couldn't do, look at my form, my posture prone and upright, whether I had a steady hand, and if I could line-up the built-in sights on the barrel to hit a target.

I called Chuck to make a time and the following morning he picked me up in his four-wheel drive. I had never been on a range before and had only shot my rifle a couple times. It was all new and exciting.

When we got to the firing range parking lot, Chuck got his rifle case and a small leather bag from the trunk and we passed through the gate, signed in, and walked down the line to an open booth at the far end of the range.

I watched Chuck, determined to not make too many foolish mistakes. He took his rifle out of the hard-shell case. I pulled my .22 out of the hand-made canvas cover I had sewn for it. He took out a box of .30-06 ammo and set it on the ground; I took my box of bullets out of my jacket pocket and did likewise. Then he reached into his leather bag and pulled out two sets of noise dampening earphones, one for each of us.

Down the line, the blasts of other marksmen were sharp and loud. My .22 didn't make much more than a loud pop when I shot it, and I clearly understood the difference in power between my rifle and Chuck's. We both put on our earphones and got ready to shoot. Chuck lay in a prone position and I followed. He pointed ahead to two paper targets attached to bales of hay.

"The targets are set at fifty yards," he said. "Take six shots and then we'll walk up and see what kind of spread we have. Rudy, you shoot at the target on the left."

Chuck fired one shot and got out his binoculars and focused on his target to see where his bullet had hit. I took a shot, but I thought I could see my hole without the glasses. I could see Chuck's hole, too. It was bigger than mine but no closer to the center of the bullseye. We each shot six rounds, taking our time. Then we went up to check the paper. Chuck had hit the target with all six shots, although some were spread within the edge of the outer circle. When we checked my target, I only counted four holes, but the spread was tight, all within an inch of dead center. I looked confused. Chuck looked closer.

"I don't believe it," he said. "Do you know why you only have four holes?" I didn't.

"I missed?"

"No. Because two of your bullets went exactly into other holes. Rudy, you're a natural!" He lifted the paper target, took out his pocketknife and dug into the hay bale and pulled out all six of my bullets. I knew they were mine because no one else here was shooting a .22. He grinned and patted me on the back. I felt good, ready to hunt. I was a natural. Who would have guessed?

We each did a couple more sets of six and he let me shoot his .30-06 a couple of times. His gun had a lot more of a kick, but I still kept my spread close to center.

I thought maybe I'd buy a bigger rifle before the hunt, but I never did. In the campus barbershop, I found a Sears catalog that had Army surplus 30.06's listed for a hundred dollars, but the postal service to Fairbanks was slow and unreliable and there wasn't time. Besides, I conjectured, I wasn't being hired to hunt; I was only hired to be a packer, to lug meat from dead animals back to camp.

Chuck said I was natural marksman. Maybe there was something else in store for me.

13: On to Anchorage

The 12th of August arrived, and my four-month wait to head out to Post Lake was finally over. I was ready to hit the road. I had no idea what to expect and I was excited. This was what I had come to Alaska for.

Since I needed to conserve money, I thought I'd hitchhike to Anchorage. It was 480 miles south of Fairbanks. It was a long way over the two-lane highway, but I figured that if I were lucky, I could get there in one or two days. Maybe I could catch a ride in an RV with tourists going all the way. Tourists tended to drive straight through. Most Alaskans lived off the road back in the woods, on a river or lake, or in one of the villages along the way.

The only way by highway from Fairbank to Anchorage was to drive south to Delta Junction at the head of the Paxton Cutoff. That was about 115 miles. Then on to the Glenn Allen junction, another 153 miles. It was not a route without challenges.

Sometimes on the cutoff, melting glaciers drifted across the road in a dangerous sloping sheet of ice. That always slowed down traffic. On the opposite side of the road was a drop off, and if your tires started to slip sideways on the slanting ice, your vehicle could slip sideways off the road into the valley below. Often tourists didn't know about the glacial creep until it was too late. I'd heard about the accidents from students who lived in or carpooled to Anchorage on weekends. There were a few deaths every year. One was reported last week in the *Fairbanks Daily News Miner*.

Another danger was that the Paxton Cutoff road passed near Fort Greeley, a military base in the middle of nowhere. This time of year, Fort Greeley territory was a popular destination for hunters lucky enough to have won a bison permit in the State lottery. I'd heard that even though there were only about two hundred bison hunting permits issued each year, every year someone got shot. Either a hunter or someone in a car passing through the area. The hunting tended to slow traffic also. The hunting season was on now.

From Glenn Allen to Wasilla and on to Anchorage was another 180 miles over roads that rippled with frost heaves and cracked and warped pavement. It never could be a fast drive. If you went too fast for too long over those spine-crunching washboard roads, one tended to puke on the dashboard.

In the morning, I gathered my gear. I had brought my heavy-duty steel-framed Army kidney buster. It fit tight and wouldn't shift around on my back when I was packing moose meat down mountains. I also had bought a mummy sleeping bag, an inflatable rubber air mattress, and a rain parka. I packed the soft stuff in my duffle along with a second pair of wool pants, a weatherproof light winter jacket, socks, two heavy long sleeve shirts, a compass, hip-high waders, a canteen, a flint and carbon block, and my hunting knife. I wrapped my Argus 35 mm camera in a towel with six rolls of Kodachrome film, a tripod, and my shaving kit. The duffle bag was even long enough to hold my .22 rifle. Except for the kidney buster, I got all that stuff crammed in.

Ready to hitchhike, I felt like an Alaskan sourdough as I stood in front of the Bunnell building bursting with hope and energy. I was wearing my new four-inch brimmed felt Dobbs hat my dad had sent me, wool pants and shirt, a khaki jacket, and my hunting boots. As I was crossing campus to walk down the hill to College Road, a former student of mine saw me and offered me a ride to Fairbanks. We walked over to the parking lot, I tossed my backpack and duffle in the back seat, and off we went. It was a good start.

"Where you goin', Mr. Rudinger?" the student asked.

"I'm on my way to Anchorage," I said. "I have a job as a packer in the Alaska Range."

"Wow! Where in the Alaska Range?" he asked, smiling in new friendship.

"Dr. Keim and I are flying into Post Lake on the south fork of the Kuskokwim River," I said. "I think it's about seventy-five miles west-south-west of Mount McKinley. We'll be in there for a couple of weeks."

"Wow! That'll be fun. The Range is perfect this time of year," he said. "The mosquitoes on the tundra are quiet and it's too early for heavy snow. My dad and I hunted near McGrath last year around this time and we got a moose and two caribou. Had plenty of meat for the winter."

"What's your name again?" I asked. We were getting close to town.

"David Harold," he said. "I was in your fall English class."

"Are you a native of Fairbanks?" I asked.

"No," David said. "I grew up in Copper Center. This is my second year at the university on a BIA grant." Bureau of Indian Affairs grants were available to any native, Eskimo, Indian, or Aleut, who had at least one-eighth native blood. That meant David was getting a four-year college education, or at least a college experience, at no cost to his family. He was driving a late model Ford and he seemed to be doing okay. I wondered where he would be in ten years.

"Are you going on to Copper Center?" I asked. Copper Center was south of the Paxton cutoff and it would be perfect if David were on his way home. It would make my trip to Anchorage easy.

"No," he said. "I'm just driving into Fairbanks to get beer. There's a party tonight and I'm buying the booze. Mostly guys from the Geology Club." We passed over the Chena River into town. "You want me to drop you off at the train station or the airport?" he offered. It was a nice gesture, but I was disappointed he wasn't driving further south.

"I'm going to hitchhike to Anchorage," I said as we came to the traffic light at the corner of Cushman and First. David stopped as it turned red.

"Wow. Really?" he said surprised. "Good luck." The light turned green and he drove down Cushman for two blocks and pulled into the parking lot of a grocery store. I got my duffle and backpack from the back seat.

"Thanks for the ride, David. Maybe I'll see you when I get back."

"Okay," he said. "Have a great time." He waived a hand over his head as he turned and went into the store.

It was ten in the morning, a little later than I wanted. I walked south on Cushman toward the Richardson Highway. It was Saturday. There weren't many cars but a guy in a rusted-out white furniture de-livery truck who I had seen on campus drove past, slowed down, and stopped. He gave me a ride to the south edge of town and dropped me off a mile past Indiantown then turned left off the main road to make a delivery. I slid on my kidney buster and slung the duffel over my shoulder. I walked a bit further and stood by the side of the road and stuck my thumb out when I saw a car coming. A few cars passed me, never slowed down. But hitchhikers in Alaska were common. It was only a matter of time.

Two hours later I was still standing along the highway when the air suddenly turned cold and a bank of clouds rolled in and blocked the sun. It was usually dry in the Interior. Fairbanks only averaged about thirteen inches of precipitation a year. But the rain began, first lightly, then in earnest. I was soaked. Also, no cars were coming so I ran off the road and found shelter under a partially collapsed wood-en fence. I was protected but off the road a good one hundred feet as two motor homes came out of nowhere heading south. By the time I grabbed my gear and jumped out into the open, waving my arms, they were far down the highway.

It was past 2 o'clock. I was hungry. I was frustrated. Okay, so I'm dressed in wet army surplus cloths, wearing a backpack, and toting a huge duffle. My hat is dripping, and no one is stopping to give me a ride.

I turned back to Fairbanks and started walking. This hitchhik-ing idea wasn't working, and I had to be in Anchorage in two days to catch my plane. I walked about fifteen minutes along the highway when a young woman in a black pick-up truck pulled up next to me. She leaned toward me with wide dark laughing eyes and a beautiful smile and rolled down the passenger window. She had dark chocolate-brown hair pulled back in a long ponytail that lay across her white sweater like a comfortable pet. I forgot my anger. I stood a little straighter.

"Need a ride?" she said. I nodded.

"Yes," I said. "Thanks." I smiled back, tossed my gear in the open bed of her pick-up and got in. She didn't seem to mind that I was soaking wet.

"Where are you going?" she asked.

"I was hitchhiking to Anchorage."

"That's in the other direction," she laughed. I laughed too and told her about my aborted try. She laughed again. I guess it was easy to tell that I was new at this.

She wasn't in any hurry because she offered to drive me all the way back to the university. I would have bought her a beer at Tommy's Elbow Room, but I was cold and wanted to find somewhere to get into dry clothes. She said her name was Mary Jane and that she was married to a Fairbanks policeman. She and her husband bred sled dogs for racing.

"We have a parcel of land across the road from Creamer's Dairy," she said. "Look. There it is." She pointed as we passed it. It was the same dog yard I had walked past a hundred times. This time the doghouse area looked a little cleaner.

Mary Jane drove me to campus, let me out near the student union, smiled her beautiful smile and drove away with a honk. That cop was one lucky guy.

August 13th.

It was still gray and raining in the morning and the time was getting short. I couldn't gamble on trying to hitchhike again so I bought a one-way train ticket to Anchorage.

We passed the section gang I had worked with. Everyone looked dirty and tired standing by the tracks, leaning on their picks and shovels. Gray figures in a gray morning. I couldn't believe that that was what I had looked like to people on the trains. The time working on the railroad was a short chapter in my life. I was glad it was over, but I knew I would never forget it.

The trip from Fairbanks to Anchorage took nearly ten hours. This was a commuter train that stopped for everyone waiting by the tracks: fishermen, hunters, families with kids on their way to Talkeetna, Wasilla, or Anchorage, or any private encampment along the way. It was the only way in or out for hundreds of miles of wilderness. Homesteaders depended on the ARR to get them to town and back home to their cabins hidden in the woods.

One family climbed on, a man and woman with three kids, all under seven. They looked and smelled like they hadn't bathed in weeks. The kids sat quietly staring out the windows while their parents fell asleep behind them five minutes into their trip. A little while later, two men carrying fishing rods and bamboo creels got on and wobbled down the aisle, each toting two large fish, banging their equipment and elbows into people as they went to the back and into the dining car hooked on behind us. They reeked of dead fish and dirty underwear.

And on we went, stopping for people needing to get to a grocery store or the post office or the bank or a doctor. One couple jumped off at McKinley Park, but most of the rail-side commuter passengers got off at the Talkeetna station while the train took on a bunch of tourists who piled into my car. Excited, they talked loudly and pointed their wide-angle lens cameras at every mountain and cabin we passed as the engine chugged forward around curves and switchbacks cut into mountainside. If a moose or bear popped out into a clearing, everyone crowded to that side of the car to take pictures.

It wasn't a smooth ride. The rail car was lurching slightly side-to-side over the uneven tracks. We were going slowly, because the whole track bed needed work. I was glad that this wasn't where our section gang had been assigned.

The train pulled into Anchorage at 9 o'clock at night, but the sky was still light. I walked over to a pay phone in the station and called Air-Sea Motives, the airline which was going to fly me to Hal Waugh's camp. There was some confusion on the other end and the man answering told me the Wednesday August 16th flight I was supposed to take had been rescheduled for the 19th. I wondered if Hal Waugh waiting out in the wilderness knew. Anyway, it put me in Anchorage for a few extra days without a plan.

The railroad station was on the far side of Ship Creek, a winding stream of crystal-clear water that separated it from downtown Anchorage, so I walked over to the embankment and sat down on a bench to figure out where I would sleep. A couple of blocks away I could see the tall Anchorage Westward Hotel. If I were lucky, Bob Larsen would be at the front desk acting as head desk clerk.

A month earlier I had caught a ride with a friend to Anchorage. I had met a girl named Joanne the week before on the UA campus. We had had a couple of beers at Tommy's before she was to get on the train to return to Anchorage where she was visiting her sister and brother-in-law, Carol and Bob Larsen. She invited me down, gave me her address, and we set up a date and time.

My taxi had dropped me off at the Larsen house two hours late. When I rang the doorbell, Carol Larsen opened the front door.

"Yes?" she said. "What can I do for you?" She looked puzzled.

"Hi," I said. "You must be Joanne's sister Carol. I'm Joel, a graduate student at the university in Fairbanks. I met Joanne in Fairbanks a week ago and we set up a date for tonight. I know I'm a little late, but here I am."

I slipped off my backpack and reached out to shake hands. Carol cocked her head and looked around. My taxi had left. I was standing on the porch as if I had appeared out of nowhere. Which I guess is what I did.

"I am so sorry," Carol said, "but Joanne is out with someone." I have no idea what my face expressed, but she apologized. "Come on in," she said. "Let me call Bob, my husband." She phoned Bob who was at work at the Anchorage Westward Hotel.

"Would you like some tea or coffee?" she asked. "I just called my husband. He's getting someone to watch the desk and is coming here to drive you into back to town. I apologize again for Joanne. Did she know you were coming?"

"I thought she did. This was the day we agreed on." I had just come 480 miles for nothing.

Bob Larsen drove up fifteen minutes later and took me back into Anchorage. He was amused that I had come all this way for a date.

"Well," I said, "What can I say? I'm a hopeless romantic."

"I guess," he said. "Too bad Joanne's flying back to New Jersey in the morning. But I'll tell her you came." He shook his head. He was not happy with his sister-in-law. "Where are you staying tonight?"

I told him I hadn't made any arrangements. I didn't tell him Joanne had told me I could stay at his house, but it worked out. Bob said he had a small closet-sized room at the hotel which he could rent to me for five dollars.

"I'll take it," I said.

That's how I met Bob Larsen.

I swung my gear onto my shoulder and walked over the Ship Creek bridge and into downtown Anchorage. Bob wasn't on duty at the hotel. The clerk behind the desk said he wouldn't be in until the next day. I thought it was too late to call him at home, so I walked up Fifth Street.

When I had ventured into town for my non-date with Joanne, in a narrow alley between Fourth and Fifth Streets I had seen a small faded sign for a cheap hotel. I laughed when I saw it because two rumpled old men came out of it and went into a bar next door. It all looked like a bad cliché from a Humphrey Bogart movie. But now I walked down the alley for a closer and more serious look. The so-called hotel was a narrow three floor rooming house squeezed vertically between two bars. I could see through the dirty front window five or six workmen in one of the bars sitting on stools hunched over drinks. The other bar looked empty except for the bartender and a blonde in a tight red dress sitting at the far end. Country music was coming from a juke box in the back.

The green door of the rooming house was narrow and warped. I saw a vacancy sign in the front window with a card taped under it: "Rooms $4." Either I could go in there or I could wander around a bit longer and try to find something else. But I was beat and dragging from that endless train ride and I just wanted to lay down and go to sleep. Anywhere. And so I went in.

There was nobody at the front desk. I hit the bell on the counter. An old man came out of a back room where he was listening to the radio. I said I needed a room for the night. "All right," he said, took my money, and asked me to sign in. He picked a key off a pegboard and led me down a dim stale-smelling corridor. He stopped at room 129, unlocked the door, and stepped back as he dropped the key into my hand.

"Toilet is at the end of the hall," he said pointing. "There's two showers and two sinks, two toilets and two urinals. Check out time is 10 o'clock unless you want to stay."

"Thanks," I said to his back. He was already walking back to the front. I put my gear in the room, locked the door, and peeked into the bathroom. It was just as he said, but it looked clean. A little pee on the floor under a urinal and a bit of toilet paper on the floor, but I'd seen worse. I went to my tiny room, got my soap, a towel, my toothbrush, headed to the bathroom, washed, and went back to my room.

I closed the door behind me and looked around. A card table chair, an end table with a candlestick lamp, a single bed, and a narrow chest of drawers. In the back of the room a window looked onto a brick wall which was almost within arm's reach. The pull-down window shade was brittle and torn. I pulled it down a little but slowly and carefully.

I took off my clothes and lay down on the bed. It squeaked under my weight and the mattress sagged. I looked around. The room itself was small. The gray plywood walls didn't go all the way to the ceiling. They were more like high partitions. When other roomers came in, it was a problem. One of them smoked and the stink rose up and over the wall into my room. When other men came in, I could hear them snoring and rolling around in their beds. The smoker was the worst. He was bouncing up and down on his cot jacking off and the springs of his bed squeaked and cracked, and, worse, his voice squeaked and cracked, and he moaned and spat as he came. Then he went silent. It would have been funny, but I was so tired that I fell asleep. What can you expect in a four-buck-a-night flop house? I chalked it up as part of my Alaskan experience.

The next morning Bob Larsen was working behind the front desk at the Anchorage Westward. I told him why I was in town, about the upcoming hunt in the Alaska Range and that I had been hired by Hal Waugh. He knew about Hal. He had a good reputation. He was said to be the best big game outfitter in Alaska. When I mentioned the mix-up in plane schedules, he smiled and invited me to stay with him and Carol. He had a job for me if I wanted it. For next two days, I painted their wrap-around porch and railing in exchange for room and board. The time went quickly and it was good to be in a home with people I knew.

In town, I discovered the Hofbrauhaus, a classy lounge on Third Street. It had an upright piano near the front window. There was no one playing so I went over and fiddled around on it. I played my jazzy version of the "Moonlight Sonata" and I guess someone at the bar liked it, because the waitress brought me a free beer.

On my last evening, Carol Larsen invited Emma Johns, an Eskimo woman, over for supper. Emma turned out to be the mother of a former student of mine. After supper, we went into town to watch Eskimo folk dancing and singing in a school gym. The loud deep slow beat of the native drum went to my heart.

14: Post Lake: The Hunt Begins

August 19, 1961. Day 1

On Saturday morning, Carol Larsen drove me to Lake Hood, the base for float plane contractors. Small hangers edged the lake. Waiting at the end of a ten-foot-wide pier was a white amphibious Cessna with Air-Sea Motives painted on its side.

A young man with a military haircut was standing by the plane. He introduced himself as Clark Engle. He had just gotten out of the navy and Hal had hired him up from Kodiak to be a guide. You could tell by his grin that he was ready to work and have a good time.

The pilot, Warren Wright, had loaded the Cessna's cargo hold before I arrived. "Are you Rudy?" he asked as I walked over with my gear.

"Yes," I said, and he took my duffle bag and backpack and tossed them in the plane.

"You're the last one. You and Engle can get in and we'll get going," he said. Sitting behind us in the plane were Jerry and Phyllis Sherman, a couple in their mid-thirties from Minneapolis.

The pilot revved the engine, the propeller blades turned over, and off we went. The pontoons under us skimmed and skipped across the water as we picked up speed. The Cessna lifted off and we settled in for a smooth but noisy ride, heading north-northwest towards Mount McKinley, towards Denali. We could see the huge mountain in the distance in the clear and cloudless day. Pilot Wright banked left leaving the Anchorage skyline behind and we were cruising above endless miles of tundra, lakes, and rivers.

We had flown about forty-five minutes when the pilot banked right and pointed down below.

"Folks," he said into the microphone strapped to the side of his head. "Look down below, to the left at about 10 o'clock."

I looked down to the ground. A cow moose and her calf were feeding on muskeg. Clark, sitting on my right, looked over and grinned with core-deep happiness.

Behind me, even in the close quarters of the plane, Jerry maneuvered a large camera out of his backpack and leaned over my shoulder to get a shot of the moose. He had a high-power telephoto lens. With my little camera, the moose would have looked like rice grains on a salad. I didn't even try. The pilot tried to keep the plane steady for Jerry but by the time he got his camera focused and his light meter adjusted, we were miles away. The plane circled around but the moose were gone. Jerry leaned back in his seat but kept his camera ready on his lap just in case.

"How far down is that tundra?" Phyllis asked the pilot. Her forehead was pressed against the window.

"Actually, that's not tundra," he said. "A lot of people think it is, but really it's taiga. Tundra is treeless with ground that's frozen most of the year with permafrost. There's a lot of tundra north of Denali, higher up in the Interior and on up to the Arctic. But this land below us is called taiga. The difference is the presence of trees." Phyllis nodded. I was glad she asked her question. The word taiga was new to me. Everyone I'd talked to so far had used the word tundra. The students at the university and the guys on the railroad called it tundra. Maybe it was a generic term of open land in Alaska. I decided to keep calling it tundra.

We banked left to get back on course and leveled out. We flew low over meandering waterways: a wide river, dozens of crooked wandering streams that sparkled in the sunlight. We were low enough to see swirling currents flowing around long thin slivers of mid-stream sandy islands carved out by the rushing water. From my angle, it looked like the whole world was flowing downhill.

We flew on, skimming low to look for animals and suddenly raising high to clear the peaks of mountains. It was all close and new and beautiful. We were flying over the great Alaskan Range, the vast string of mountains with their long patches of lichen, gray shale slopes, and vertical cliffs.

"Post Lake ahead," the pilot announced. We all looked forward over the nose of the plane. Directly ahead was a small circular lake, blue-black and welcoming. I felt like I was coming home, that I was in the right place at the right time.

"Okay, we're going in," he said. "Make yourselves secure," and we began our descent. I felt a shift in the engine as we glided towards the lake.

It was a perfect landing. The pontoons skimmed the surface of the water and we settled down, slowed, and taxied toward a dock. It was 2:00 p.m.

Hal Waugh and two other guys were on the dock to help secure the plane. I saw a yellow raft tied to one of the pilings.

Clark was first off. I followed. Behind me came Phyllis and Jerry. The pilot jumped out last, opened the cargo doors and handed out our gear. Hal Waugh came over to greet us.

"Welcome to base camp," he said and stuck out a hand. Hal included me in his greeting. This was the first time we had met.

Then Hal, Clark, and I unloaded supplies: loaves of bread, cartons of eggs, cans of coffee, slabs of bacon, sacks of beans, butter, rock salt, coils of rope, a box of hooks, and ammunition.

Standing by the plane, the pilot was talking on his two-way radio to someone back in Anchorage. He said something about another round trip and climbed back into the cockpit. I helped untie the plane, the pilot started the engine. I watched the little plane roar away over the still water, build up speed, and lift off. A minute later, the whine of its engine passed over the top of the mountain and the sky went silent.

Hal took Jerry and Phyllis over to their personal tent. It had a private outhouse next to it. Clark and I tagged along and waited for them to store their gear, then Hal took all of us on a tour of the campsite.

Base camp was about the size of a football field. On the north side was Post Lake, a small oval body of clear and quiet water about quarter a mile across. To the south and west was tundra with sparsely scattered low bushes and an endless network of muskeg growing out of a water-filled swamp that ended at the foothills of the line of mountains. On our east, the ground rose in a series of low wide mounds. About four hundred yards away, a clump of leafy birch trees rose up. The earth looked dry on the east side of camp, and I could make out a path worn into the waist-high brush.

Across the compound from the Sherman's tent was the cook tent where the food was prepared and where we ate at two wooden picnic tables. Inside was a wood burning stove, a metal slop sink, and shelves made of wooden boards to store the plates, mugs, and silverware. Next to a wall behind one of the long table benches was an army cot.

Hal's private tent was behind the cook tent. Off to the left was a four-man tent for Clark and me and Larry Keeler — Hal called it the Bull Tent — and a six-man tent for the senior guides. The largest tent in camp was a 15x20-foot tent for the paying clients, the hunters. This was the only one with a canvas floor and was furthest from the edge of the lake. The outhouse for the male workers and hunters was between the guide tents and the client tent.

The only other structures in the compound were two enclosed log caches for food and supplies. Each one was raised twelve feet in the air on support poles eight inches in diameter with strips of sheet metal wrapped around them from the ground up to keep bears, wolverines, and other hungry animals from climbing up. A wooden ladder was tied to the top of each cache by a rope and leaned back and away from it, again to foil climbing animals. A tall free-standing bleed rack used to drain the blood from fresh animal meat stood behind the Bull Tent.

Clark and I didn't stay long in base camp. As soon as we crawled out of our tent after stowing our personal gear, Hal had an assignment for us.

"Clark, Rudy," Hal said, "I need you to take some equipment and supplies up to a spike camp, set up tents, make a fire pit, and cut some firewood. Store these boxes of food in the cache there and come on back for supper." He pointed to four small boxes of supplies which had come on our plane. "We'll cook supper for you when you get back."

"Where's the spike camp?" I asked. Hal pointed towards a mountain range.

"At the base of that third mountain," he said. I looked at the line of mountains stretching as far as the eye could see and the immense tundra between our camp and the foothills. The grass on the tundra was tall and turning gold. It was beautiful.

"So, how far is it to the spike camp?" I asked, staring at the panorama before us.

"About three miles," said Hal. "Clark, take your rifle. We'll keep you in our scopes as you go." I had seen military binoculars mounted on a tripod at the far edge of camp and now I knew why. If we got into trouble, they'd see it and come out to help us get back.

We tied a four-man tent to my backboard kidney buster. On top of that we attached a duffle filled with food and camping equipment. Clark's load included two smaller tents, binoculars and more food and tools to set the tent up and cut wood. He also took several canteens of drinkable water to leave at the site. From my experience on the railroad, I had learned the importance of mosquito repellent. I had a bottle of it in a pocket of my hunting jacket along with a waterproof matchbox and a flint just in case we needed fire. Clark had his .308.

We left camp mid-afternoon and started walking in a direct line for the foothills. Clark had just come out of the Navy and had never walked across rough tundra like this, nor had I although I had seen it close-up on the railroad. The predictable clouds of mosquitoes had kept us close to camp.

The grass we had admired from the plane wasn't growing out of solid ground. It was growing out of clumps of muskeg, raised mounds of soggy earth covered with spongy moss sitting in six to ten-inch-deep stagnant water. We had to wobble and hop from one clump to another to avoid stepping in water over our boot tops. It was slow going and the thought of walking through this stuff for a mile or more before we reached the shale base of the foothills was daunting. I would like to say that we were too focused to think about it, but that would be a lie. Clark cursed every wobbly step. I just silently tried to keep my balance.

I thought of Hal and the others back in base camp possibly watching us lumber forward like bow-legged circus clowns. If they were watching, they were probably laughing. And the thought of them laughing made me smile and then I chuckled out loud.

"Rudy, what the hell are you laughing at?" Clark growled over his shoulder.

"Just the fact that we're stepping around on this crazy muskeg like two cats on a hot tin roof," I said. He didn't get the Tennessee Williams allusion, so I followed him in silence till we stepped onto dry land. It was important that we not twist or sprain our ankles. This was tough walking.

When we finally got to solid ground, we dropped our packs to rest. I looked back towards base camp. It was out of sight even though we were on a rise. We both took a swig of water from our canteens and ate a couple of candy bars Hal had given us. It was ironic that I had a Clark bar, but Clark had a Milky Way.

Clark pulled out a rough, hand-drawn map Hal had given him showing the spot where we were to set up the spike camp. The trek across the shale and stony edge of the range was easier than crossing the muskeg and, although it was three mountains over, it only took us an hour to get to it.

We found the cache. It hadn't been used in a while, but it was in good shape. We dropped our gear, set up the tents, then stashed the food up in the cache and pulled the ladder back to lean it away from it. Clark took the hand axe and headed toward some trees. The last of Hal's hunters to use this site had left some rocks from a fire pit scattered around, but I thought we could use a few more so I went searching in the other direction. I could hear Clark chopping wood behind me out of sight.

Finally alone, I sat down for a minute to feel the mountain. The sun was high above the western peaks. But for the chopping, the world was silent. Twenty yards from me was a patch of blueberries. I picked a handful. They tasted sweet and fresh. I felt a rush of contentment as the sugary pulp burst open in my mouth. I was alone surrounded by pure beauty, and I thought, "No man since the beginning of time has ever stood where I am standing now."

Chop, chop, chop. Clark's axe sounded far away.

I saw six or seven brick-sized rocks below the blueberry patch, and I side-stepped down the shale slope to get them. The shale was loose. I had to be careful not to slip and fall, but I got the rocks and put them in my backpack.

As I rounded the curve of the mountain towards the camp site, I looked up in the direction Clark had gone. There was no chopping. Near the top of the next mountain over, in full view, were four snow white Dall sheep, three ewes standing still as statues, glowing in the sun, and on a ledge above them a large majestic ram, his curled horns powerful and menacing. I stood still and stared at them in silence. I didn't want to spook them.

Clark came down around the bend quietly with wood in his arms. I pointed up.

"I saw," he said quietly. "It will be a good hunt tomorrow. They're up wind."

As we made our way back to base camp, we heard the whine of a plane. It was the Cessna from Air-Sea Motives returning from Anchorage. We watched it splash down and taxi to the dock. Five people got out. A few minutes later, it took off and headed back to Anchorage. The hunting party from Michigan had arrived.

It took us less than three hours to get back to camp. It was easier since our backpacks were empty. High stepping from muskeg clump to muskeg clump still wasn't easy, but it was less dangerous than before, although I did slip off once and wound up knee-deep in cold water.

When we got to camp, the hunters from Michigan were sitting in front of their tent in canvas folding chairs. As Clark and I approached, they waved us over.

"Hi, you must be Rudy and Clark," said one of the men. "Hal said you were setting up a spike camp for us tomorrow. I'm Erwin. This is Howard and Leo." We shook hands and Erwin settled back in his chair. Within seconds, he was totally focused and absorbed bent over a stick of wood, whittling its end to a sharp point with his hunting knife. Leo and Howard had questions about the area and Clark described the terrain we had just crossed and told them about the sheep on the mountain.

Howard and Leo walked with us to the cook tent. Inside was Hal, Chuck Keim, and Fred Boyle, the ski coach from the university who was hired as a guide and cook. Larry Keeler was there, too. Larry was a spotter. Hal bragged that Larry had telescopic vision and could spot animal movement on the tundra a mile away. By its movement, he could tell what kind of animal it was, a moose or sheep or caribou or wolf, a black bear, or a grizzly.

At supper, Erwin told us that he was the son of Charles Erwin Wilson, the United States Secretary of Defense under President Eisenhower, and that Leo and Howard owned a men's clothing store in Birmingham, Michigan. I told them my father had a men's clothing store in Toledo. Small world.

Around 10:30 p.m., everyone disappeared into their tents, and I climbed exhausted into my mummy bag. Day one of this hunting trip was over and we had done a lot.

August 20, 1961. Day 2

Fred Boyle woke us around 6:00 a.m., then made the rounds to get everyone up. Hal wanted to get an early start since the animals would be up and grazing. By 6:30 everyone was huddled in the cook tent for breakfast. Fred had made a pile of bologna sandwiches the evening before. We each grabbed a couple as well as an apple from a basket on the table for lunch on the trail.

Hal gathered the hunters and guides in front of the tent. "It's best to go in pairs and keep separated," he said. "If you hunt as a bunch, the animals will see you or hear you or smell you. If you hunt in pairs, you'll have a better chance to make a kill."

I saw Erwin move away impatiently. Both he and Leo were experienced hunters. Leo told me the two of them had hunted in Alaska before, but after Hal's directions, Erwin was silent. Howard was new to this and Erwin probably understood that Hal's comments were meant for him. Chuck had told me that one of the reasons Hal was respected as a big game outfitter was that he was also a teacher. Many of his clients were inexperienced and needed a little perspective on the dangers as well as the methods of an Alaskan hunt.

"Clark, go with Leo. Fred, you go with Erwin, and Chuck can follow and split off with Howard," Hal said.

A new guide, Dick Pometer, showed up in base camp that morning. I had no idea where he came from or how he got there. Hal assigned him to the Shermans. Phyllis had a high-end Nikon camera hanging around her neck. She had said yesterday that she was interested in taking pictures for a gallery back in Minneapolis. She and Jerry both carried rifles. Pometer stood by until they were ready with their backpacks and then led them onto the tundra in the direction of a stand of trees on a line running parallel to the mountains away from where the other teams were headed.

Each group left the camp dressed in full rain gear. It wasn't raining, but the clouds were gathering over the mountains and Hal said, "Better safe than sorry. Especially if something happens and everybody doesn't get back to base camp." If there was danger out there, he wasn't making a big deal about it, but I knew accidents could happen, especially if you're crawling around on steep slippery shale.

Hal and Larry Keeler didn't take any clients. Hal said he and Larry were rowing the raft across Post Lake and over to the Kuskokwim River to check the southern spike camp and look for game.

"What about me?" I asked.

"You stay here to guard the tents, Rudy. Keep away bears or wolves if they show up. I left a loaded .308 in the cook tent for you. Wash the breakfast dishes, chop some wood for the stove and keep it stoked, and get a campfire started when the first group gets back." He pointed to the Michigan group's tent, "If you spot any game, like a moose or caribou, don't go after it. You're a packer, not a hunter."

The hunting parties walked out into the muskeg headed towards the mountains where Clark and I had gone yesterday. Hal and Larry watched them leave then loaded their gear and weapons into the raft. Larry rowed and Hal sat low in the back. Twenty minutes later, they tied up to a dead tree on the far side and I watched them disappear into the birches at the base of a mountain. I was alone in camp in the midst of beauty and perfect silence.

I walked past the Sherman's tent and their private privy, and over to the edge of the lake. The water was clear and rippled in the steady breeze. The cloudy sky made the water dark. I leaned over and peered into it thinking that maybe there would be fish, but I saw none.

I had no idea how long the hunting parties would be gone. I knew how long it had taken Clark and me to reach the base of the mountains to the north, but we'd been carrying heavy packs.

I looked back to the tundra. There were Clark and Leo, keeping low but moving steadily. The other pairs kept about a football field's length apart. Then Fred and Erwin split off to the right, away from the others. Erwin was leading with a head-down sense of urgency. I went into the cook tent to find the axe and check out the rifle Hal had left for me. The stove was still warm, and I tossed in a few small logs.

The stand of trees where Pometer had led Phyllis and Jerry looked like a good place to get wood so I grabbed the gun, a handful of shells, the axe, and an empty packboard from the cook tent and headed out.

The most notable thing about the land between camp and the stand of trees was that there was almost no muskeg. The land rose a little and was drier. It was easy walking. I saw some narrow animal paths in the high grass, so I knew there was game of some sort in the area. I noticed little prints in the dirt which seemed to be too small for a moose. I stopped and looked around. I wished I had brought my binoculars.

When I got to the trees, I was in a shallow wood of white birch. Birch was soft and would be easy cutting. But there was something in the air. Something moved. It got my attention. I stood still, breathing in and out with slow deliberate quiet. I froze and waited like a stone for several minutes, then came a rustling in the brush. And suddenly I saw them, a dozen ptarmigans hiding in the shadows. They looked like little partridges.

They moved an inch and froze, moved an inch and froze, almost invisible in the shady woods. Other than the intermittent off-on rustling of grass or leaves, they moved in silence. Until I lifted my axe. They burst up from all sides in a sudden panicked flurry of wings. Then they were gone. Maybe I'd come back with my .22 and shoot a few for supper. I'd ask Hal about it.

The woods were beautiful and again I felt the deep private happiness of being alone in the Alaskan wild. There were so many places you could be alone.

I leaned my rifle against a tree. For next hour, I chopped down and trimmed three or four small trees, cut them into two-foot logs, tied them to the packboard and walked back to camp. It took several trips, but I stacked most of the wood by the fire pit near the center of camp and took an armful into the cook tent for the stove. There were still hot embers in it, so I got the fire going, heated some water, and washed the breakfast dishes. By this time, my watch said it was just past 1 o'clock, and so I grabbed a bologna sandwich, an apple, and my canteen and sat on the dock to eat lunch.

At 5 o'clock, Leo and Clark returned with nothing. At 5 o'clock, Fred and Erwin returned with nothing, but Erwin's left hand and arm were badly swollen from a bee sting, his second one in two days. Yesterday his right hand had gotten bitten when he went exploring alone after supper and it puffed. Because of the pain, he couldn't stay still. He paced back and forth in front of his tent, then to the edge of camp, back to the tent, back and forth like an angry tiger trapped in a cage.

Half an hour later, Chuck and Howard Fitzgerald walked into camp. Howard had seen a bull moose with a huge rack.

"It was big enough to get into the Boone and Crockett record book," he said. He was happy and excited even though he hadn't shot it.

Pometer's group got back soon after. Phyllis and Jerry disappeared into their tent.

"Look over there," I pointed. Hal and Larry were rowing back across the lake.

As soon as Howard returned, Erwin stopped pacing and got a bottle of Dewar's scotch from his backpack in the Michiganders' tent. Hal went for plastic cups and Erwin poured us all a shot. Pometer went over to Phyllis and Jerry's tent to ask them to join us. It was the first time I had tasted scotch. It was good. Erwin poured us all another. After a third shot, he started to calm down and put the bottle away. My guess was the booze was killing the pain in his hand. I know I wasn't feeling any.

Fred and Pometer went to get dinner ready and around 8:00 p.m. we got the call to gather in the cook tent. There wasn't enough room at the table for everyone, so Clark and I sat on the army cot. By the time dinner was over and the dishes washed, it was after 10:00 p.m. and we were ready to sack out.

August 21, 1961. Day 3

Instead of getting us up at 5:00 a.m. as planned, Fred got us up at 6:00. Erwin had had a bad night with his swollen hand and arm and said he couldn't sleep because of Leo's snoring.

At 8:00, all of us, except Erwin, crossed a small creek that separated camp from the tundra to "glass" the mountains. Two mountains over, we spotted two rams. With Hal's 20X power scope, we could almost see the ridges in the curls of their horns!

Erwin was ready to go around 9 o'clock. Hal handed me a list of projects and told me to stay in camp again to keep things safe. When the hunters left, Hal and Larry went scouting and I settled down to my chores. I put up boot racks for each tent, cleared away tree stumps, cut down a couple more trees for firewood, and got a tent out of the cache. I tried to set it up, but it was a two-man job.

When my chores were finished, I got to thinking about those ptarmigans. I took my single-shot .22 rifle and walked silently back to the stand of trees. This time I would be ready. I crept slowly into the underbrush and waited.

Then came the movement. A quick busy rustle in the grass, then silence. I moved my gun around and pulled open the chamber for a bullet and snapped it shut. The startled ptarmigans flew up into the tops of the trees. I shot at one as it rose, and it dropped like a stone. I waited and they returned as I knew they would. I shot again and again they flew up in panic. I aimed and pulled the trigger and another one fell. I had to reload after every pull, the birds always flew away in panic, but minutes later they came back. I brought six birds back to camp. If the hunters returned empty-handed, we could eat my birds. Otherwise, we could cook them for breakfast.

When it started to get dusky, I lit a lantern for the hunters and put it out by the fire pit to help guide them back. I thought some of them might go to the spike camp Clark and I had set up, but by 9:00 p.m., all the groups had returned. Erwin had shot a Dall ram with thirty-six-inch horns and a thirty-inch base. He carried the cape and rack back to camp himself—"hunter's pride," he called it—while Clark packed the gutted carcass, plus his daypack and weapon. We sat around the campfire and roasted the sheep's liver over the fire.

After dinner, Erwin sharpened his hunting knife on a whetstone and started to scrape the fatty tissue and muscle from inside his sheep skin. Chuck hung the meaty carcass on the drying rack to let the blood drain. Then he and I covered it with sheets of plastic to keep off the black flies. The smell of raw meat attracted thousands of flies just like those bloodthirsty mosquitoes on the railroad. Hal brought over a bag of salt to rub into the skin to preserve it. Erwin rubbed it in, then rolled up the hide in plastic sheeting, again to keep the flies away. The last thing he wanted was a trophy crawling with maggots, and it wouldn't take long for that to happen out here.

We passed around Erwin's bottle of scotch and drank to the spirit of the ram and to Erwin's success. His arm wasn't bothering him anymore. We all went to bed a little after midnight and let the campfire burn itself out.

August 22, 1961. Day 4

The next day, Fred cooked up the sheep's liver and coffee for breakfast, then Leo, Clark, and I went out to scout. After hours of stalking, we spotted a ram with three ewes and, an hour later, a huge bull moose. We got back to base camp around 6:00 p.m. and took hot showers.

The shower was a ten-gallon canvas bag with a shower head attached to the bottom. The bag hung from a tree limb about eight feet off the ground with a few wooden boards underneath to stand on. We'd heat up a couple of gallons of water over the campfire and, when the water was hot, we'd pour it in the bag, hoist it up, strip down, pull a rope attached to the showerhead, get wet, soap up, pull rope, rinse off, grab a towel and the next guy would do the same. It was a little awkward with Phyllis in camp, but she didn't seem to mind. Her husband Jerry thought it was funny. I was hoping Phyllis would try it, but she didn't.

We had a few more scotches from Erwin's stash and around midnight we all turned in.

August 23, 1961. Day 5

In the morning, Leo, Clark and I packed enough gear on our backs to spend the night in the mountains. At last I was doing what I was hired for. When we got to the camp we had set up on day one, it was around 1 o'clock. Leo and Clark took off for the top of the mountains to hunt for sheep. I, being the packer, stayed in camp to set up the tent, gather wood, and pick blueberries for supper.

I took the coffee pot to gather berries. The sun was overhead, and the sky was streaked with wispy clouds. It was a beautiful day and I took my time. Pick a berry, eat a berry, sit on a rock, breathe deep the air, silence above, silence below, face into the sun and close my eyes. It was heaven. When the pot was full, I went back to camp, then got more wood and started a fire.

"It was fantastic," Leo said with a grin when he and Clark came back. "We spotted two rams with a dozen ewes.

Clark went over to the campfire and pulled dinner fixings out of his pack: sheep steaks and a can of stewed tomatoes. I set out my pot of berries. We sat cross-legged by the heat of the crackling fire, ate supper, and shared stories. I asked Clark about his adventures in the Navy, but he didn't have much to say about that and changed the subject. He talked more about hunting bears on Kodiak and fishing for halibut off the coast. Then he asked me why I had come up to Alaska. I told him my story of the crazy photo in the *Time* magazine, about some of the people I had met at the University of Alaska, how Chuck Keim had hooked me up with Hal, and my short stint on the railroad.

"Great stories," Leo said.

"What drew you to Alaska, Leo?" I asked.

"Me? I came up to get some trophies to hang up in my store. I have an empty wall opposite a big picture window ready for some new heads. I already have a dozen Erwin brought back from Africa. He's a good hunter. We'll get some big ones here."

During the night, it rained. I was cold even in my mummy bag. It was a bad night. A bunch of stones under the tent floor were scattered beneath my sleeping bag and, in shifting around to avoid them during the night, I had wriggled my way to the front of the tent. In the morning when I woke up, I was halfway out.

August 24, 1961. Day 6

After breakfast, Clark asked me to hike back to base camp and bring back more food. Since I had an empty backpack, it only took me two hours to get there.

No one was in camp when I arrived. They were all out in their separate hunting parties. I spent the next two hours rounding up food. I took a loaf of bread and some apples from the cook tent, a fresh canteen of water, a few potatoes, and after I did a fast sharpening of my hunting knife, cut off a healthy chunk of meat from the hind quarter of the hanging sheep.

On the return hike, once out of the muskeg, instead of following cut trails, I made a beeline up the mountain. It took me about two and a half hours to get back to the spike camp. Leo and Clark were away so I dug the annoying stones out from under the floor of the tent, cut more wood, consolidated our trash, and got things in order. The guys returned empty-handed again, but Leo was enjoying the hunt.

"These mountains are fantastic," he said.

"Yes, they are," I said.

Clark fried up the meat and potatoes I had brought back.

Our spike camp was a good four thousand feet above sea level and the sun was hidden by clouds. It was getting dark earlier and the air was damp and chilly. We stood around our campfire talking about the next day's plans. Around 8:45, we hit the sack.

"No rocks tonight," I thought.

August 25, 1961. Day 7

It rained all that night and morning. The mountain shale was too slippery for safe footing. It was too wet to go after the sheep. Looking across the way, we could see new snow on opposite peaks. "That's 'termination dust'," Clark said. "When summer tourists see snow like that, they skedaddle home to the Lower 48."

As we ate breakfast, our breaths came out in thin white puffs. It was 10 o'clock by the time we broke camp to hike back to Post Lake.

When we arrived, Hal was there. Something was wrong with his foot. It had swollen so badly that he could barely walk. We could tell by his limp over the uneven ground that he was hurting. But he never complained. Erwin and Fred got back around quarter after five. At dinner, we discussed the barren game situation. Erwin was getting impatient.

The clouds had disappeared, and the moon was almost full and blazing white in the star-filled sky. The temperature was around 40 degrees when Erwin left the cook tent to take a shower. Fifteen minutes later he returned with a craving for Dewars.

Jerry and Phyllis didn't mingle much with the Michigan group except for dinners in the cook tent. But when she heard there was a card game going on, Phyllis wanted to play. She said she liked to play Canasta, a four-person game.

"That's one of my favorites," I said. "When I was a kid, we used to play that on our back porch in summer."

"Why don't you play with us, Rudy? Here, sit next to me." She patted the bench next to her. I scooted up and sat close on the picnic bench as she shuffled and dealt the cards.

Hal sat behind me on the army cot drinking a beer. All that rich sheep meat I'd been eating came to a head and suddenly I farted, a deep, long, ass-blasting fart that made everyone look up. Phyllis almost fell off the bench laughing. Hal, however, was not laughing.

"RUDY!" he gasped loudly. "Jesus! WHAT DID YOU DO?"

I was embarrassed. I turned red, excused myself, and left. Hal and Chuck Keim opened both ends of the cook tent to let in the fresh air.

August 26-29, 1961. Days 8-11

Hal wanted me to go with Clark and Leo up the mountains again after sheep. This time we would be gone two or three days. We spent the evening getting our tent, gear, and food supplies ready, and left after breakfast the next morning.

Once we got to the mountain's base and the ground began to steepen, we found a stony creek bed that zigzagged up the slope. At the top, we scoped out the opposite hillsides, saw nothing, and retreated a few hundred feet to a flat area to set up camp. Clark started a small warming campfire, but we didn't want to cook on it. Here the smell of cooking food could attract bears and scare away sheep downwind. We kept silent also. If we needed to communicate, we whispered or signaled. We turned in to get an early start.

We got up in the dark. A pre-dawn start would give us a better chance to find rams. After a cold breakfast, we set out. Clark said he thought the sheep would still be close.

We moved single file up the creek bed, Clark in the lead. It had rained again in the night. The creek bed was slippery and the small rocks in it made for dangerous and unsure footing. We went slowly and deliberately because we didn't want to make any sounds to spook the animals.

Leo was watching his feet so he wouldn't stumble, but when he turned a bend and looked up something caught his eye. He pointed up the mountain. Two mature rams were silhouetted in the early dawn, down-wind from us, unaware that we were there. We backed out of sight around a pile of boulders. Clark put his fingers up and signaled to slip out of our packs so we'd be free to move fast. Clark and Leo got out their binoculars and studied the sheep for several minutes. I marveled at their patience. I would have checked them out for thirty seconds and gone after them.

The sun was coming up over the mountain. It was bad for shooting since we'd be facing into it. Clark motioned for us to go back down to the creek bed and creep around the curve of mountain to get a better angle.

"Three of us make too much noise," Clark whispered. "Rudy, you stay back. When you hear a shot, then come up."

I hunkered down in a crevice out of sight. As soon as Clark and Leo rounded the next curve, it was as silent as death. The sun had fully risen above the top of the mountain and glinted off the stark gray, wet shale.

The minutes seemed like hours. I started to doze off when the sharp crack of a rifle snapped me to my feet. I looked up and saw Leo with his rifle in hand, sweeping it to the right. Then he disappeared. I started running up the slope, fighting the slippery shale and noisy loose rocks all the way. I grabbed at pieces of brush when I could, but when I got to the place where Leo's shell casing was laying, he was gone. I climbed up the slope to get a downward view, but neither Leo nor Clark was in sight. I couldn't hear a sound. I went back down to the packs and waited.

"Ruuudddy."

Leo was looking down at me from the top of a ridge. I waved. "Rudy, bring my cap and scope. I left them where I took my shot."

"Okay," I called back. "Did you get one?"

"Yeah, a beauty!"

I grabbed all three packs and found Leo's cap and binoculars. When I got to the others, a ram lay on the ground already half gutted. Leo was bent over rolling up the cape and horns to pack out. Clark cut out the sheep's heart and liver and bagged them. The rest of the sheep meat, minus the lungs and guts, we backpacked to the spike camp. The lungs and guts we left for the wolves or bears or birds, whoever got there first.

It got cold fast as the sun passed beyond the mountain tops. Shadows fell quickly. We were in our sleeping bags by 7:30 p.m.

In the morning, we tied our gear and sheep parts to our pack-boards and started the hike to base camp. My pack weighed at least seventy pounds and trekking up and over the slippery mountains and back through the muskeg was hard and tricky.

In the distance, I heard the whine of a small plane and saw a Widgeon glide down and circle Post Lake. It skimmed the water near the dock, slowed, and stopped, but only for a few minutes, then pulled away, picked up speed, rose, and headed back to Anchorage. "What was that about?" I wondered.

When we got to base camp, Hal saw us coming in with the sheep and grinned. Clark's success was his success. A good trophy made a happy client. Leo's ram measured a curl and a half, a great trophy for his store.

Soon after we got back, Erwin, Dick Pometer, and Fred marched into camp with a grizzly pelt.

"Erwin," smiled Hal. "It came."

"Where is it?" asked Erwin.

"In your tent. Nothing broke."

"What came?" I asked.

Erwin went into his tent and came back with a virgin bottle of scotch whiskey.

"Air Sea Motifs brought us a new case of Dewars," he smiled. "Thank god for two-way radio."

Forty-five minutes later, Larry Keeler, Chuck Keim, and a grinning Howard Fitzgerald came in from a different direction carrying two rams' horns and the pelt of a black bear. Hal was almost dancing with excitement even with his bad ankle. This was what his clients had paid their big bucks for. He was happy.

While we were gone, Jerry and Phyllis had caught a dozen graylings in the lake and Hal, himself, fried them up for dinner. I made a batch of butterscotch pudding for dessert. Fish and pudding and a tumbler of scotch. Even Phyllis had a glass. A great meal after a great hunt.

When all the meat from the animals was hanging on the bleed racks and covered with plastic, everyone turned in. It was good day.

Aug. 30-31, 1961. Days 12-13

Everyone was up and in the cook tent for breakfast at 7 o'clock. Hal, Larry, Clark, and I stayed in camp. I spent most of the morning washing dishes and later went down to the edge of the lake to update my hunting journal and write a letter to my folks. The air was cool and the sky was clear. The mountains on the far side of the lake were glowing with color. The trees near their bottoms were turning red and gold and beautifully outlined and framed wide areas of dark gray shale. I got out my camera, set up my tripod, and took some pictures.

The rest of the day, I stayed in camp to chop wood. Larry came over to help. Somewhere I had heard that a karate move could be intensified if you used an explosive sound with it, so I tried it. I lifted my axe and came down with power, swift and hard on the end of a log.

"Ky-ii," I yelled. Larry thought it was funny and laughed. The log exploded. I did it again, "Ky-ii." The axe slammed down. The wood split neatly apart. Again. "Ky-ii" and again. It was true. Ky-ii worked.

It tightened my abdominal muscles as I came down with the axe and doubled my power. Chop. "Ky-ii." Chop. "Ky-ii."

"Rudy!" I looked up. It was Chuck Keim. He had just come back into camp and sounded angry. "Why are you yelling my name every time to slam down on the wood?" he asked with a frown. "Is that supposed to be me?"

I was surprised. "I wasn't saying your name," I said. "Why would I do that? It's a karate sound I learned to give me power."

Why would he think I wanted to hurt him, or insult him? He was the man who got me this job. He was my friend and mentor at the university. I'm not sure why he thought I was visualizing his head as I came down on a log of wood with an axe, but I guess he did. He turned away angrily and went back to his tent.

Chuck was in a better mood by suppertime. He and Fred Boyle were leaving in the morning. It was the end of August and they had to get back to their university jobs. But the plane which was scheduled to arrive around 9 o'clock didn't come. Hal radioed the dispatcher at Lake Hood. Anchorage was weathered in.

An hour later, Clark, Leo, and I left for spike camp number two. When we got there, Clark told me Hal wanted me to pack out a hide and skull from a brown bear that was shot the day before, along with some canned food from the cache, and bring them back to base camp. The first part of the walk back was easy, but the putrid bloody hide on my packboard stunk like rotten, week-old garbage.

While I was hiking back to base camp with my stinky load, Erwin and Howard had bagged a young caribou and buried its remains on a mountain. The next morning, the first day of September, Larry Keeler and I went in search of the carcass. Erwin got out his binoculars, pointed to a vague spot a mile away, and gave us directions.

When Larry and I got to the mountain, we searched the area looking for the sign Erwin said he had left, some toilet paper on a forked stick on the top of a hill. The meat was supposed to be about a hundred yards beneath it. Larry and I didn't find the stick and after a while we started back. Given the fact that it rained in the mountains a lot, I thought using toilet paper as a marker was a dumb idea, but Erwin was the experienced world hunter, so neither of us said anything.

On the way in, we spotted a bull moose feeding in a creek bed about four hundred yards below us. Larry wanted to take some pictures, slipped off his pack, got out his camera, and started down the hill after it. While he was concentrating on that one, he didn't see a second moose coming up on us on the left.

"Larry!" I yelled. "Moose coming from the left!" I had my rifle loaded and ready if I had to use it. Luckily, when I called out, the moose swerved to the right and broke into a run, heading downhill. Larry didn't get his picture.

We came onto a long-abandoned camp which might not have been Hal's. If it wasn't his, it was illegal since Hal had sole hunting rights for the Post Lake region. We collected and packed out a cast iron fry pan, a rusty saw, an Army canteen, and a ball-peen hammer.

It was getting dark and we began to stumble around as we came down hill towards the tundra and the muskeg. Larry had a flashlight so at least we could see where to put our feet. He had hunted with Hal in this area a number of times and knew the terrain. Even so, by the time we got into camp, it was almost midnight.

The next day, my feet were blistered and painful and one of Larry's eyes was giving him trouble so we both stayed in camp. I chopped more wood, quietly this time, even though Chuck had taken Phyllis out to hunt. Still no word of a weather change in Anchorage. Larry helped Hal inventory and reorganize the cache to see how much coffee, sugar, salt, eggs, flour, bread, and cheese we had left.

Phyllis had shot and killed a ram and was excited and glowing. She had even helped Chuck hang the meat on the bleed rack. It was the first time we heard the chorus of wolves.

In the morning, Leo, Clark, Erwin, and I packed food up to the spike camp where we had left Howard. The guys said they didn't need me, so I left them for base camp with only my rifle. Near the bottom of the mountain, I saw a cow moose eating grass in a creek bed. She was out in the open. "What the hell," I thought. And I pulled a sneak on her just for fun. Legally I couldn't shoot her unless I was in mortal danger, and I wasn't. This was a pretend hunt.

My feet hurt but it was exciting anyway. I crept forward, hidden by the high weeds. I was back in the muskeg again but was careful not to make any noise to alarm her. I went low and slow. As I got closer, I could hear the crunch of creek bed stones and stopped. Then nothing. I heard nothing. I raised my head to take a peek. The moose was gone. How could something so large disappear so quietly?

I heard a wolf call coming from up the hill in the brush behind me. I stayed low just in case. Was I prey or was I a predator? After waiting a minute, I stood up to be visible and climbed back up to the path. I got back to base camp before dusk.

After supper, we made a blaze in the fire pit and Phyllis set to work happily scouring her sheep horn. Jerry came over with a cup of coffee and sat for a while, stared at the fire, then wandered off. I wondered if he even wanted to be here. His wife was having all the fun. It was none of my business, so I thought about other things. Clark stayed away from the group. He said he thought he was getting a cold.

Hal came over when the Michigan gang had finished their last scotch and went to bed. When it was only the two of us left by the fire

"You're doing a good job, Rudy," Hal said. "The wilderness agrees with you. I don't know what your plans are when our hunts are over, but on the way back to Fairbanks I'm going to Copper Center to check on my new boat and maybe do some hunting. Would you like to come along?"

Up to this time, I hadn't thought about what I would do when Post Lake was over. I had no plans. Having dropped out of the university, I wasn't even sure I would stay up north. But I liked Hal. I admired his reputation and his care for his clients. And I thought, "Okay. This is my life. Nothing is tangible, nothing is fixed. My life is evolving. Things will work out. This is Alaska, the last frontier."

"Yes," I said. "I would really like that. Thanks."

15: The Day the Mountains Moved

September 5, 1961. Day 18

The next morning, Hal called me over. "Rudy, I got a message from Anchorage that two clients have booked a two-week hunt here when this group leaves. I need you to hike out to south camp and bring back the canned food from the cache." We went to the table in the cook tent where he penciled out a rough map.

The south spike camp was on the far side of the south fork of the Kuskokwim River. This solo trip would take a full day. Most of my work had been in the other direction, into the mountains behind us. The only people out of base camp to wander south had been Hal and Larry when they had gone scouting weeks before. They hadn't seen much game in that area which was why most of the attention was directed to the north and east. Besides, south camp was in flat land and Erwin had been hot to get mountain dwelling Dall sheep.

After breakfast, I organized my kidney-buster packboard, checked its webbing and straps, and tied on an empty duffel bag.

"Rudy, take this with you in case you come across a bear," Hal said. He handed me his own .300 Weatherby Magnum. It had a beautiful walnut stock with detailed crosshatched etching. I loved it. When I held it in my hands, it felt like power, like safety. It chambered three rounds, one of which could knock over a bull moose. It made my own rifle feel like a popsicle stick. Even a 30.06 was puny by comparison. I made one last check of my gear: pack, gun, ammo, food, water, hunting knife, and I was ready.

Hal said that south camp was about four miles from base. The best way to get there was to walk around Post Lake and pick up the trail on the other side.

The trail was a narrow steady climb that wound through a dense thicket of evergreens and birch. The path I was on was made by animals, probably wolves and bears. I had to twist my body sideways in places to squeeze between close, low-growing branches. It was not an easy trail even travelling lightly. I wondered about my return trip carrying a heavy backpack bulging with supplies.

There was one spot where the undergrowth was such a thick tangle that it ripped the pack off my back and sent me sprawling. It

94

only happened once, but it made me realize that I was out here alone. If I broke a leg or got stuck and couldn't get back, I could be dead by morning.

At last, I emerged from the tree-line and found myself facing the wide Kuskokwim River. I had stepped out of a shadowy forest into a beautiful open landscape of river and rolling tundra with the high mountains of the Alaska Range to the north, beautiful and topped with fresh snow.

The section of the river in front of me was fast-moving and shallow with dozens of long, narrow, irregular, disconnected, sandbars which lay between me and the opposite shore. I looked up and down the river. I had to get across and I could see no place to do it. The river's rushing waters funneled noisily into narrow channels. White water splashed over the edges of the sandbars and no sandbar looked solid, dry, or safe.

All I could do was walk along the riverbank until I saw a reasonable fording place, so I followed the shoreline north. Ten minutes later, I came to a bend where the river widened and slowed. It looked a bit shallower here and I thought it might be possible to leap from sandbar to sandbar to get across.

I had a red bandana tied around my neck. I took it off and tied it to a bush that jutted out from the tree-line behind me. This would be my return marker. I tightened the straps of my packboard, took a running jump, and landed on the nearest sandbar. It was soggy but firm. I was feeling a little more confident. I got my bearings, watched the action of the oncoming current and the density of its waves, and leapt to the next sandbar. I could do this. Fifteen minutes later, I was on the other side.

The tundra before me was a rolling landscape with small bushes and scattered trees growing here and there. There weren't many landmarks except for bends in the river which were marked on Hal's map. I stayed by the river because the ground was level and it gave me a clear vision of the land. I stopped and looked around for bears. I saw none, but I had Hal's rifle ready just in case.

In the distance to my left, I spotted a cylindrical mound of dirt about six feet high. Hal had an arrow pointing to it on his map. I hiked over to the mound. South camp was just beyond it.

The cache at south camp looked like a miniature cabin on stilts. The wood sides made of peeled logs were smooth and bleached from the sun. Its thick support poles were protected by metal sheeting, like the ones at base camp, wrapped around and nailed down. The floor of the cache was at least fifteen feet off the ground. Attached by a rope to a hook under the edge of the roof was a ladder made of two twenty-foot narrow tree trunks with steps connected with nails and construction wire. The ladder, which leaned away from the cache at a forty-five-degree angle, was attached by a chain to a rock dragged up from the river. The chain kept the ladder from blowing back onto the cache in case of a strong wind.

I unchained the ladder and leaned it against the front of the storage cache. I released the deadbolt, pulled open the door and looked in. I couldn't believe it! It was packed full, from floor to roof. Stacks of canned beans, soups, and fruit and vegetables. I could never carry it all back to base camp in one trip. "Okay," I thought, "be realistic. I can only do what I can do. There is always tomorrow."

The opening to the cache was small, but I climbed in. There was just enough room inside to turn around. I grabbed what I could and tossed cans out the door one at a time. When I thought I had my limit, I got my butt out the door and climbed down. I packed the food in the duffel, tied it down on my packboard, and sat on a rock to eat some lunch.

I took a can of pineapple chunks and reached for my hunting knife to open it, but my sheath was empty. My knife was missing. I had lost it, probably when I was worming through the tangle of trees before I got to the river. Anyway, it was gone. But I did have a Swiss Army knife in my jacket packet. It had a can opener. After I had eaten, I rested a few minutes, looked around one last time, and started back. The pack I hoisted onto my shoulders was heavy. It must have weighed more than eighty pounds.

I retraced my steps to the edge of the river where I thought I had crossed, but the river had risen and had washed away my foot-prints in the sand. Nor did I see my bandana marker on the other side. I took off my pack and set it down to think.

Off to the right, four mountains with snow-capped peaks glistened in the sun. I stared at them rising silently into the sky. Minutes passed. I felt alone in time and space. I didn't want to move. I wanted to sit there, that silent beauty before me shimmering high above in the thin crystal air. Then something happened.

I saw and felt a sudden flash of light. The mountains shifted— *kathunk*—a fraction of an inch. What had just happened? It was as if something below the surface of the earth had suddenly jerked awake.

In that epoch moment, I had touched and seen the spiritual essence of Alaska. I had fallen in love with its soul.

What was that brilliant, microsecond, visible flicker of light? I had never been religious, but I felt that this was a profound spiritual moment. I, now and forever, would be a part of this wild land. I looked up. A golden eagle appeared from nowhere and circled above me. As I watched it, I remembered that I had miles to go before I could get back to base camp.

*   *   *

I shouldered my heavy load and started back to the edge of the river. The sun was getting low in the sky and shadows were growing below the outcroppings of the slopes.

The sandbars in front of me were not the same ones on which I had crossed over, but they looked reachable. However, now weighted down, I was anything but nimble.

On a soggy sandbar halfway across the river, under the heavy weight of my load, I stumbled over a small pile of rocks and landed sideways in the water. The rush of the current caught me and pushed me headfirst downstream. Another white frothing wave flipped me onto my back, and I found myself face-up with my load strapped under me. The power of the Kuskokwim pushed and sucked my body past one sandbar after another. Downstream fifty yards, my backpack got wedged in a dead tree sticking out from the shore. I struggled and pulled myself out.

I was soaked. The duffel bag strapped to my packboard was soaked. But through all of this, somehow, I had kept Hal's rifle dry. Somehow, I had kept it above water. But the beautiful fine cross hatching on the stock was gouged from scraping across a rock. The thought of Hal getting pissed and the uncertain hike back to base camp brought me back to the present and my need get on solid land for my own survival.

I had twisted my upper right thigh struggling to get out of the river. With a piece of driftwood I found on shore, I made a little crutch, a walking stick. I was thankful that I hadn't broken any bones as I was being dragged over rocks and submerged limbs.

I turned back into the woods. Hal's little map was worthless now. Not only was it a just soaking wet wad of paper in my pocket but its directions no longer applied.

Then through a thin spot in the canopy of the trees, I spotted a familiar mountain peak I knew was on the other side of base camp and I headed towards it.

When I came to a narrow clearing, from my position above—thank god—I could see the far edge of Post Lake and the campfire near the Michiganders' tent flickering like a welcoming star. I limped and staggered slowly down the hill, maneuvering my heavy pack and my aching, exhausted body back through the evergreens and birch, down to the edge of the lake and finally, an hour later, into camp. I limped over to the fire, dropped my load, and fell to my knees exhausted. Chuck Keim saw me and trotted over with his camera. He took my duffel off my packboard and took a photo of me sitting on the ground surrounded by piles of the food and gear I had brought back.

"That's impressive," Chuck said as he snapped a few more pictures.

Hal came over too. When he saw the scratches on his Weatherby, he was pissed as I predicted.

"Damn it, Rudy!"

Chuck reminded him I could have died and the rifle could have been lost altogether. Hal calmed down. A little. He still wasn't happy.

I could barely move. My knee was red and beginning to swell. I was almost too tired to know I was in pain.

After I had some supper, I crawled into my mummy bag and fell into a deep and dreamless sleep.

16: THE BAD LEG

September 6, 1961. Day 19

The next morning, I was still worn out and hurting, but I took off for the north camp anyway with Fred. He hadn't flown out with Chuck yet because Anchorage was still weathered in. We were to take food and ammo to Pometer, Howard, and Erwin. It rained steadily all the way. To make matters worse, when we arrived at their campsite, they were gone and had taken everything in camp with them. Fred and I ate a couple of sandwiches and some dried prunes and started back.

The leg I had hurt yesterday on my return from the south spike camp began giving me a lot of trouble and by the time we were halfway home, it was useless. It was pure stabbing pain, pure dead weight. I had to lift it with both hands and swing it forward to use it for support.

About three quarters of the way back, I fell to the ground. Overwhelmed by pain and knowing how far we yet had to hike over slippery terrain, I started to sob. I couldn't control it. Boyle stood there staring at me. He said nothing. What could he say? The pain was shooting through my leg from my calf to my groin. I couldn't stand. There was a boulder nearby and I pulled myself up onto it and sat bent over from the pain and the weight of my backpack. I was ashamed of my weakness and uncontrollable sobs.

"Fred, I'm sorry." I looked away.

I could tell he was uncomfortable and had no idea how to cope with my physical collapse. He sat on rock nearby and looked around, avoiding me.

"Fred, you go on back to camp. I'll follow you when I can," I winced between words.

He sat there for a minute more and then stood up, adjusted his backpack and grabbed his rifle.

"Okay," he said. "I'll take your pack back to camp for you."

I slipped off my pack and he hoisted it up onto his shoulders along with his own. I watched him hike away down the hill, getting smaller and smaller the further away he got.

After a long ten minutes, I tried to stand, winced in pain, and dropped again to the ground. I knew I couldn't remain here. I willed myself to my feet again and slowly started to follow him. I had to lift my right leg with both hands and heave it forward. Balance and lift, balance and lift. Every move was stabbing pain.

Fred was far ahead and there were long minutes when he was out of sight around a bend or below me on a lower slope. Finally, he was so far ahead, he and his hat disappeared altogether. Not once did I see him turn around to see if I was following. Which is just as well.

I had to get down off this mountain. It wasn't steep where I was, but it was rocky and slippery from the rain. Then there was the muskeg on the tundra when I got down to level ground. The only thing I had with me was my rifle. Fred had my canteen. It was in my backpack. It would be a long and painful two miles back.

The agony was now centered in my groin. I figured I hurt because of the eighty-pound load I had carried yesterday from south camp after banging my knee, my balance thrown off by using the walking stick on the slanted hillside, my left foot always higher than my right. Something inside of me must have ripped. Maybe I had torn something when I got washed down the rushing Kuskokwim.

I dragged my aching body back into base camp an hour and a half after Boyle got back. Half an hour later, Pometer, Erwin, and Howard came back with a sixty-three-inch wide moose rack. We all had some of Hal's hot vegetable and sheep-meat stew and then I dragged my sorry ass off to bed.

The next morning, Larry came into the Bull Tent where it was warm to flesh out the moose cape. Pometer came in as I was getting dressed. There was a look of worry on his face and he left. Two minutes later, Howard Fitzgerald walked in with a cup of water in one hand and a medical kit in the other. He sat down, laid open a metal case with pills, and gave me five codeine tablets for pain and three Aureomycin which he said would help me sleep. The pain had kept me up all night. I took a codeine, washed up, had breakfast, and helped Hal with the dishes. Then I went back to the Bull Tent and fell asleep. The codeine was kicking in.

Later, Hal asked if I could climb up into the cache behind the cook tent and turn the eggs. "When you order twenty cartons of eggs and you're out here in the bush for a month, you got to turn the eggs over every so often. It keeps the yokes from settling and going bad," he said. After supper, I climbed the ladder into the cache and flipped over the egg cartons. I think it was a test to see what I could do. My groin was throbbing, but I kept quiet about it and did my job.

The next several days it rained, and everyone stayed in camp. On September 9, the twenty-second day in the bush, Jerry and Phyllis were supposed to fly out but the planes on Lake Hood were still weathered in.

Finally, at 7:00 a.m., we got word by radio that an Air Sea Motives Cessna had left Anchorage. Everyone sat around waiting for it.

The Shermans had all their gear out of their tent ready to load. It was one of the few times I saw Jerry smile. But around 9 o'clock the rain returned, Air Sea Motives radioed Hal that they had to scrub the flight, and, for another day, the clients were stranded.

The weather stayed bad for the next four days and on September 13, our twenty-sixth day, exactly at noon, a plane arrived and with it the new two clients, Floyd D'Angelo and Dick Cook. The plane brought the hunters and their gear but no food. Phyllis, Jerry, Chuck, and Fred climbed on board and the plane revved up, pulled away from the dock, screamed across the lake, and lifted off. The plan was for the Cessna to return with supplies.

I was feeling better after a couple days of rest. My groin no longer hurt, the leg was moving on its own, and I felt stronger. In the afternoon, Clark and I took Floyd through the muskeg and part way up a mountain to give him a sense of the terrain. When we returned to camp, Hal, Erwin, Leo, Howard, and Dick were finishing Floyd's two bottles of Seagram's whiskey. They were as happy as they were hungry and, in their joy, they fixed everyone dinner.

The plane did not return that day.

17: A Promotion

September 16, 1961: Day 29

Early in the morning, we got a call from Air Sea Motives that a plane was finally on its way. Hal told me go up to north camp again to bring back the rest of the leftover food. Before I left, I said goodbye to Erwin, Howard, Leo, and Pometer. An hour later from the trail, I saw the floatplane fly in and soon after leave. I filled my packboard, tied the food down, and sang my way back home.

After drinking a glass of scotch — Erwin had left behind a few bottles — a different floatplane returned with more supplies. The pilot had dinner with us and left. The five of us remaining — Hal, Clark, Dick Cook, Floyd, and I — sat around the campfire until midnight. Hal was relaxed and in a good mood. The first long hunt was history. This smaller group of two would be easier to handle.

As we sat around the fire basking in its flickering warmth, Hal looked over at me and said, "Rudy, I think you've earned a promotion. You've survived some difficult times. You are now officially an assistant guide." I couldn't believe it. This was something I never dreamed of. The guys around the campfire raised their tumblers of scotch and applauded. I went to bed happy.

September 17, 1961: Day 30

BANG! A gunshot! I looked at my watch. It was 6 in the morning. I scrambled out of my sleeping bag and jumped barefoot out the front of the tent. Floyd had gotten up to pee and had seen a bull just two hundred yards from camp. He shot it.

The dead moose got us busy. We spent all day hauling hundreds of pounds of meat sliced and hacked from the two thousand-pound carcass. Its rack measured sixty-five inches. It was huge and heavy. Towards the end of the afternoon, Clark looked tired and fell asleep while scraping the moose hide but woke up just as Hal came back into camp with Richard Cook. They had gone out to look for game.

We woke up the next the morning to an inch of snow on the ground. Clark was sick and weak with the flu. Now that I was an assistant guide, Hal asked me to take Floyd up on the ridge to hunt some caribou we had spotted from camp. We were on our way by 8:30 and reached the foothill of the mountain two hours later. We walked across the slope keeping low and into the wind. I spotted fresh bear tracks so we diverted and followed them until we came to a dense patch of spruce. Not a good place to go after a bear. Off to our left was another bull moose, head down, grazing. His rack was smaller than the one Floyd had just shot, so we continued up the hill after the caribou.

Floyd's leg started to bother him, and he was limping a little and having a hard time keeping up. At 11:30, we stopped for lunch, but we didn't see the caribou.

"I think they're on the next mountain," I said. I pointed to the mountain beyond.

"No, I don't think so," Floyd said. "I'm sure that they're on this one."

He pulled out his binoculars and scanned the rises around us but saw no caribou. He didn't want to keep going. He was exasperated and wanted to return to camp.

I was disappointed as well. I knew I was right, but Floyd was struggling with the climb. He was the client, so we turned around and headed for base camp.

An hour after we returned, Hal and Dick came back with moose antlers. Dick had shot a large bull and had left him on a hill about two miles away. Hal had carried the rack back on his shoulders and had almost become ill because of the smell of rut. It was bad. A horny moose stinks worse than a rotting bear. I had to drag the rack out of camp and left it downwind about a hundred yards away in a buzzing vortex of hungry black flies.

After supper, Hal asked Floyd about the hunt. I told him we came back early because we couldn't find the caribou.

"I know," said Hal. "I was following you with my binoculars. You stopped a mountain too soon. There was half a dozen of them grazing on your level. You should have kept going, Rudy. You and I both saw them before you took off."

Floyd interrupted. "Hal, it was my fault," he said. "Rudy said they were on the next mountain and I didn't believe him. He was the guide and I should have. Rudy, I apologize. I'm sorry." He was sincere. Floyd was a good man.

Floyd was a wealthy, experienced world traveler. He had arrived at Post Lake direct from a safari in Kenya where, he told us, he had killed a leopard and a rhino, and had the trophies sent back to his office in Los Angeles. And here I was, a twenty-two-year-old newly appointed assistant guide telling him, "No, the caribou are on the next mountain, not this one" I could understand why he would doubt me.

18: Can of Stones

September 21, 1961: Day 34

Clark felt better after a day of rest, and he and Floyd went off towards the mountains with Floyd's movie equipment. Floyd wanted to carry his camera and tripod himself.

Later that afternoon, Hal asked me to go out to a temporary campsite he had set up earlier that summer. "I left some tools there," he said, "and since I'm not going out there again this fall, we might as well bring them back to base. I'd like you to go and get them this afternoon. It's about three miles. Once you get past the edge of the lake, you'll find the path. It's blazed. I put up markers every two hundred yards or so. I was going to send Larry, but he has the shits and it's better he stay in camp. He spotted a brown bear out there earlier, so be alert. You'd better take this." He handed me an empty tin can. I had no idea what it was for.

He anticipated my question. "The can is for bears. If they know you're there, they'll avoid you. Put some stones in it as you walk and shake it like a rattle now and then. If a bear hears you, it'll go the other way. But take this 30.06 with you just in case."

Larry Keeler was a spotter. Hal said he had telescopic vision. That's why he was hired. He could see an animal half a mile away without binoculars. That's no small feat when the animal's fur is the same color as the land. If Larry had told Hal there was a bear out there, there was. Usually wherever Hal went, Larry was nearby like a quiet shadow. I hardly ever heard him talk.

I pulled my hip boots on over my Red Wings in case the ground was wet. Half an hour later, I was on my way. Past the edge of Post Lake was the tundra, the first mile or so of which was boggy muskeg. I had gotten good at hopping from clump to clump and moved forward at a steady pace. My leg and groin were now pain free.

When I got to an elevated ridge, the ground was dry, and I saw the path Hal had mentioned. It zigzagged through knee high brush. Clearly it was animal made, but what animal I wasn't sure. I didn't think it was a moose run since adult moose tend to be solitary and wander as they feed. But this was clearly a trail. I hoped it wasn't a bear trail.

When I saw a stone or pebble, I picked it up and dropped it the can. In a few minutes, I had collected a dozen stones and when I shook the can, it rattled loudly. If this would keep bears away, great. Every fifty paces I shook the can. It was surprising how safe that little noise made me feel. I wondered why Hal hadn't clued me in on the anti-bear rattle before, like when I had gone alone to south camp across the Kuskokwim. Here, out in the open, I was on high alert. Sparse stands of scraggly trees grew scattered in the distance breaking up the landscape. They could hide large animals.

What I didn't expect were small animals. That's why my heart skipped a beat when I saw something low to the ground dart out of the weeds ahead of me as I came around a bend in the path. It wasn't a bird and it was too small for a wolf. I knew that wolverines, while fearless and ferocious, avoided humans unless they were trapped or surprised. I had rattled my can every fifty steps. Any animal that wasn't deaf would know I was here.

I readied my rifle just in case. I waited. Maybe it would reappear. And it did.

A skinny red fox popped out from the weeds and stood in the middle of the path. It stared at me for ten long seconds, then, without hesitation, started to trot toward me, head down. It didn't make eye contact. It didn't slow or change its line of approach. In fact, as I stood there, it passed by within two feet of my boots and continued on as if I didn't exist.

I turned and watched it disappear into the growth behind me. What had just happened? What was I to this hungry fox that I was not a threat? Did I not matter? Why wasn't I a threat? Did it want anything, expect anything? Was my body scent attractive to it? Or was it, like me, curious and looking for adventure?

I found Hal's campsite, collected the gear, and was back at base before supper.

19: Leaving Post Lake

September 22, 1961. Day 35.

The rain began before sunrise. The cloud ceiling at noon was still too low for a plane to fly in. In the afternoon, Clark and I cut down and threw away the spoiled meat on the bleed rack. The black flies had gotten to it, and the flesh was crawling with maggots. From day one with Erwin, Leo, and Howard, we had been careful to cover all hanging meat with sheets of tied down plastic to keep the flies off. That was a month ago. Now the plastic had gotten brittle. I noticed small cracks in it. It was only a matter of time. How long can you keep a thousand flies from fragrant bloody flesh? It was a gross, messy task.

At dinner, Floyd told us that Squaw Valley in California was passé and that the new crowd was going to Mammoth or Tahoe. The ratio of women to men was high in Sun Valley so that was another favorite spot of his. He passed out his business cards. His company was "Aluminum Skylight and Specialty Corp.," in Los Angeles, California. Everything about Floyd had the sense of comfort and money. Everything he wore at camp was new and he told us that we could have it all, or burn it, when he flew out. He didn't carry dirty clothes.

He showed me a flier of one of his recent projects, an aluminum house built on a round platform that rotated with the sun. He said the energy was produced by something called a solar panel, a new invention. He had a picture of his own rotating mansion in the Arizona desert. It was circular, huge, and silver, the color of aluminum, with floor-to-ceiling windows.

Hal changed the subject back to the hunt and asked Floyd what he wanted to do with the moose rack. "That," he said, "I'll take with me."

In the morning, everybody was disappointed that we couldn't get out because of a heavy fog, but in the middle of the afternoon, the clouds parted and the sun came out. Hal, Clark, Floyd, Dick, and I made plans for the next day's hunt. Then the clouds and cold air blew in again. "It comes with the territory," said Hal, so we went into the cook tent and played gin rummy.

Before dinner, I went off alone to set up my camera and tripod on the banks of Post Lake. The sky was gray, the wind rippled water steely blue. Sections of the foothills still looked red orange from the autumn muskeg, the forests climbing their steep slopes were glowing blue purple, but above the tree line, the rocks and peaks were topped with glistening snow.

September 27, 1961. Day 40

Five days later, we heard a buzz in the air. Air Sea Motives finally got a plane to Post Lake. It was my fortieth day in the Alaska Range at Rainey Pass.

20: Back in Anchorage

September 27, 1961

Dick Cook, Floyd, and I climbed on board the plane with our gear while Hal and Clark loaded the hunters' animal-head trophies. They stayed behind to finish shutting down the camp. The weather forecast was good, so they knew the plane would be back and that they'd be in Anchorage that evening. Hal gave me the name of his motel and told me to call him that night.

Floyd was booked into the Anchorage Westward Hotel. He invited me to share his room and then have dinner with him in the restaurant. I welcomed the chance to sleep in a real bed between clean sheets, and take a long hot shower with soap and shampoo.

The first thing he did when we checked in was to phone a local clothing store and order new clothes to be sent over to the hotel. New shirts, pants, socks, underwear, and a lightweight jacket. He didn't get new shoes, though. He liked his hunting boots and the front desk sent room service up to give them a good buffing. He also ordered from room service a new razor, a comb and hairbrush, two toothbrushes (one for me), and a tube of toothpaste. Floyd took a shower first then went over to the window to look at the mountains beyond Cook Inlet. When I came out of the bathroom after my shower, I couldn't believe it. All his new stuff had arrived. I must have taken a long shower. He was dressed and ready for dinner.

"Rudy, do you want any of my clothes?" Everything he had worn at Post Lake lay in a neat pile on one of the beds. All his blood-stained hunting clothes he had left behind. The clothing on the bed was good quality stuff and I wish I could have used them, but Floyd was five foot six and slight of build, weighing maybe 130 pounds. I didn't weigh much more, maybe 140, but I was six feet tall and nothing he had would have fit.

We didn't go to the restaurant right away. We headed for the bar. A pretty waitress in a lacy black apron and laughing dark eyes came over.

"Order what you want, Rudy," he said. "You deserve it."

"Thanks," I said, and I turned to the pretty waitress with a grin, "I'd like a Dewar's on the rocks."

"Yes, sir," she said.

Those beautiful eyes. I noticed she kept looking at me. Floyd saw her staring at me too and leaned in and whispered, "Rudy, there's a piece of bloody tissue sticking to your face." Oops. I rubbed it off. Floyd had lent me his razor, and while I was shaving I had cut my chin and had folded a small piece of Kleenex over it to blot up the blood.

"And you, sir?" She turned her attention to Floyd. Clearly, he was the one paying the bill. She was looking at his expensive, sporty, wrinkle-free clothes, totally out of place in this bar.

"I'll have a double Seagram's VO neat and a bowl of mixed nuts for the two of us," Floyd said. He laughed and then said to me, "Erwin and Hal drank all my Seagram's the first day. I've been waiting for this." He didn't get upset about it at camp. That was one of the things I liked about him, that and his willingness to admit a mistake. He knew how to navigate the world.

The waitress came back two more times with fresh drinks, and by time we decided to go to dinner, we were both a little tipsy. We weren't loud or out of control. We could walk, but not necessarily in a straight line. The bartender phoned the dining room that two customers were on the way and the maître d' met and guided us to a white linen-covered table. I ordered the clam chowder and a main course of broiled lobster and steak with a side of asparagus because that was what Floyd ordered. I really wasn't focusing on the food. I was just happy to be here.

When dinner was over, we took the elevator up to our floor. I went into the bathroom, washed, came out, and fell onto the bed by the window. I was asleep before I hit the blanket and when I woke up it was 9 in the morning. Floyd was up, dressed, and packed ready to get a cab to the airport. He had booked a first-class seat on an Alaska Airlines flight leaving at noon for Seattle.

"Thanks for the company, Rudy," he said. "If you ever get out to L.A., give me a call." He handed me another of his business cards. "I'd like to show you my rotating sun house in Arizona." There was a knock on the door, Floyd opened it and motioned for the bellhop to take his suitcase. He turned and smiled, "Oh, Rudy, by the way, don't forget to call Hal. He said he was at the Sunset Motel."

"Thanks, Floyd," I said. We shook hands goodbye.

"Good luck, Rudy."

The bellhop closed the door behind him.

21: Copper Center and Lake Louise

I sat up in a panic. Sunset Motel. I was supposed to call Hal last night. I got the motel number from the phonebook and called Hal's room. It took six rings before he picked up.

"Hello?" A tired voice. I had woken him up.

"Hi, Hal. It's Rudy. Sorry I didn't call last night. Floyd and I had a few drinks in the hotel bar before dinner and I forgot."

"Thanks okay," he said. "The plane didn't come back for us till after 5:00 and when we got into Anchorage, we went out for drinks ourselves. Didn't get back in until after midnight. Get some breakfast and meet me here at the motel around noon. We'll talk about our trip to Copper Center then."

I took another hot shower, got dressed, jammed my dirty clothes, hunting gear and rifle into my duffel bag, and lugged it down to the lobby.

The hotel restaurant was busy, but no matter. It was too expensive for me anyway. Hal hadn't paid me my salary.

I saw a little café down the street, so I headed there. I bumped my bulging duffel against the door frame as I went in and knocked the Open sign off the door window. The cook behind the counter gave me a look but said nothing. I picked up the sign, rehung it, and went over to a table against the far wall. A waitress came over with a cup of coffee and a menu, then walked back to the counter. When I looked up from the menu, she came back and took my order.

Two men were sitting at the counter with mugs of coffee and donuts on napkins and a couple was sitting at a table by the front window. They were kind of raggedy like me, so I figured I was in the right place. A few faded photographs hung on the wall, mostly pictures of Anchorage street scenes before statehood. There was a black-and-white photo of the Iditarod dog race starting on Fifth Street in front of City Hall, and an 11x14 photo of an engine from the Alaska Railroad that made me smile. Behind it some track laborers were posing with their crowbars and leveling shovels. The waitress came back with my order, refilled my coffee, and left. The clock on the wall read 10 o'clock so I took my time, and watched a few people come in and sit at the counter. When I leaned back in my chair, the waitress came over with the bill. She was good at reading body language.

"Do you know where the Sunset Motel is?" I asked.

"Oh sure. Go about five blocks south on Fifth, then go right two blocks," she said. "It's on the corner." That wasn't too far away, so I thought I'd walk it. I paid the bill, gathered up my stuff, and left, careful not to bump the door again on my way out.

A military convoy from Fort Richardson of a half dozen transport trucks full of uniformed soldiers in combat uniform passed by.

The Sunset Motel was small, only about ten units, with beige peeling paint. Not a classy place, but for a one-nighter it was okay and cheaper than a hotel. Hal said he usually stayed there because he knew the woman who owned it.

Hal was in room seven. A 1960 blue Ford pick-up was parked in front. Since there were no other cars in the lot, I figured it was his. I knocked and Hal opened the door. He was packed and ready to go. He told me to toss my gear in the truck bed, he did the same, and we headed east out of town on the Glenn Highway towards Glennallen and Copper Center.

Hal hadn't eaten so about fifteen miles out of town we stopped at a diner, which was good because he was driving fast over roads that buckled with frost heaves and potholes and I was getting carsick. Hal had hold of the steering wheel so he could brace himself, but it was bronco-riding rough on the passenger side. I was hoping our gear wouldn't bounce out of the truck bed. He'd glance over at me and grin and, if I didn't know better, I'd think he was having fun watching me bashing my head against the roof. It felt good to have my feet back on solid ground when we got to the diner.

It was lunch time so we both had cheeseburgers and fries. I had a Coke and Hal ordered a Budweiser. Separate checks. When the waitress came over and put them in front of us, I stared at mine for a few seconds. Hal noticed, opened his wallet, and counted out twenty-five ten-dollar bills. I knew the Post Lake experience was priceless, like Hal had said, but, even so, I needed money to buy food. He still owed more for the second hunt, but I would ask for that later.

While we were eating, Hal told me again why we were going to Copper Center.

"I bought a twenty-two-foot jet boat in June," he said, "and I've only had her out once. I want to take her on the water and give her a run. Need to burn some gas." He had mentioned a new boat back in base camp, but this was the first time I had heard it was a jet boat. I had never seen one.

"Sounds like fun," I said and took my last swig of Coke. "What does a jet boat sound like?" I asked.

Hal grinned. "You'll see."

We paid our bills at the register and headed back to the truck. This time I kept my window open so I could wedge my elbow into the window frame at the bottom and brace my hand against the top. It was chilly, but it kept me solid. Hal turned up the heat in the front, so it worked out and I didn't feel like I had to puke. Bracing gave my head and neck a lot more stability.

We drove east on the Glenn Highway until it joined the Richardson. Then we turned south towards Copper Center about fifteen miles away. Hal turned onto a gravel road badly chewed up by the weather. It led down to the Copper River where his boat was stored.

The boat was wrapped in canvas. It was on a two-wheeled trailer that we had to hook onto the towing hitch attached to Hal's rear bumper.

The boat ramp into the river was concrete. Hal had to drive along the bank and jockey the truck around, then back the trailer down the ramp into the water. My job was to stand near the bow and hold the lines as the boat inched backwards into the river. It slipped easily off its cradle until it was fully afloat. Hal drove his truck back up the ramp and parked it off to one side. He came loping down the ramp and took over the lines.

"Climb in, Rudy," he said with a grin. He was proud of this boat.

I stepped into the freezing water up to my knees and pulled myself up over the side. Hal climbed in and slid behind the wheel and sat high in the captain's chair as he turned the key in the ignition. The jet engine thundered to life.

"Put this on," Hal said, and he tossed me a life jacket he pulled out from under the console. "No telling what might be floating down the river."

I strapped on the vest and he did the same, then he slowly backed out about thirty yards, rammed forward on the throttle and we spun around on the tail end of the boat at nearly a forty-five-degree angle, from zero to twenty in seconds. The single jet roared and thrust us forward while a rooster tail of water six feet high shot up behind us. It was exciting. There were no other boats on the water. Just us.

The riverbank was lined with autumn trees turning yellow and gold and red. Hal throttled past a half-mile of them.

We came to a flock of Canada geese floating mid-river, hundreds of large dark birds bobbing on the dark water. When they saw and heard us coming, they rose in wild honking flight over the golden trees. It was beautiful.

Hal was happy buzzing up and down the river, eyes ahead, smiling, sitting tall. Sometimes he had the jet boat racing full throttle. I had no idea how fast we were going. He'd bank off and turn in tight circles. It felt like being on a thrill ride at the Cedar Point fun park back in Ohio. He would pull back a little and the bow would settle down and we'd cruise on, throbbing straight ahead past trees and empty spaces and an occasional cabin. And then he put the boat in idle and we sat quiet on the water, floating with the current, and then, *BANG*, full throttle again up on our tail. It was pure play, pure fun. Hal laughed and grinned.

Finally, he turned around and said, "Time to head back, Rudy. She's running good. That's what I needed to know." And he aimed the boat back upriver.

We coasted in towards the ramp. "Rudy, when I get near the bank, I'll jump out and you hold the boat steady until I back up the trailer."

He approached the ramp slowly and, when we were a few feet from the shore, he put the boat in neutral. The engine throbbed slowly under me. He turned a knob and an anchor the size of a football dropped from a hidden compartment at the front tip of the bow. Hal grabbed it and tossed it onto the shore. That was good. I felt confident that the boat wouldn't float back into the middle of the river.

"Okay. Now slide over and grab the wheel," he said. "With two hands."

I could feel every tiny movement under me, the rocking, the swishing, the stern pulling slightly to the right as the current flowed against it. I could feel the steering wheel vibrate in my hands as I gripped it. And the next thing I knew, Hal was in the water up to his knees. He was up on the ramp in seconds and jogged back to the truck. I didn't hear him start the engine because the jet under me was rumbling, but the pick-up with the boat trailer started to back towards the ramp and down until the rear two-thirds of it was under water. Hal put the truck in park and jumped out, went over to the onshore anchored line, and held it taut.

"Okay, Rudy. Give it a little gas and aim for the center of the trailer. Try to fit the bottom of the boat into the groove." He pointed to the V-shaped frame of the trailer. I pushed forward on the throttle and the engine roared. "Too much gas, too much gas," he yelled. I pulled back on the handle. "Okay, less gas. And you have to take it out of neutral." I pushed the handle into forward, tapped the throttle gently, aimed the front of the boat towards the middle of the trailer and inched forward. I inched and inched until Hal had guided the boat with the rope fully onto the trailer's rack. When I saw it was totally on, I shut off the engine. Meanwhile, Hal was busy moving from one side to the other tying down the boat. I climbed out over the side to help.

The flock of geese flew over honking loudly. Behind us in the middle of the Copper River, a fish leapt out of the water. A scattering of yellow leaves floated down from the trees onto the bank as Hal climbed into his truck and pulled the boat up the ramp to dry ground. I got in and we drove back to his storage spot where we put the canvas cover back on, unhooked the trailer from the truck, and drove up the gravel path rocking and bumping back onto the paved Richardson Highway. Hal was grinning. He loved his toy.

"On to Lake Louise," he said. "Good hunting there."

I grabbed the window frame and held on.

A map on the dash showed Lake Louise to be about sixty miles from Copper Center. When we got back to the Glenn Highway with its gut-bouncing frost heaves and potholes, we turned west. Even though the suspension coils on the truck were new, Hal now drove slowly. He respected his equipment because it was expensive to repair. The road to Lake Louise was thirty miles from where we had turned off, but it took us an hour to find a place for the night.

Hal pulled up to a six-unit, weather-stained, log cabin motel with a vacancy sign in the front window. We went in. The motel owner knew Hal and rented us a room for just five dollars. He offered to whip up some supper for us as well, no charge. I think he was glad for the company. There were no other cars in the parking lot. He reminded me of the stereotype Alaskan sourdough, an old guy in a sloppy wool shirt and stained canvas overalls, worn battered hunting boots, and a graying beard. And friendly.

Behind the counter was a gun rack with a rifle in it. A moose head with a huge rack stared at us from the wall across the room and an aged black bear hide was draped over a sagging leather sofa. In front of the sofa was an unlit fireplace and two card tables with folding chairs. It looked like the local homesteaders came here to play cards.

The owner, who Hal called Henry, left to cook us some supper and Hal and I got our gear from the truck and put it in our motel room. A quick pee, a splash of water on our faces, and we went back to the lobby. Henry had cooked up corn beef hash and fried potatoes and a fresh pot of coffee. He put places for three at the table and sat down to eat with us. Corned beef hash never tasted so good.

"So, Hal, what are you doin' here this time of year?" Henry asked. He leaned forward anxious for details.

"I was showing Rudy my new jet boat over at Copper River and we stopped by to get a few caribou before we head back to Fairbanks. Good to see you again, Henry. How's the wife?"

Those were the last words I heard before Hal shook my shoulder. I had fallen asleep. I had been up since early morning and the day had been full of crazy truck rides and a jet boat adventure. Plus, I had gotten paid and that was a load off my mind. Hal gave me the key to the room and told me to leave it unlocked. He'd be in later. I thanked Henry for the meal and left.

22: Moose Threat

We slept until 9 o'clock, then stopped to say goodbye to Henry. He had a pot of hot coffee ready and a tray of thick, soft, peanut butter cookies he had made that morning. Hal and I sat for few minutes with coffee and cookies, paid him for the breakfast, said goodbye, and then drove deeper into the Lake Louise area to hunt.

We were alone in the park, no other cars or trucks on the roads or in parking areas. We stopped along the edge of a pull-off, got our rifles out, put extra ammo in our jacket pockets, and headed off. Hal led the way. Half an hour later, our winding path opened onto a field. Hal pulled up his binoculars to scout the area.

"I don't see any caribou," he said. We were standing halfway up a hill about a hundred yards above the field, part of which was obstructed by a few birch trees. Hal turned and focused on the trail ahead up the hill from our current elevation. Something caught his attention.

"Rudy," he said in a low whisper, "I think I see movement up ahead. Go down and look around. Maybe there'll be a couple of caribou back in where I can't see. I'll go up the path and check what's there."

He lowered his binoculars and slipped his rifle off his shoulder. I did the same, holding my rifle in my right hand, using my left to grab onto trees as I sidestepped carefully down the hill. It was steeper than it looked.

When I was standing on flat ground, I looked up to signal Hal, but he was out of sight. It was just me in the open field. I walked slowly towards the middle, rifle ready, left hand cradling the barrel, the right with fingers by the trigger guard.

When I was well into the open area, I stopped and looked around. I didn't have binoculars with me, but evergreens around the far end of the field formed a dark wall, so glasses from my spot wouldn't have been helpful anyway. Caribou are tan like deer and I didn't see anything pale moving against the dark background. The ground cover was a foot high at best, so they would have stood out. Then I saw some kind of animal feeding silently about three hundred yards away. It was chocolate brown and large. Very large. A bear alarm went off in my

115

head and I froze, staring hard in its direction. Then it moved. When it turned sideways, I could see it wasn't a bear. It was a cow moose. I hoped there was no calf nearby that she felt she had to protect.

Joel in hunting gear ready to descend the hill into moose territory.

Moose are fearless. They attack anything without cause or reason. She saw me. Without hesitation, she started to charge. That's when I saw she was hurt or wounded. Her rear left flank jerked stiffly as she ran towards me with thumping unstable strides. I didn't want to shoot her, but she was coming fast.

I saw a single birch growing nearby in the middle of the field and I made a dash for it, thinking to get it between me and the moose. If she ran into the tree, it would slow her up if not completely stop her. The problem was its trunk was only six inches thick. If she ran into it, would she knock it over? But I had no other choice.

I got behind the tree and stood sideways. The moose was now barely a hundred yards away. Of course, she could see me, at least part of me. But luckily the tree was enough. With only that narrow trunk between us, she veered off to the right, stopped in her tracks, and started to feed as if I didn't exist. But as I said, moose are dangerous and unpredictable. I wasn't going to take a chance and head back to the hill with her so close. Luckily, in her apparent boredom and lack of focus, she slowly wandered away as she fed, her large hind quarters jerking as she moved. After a few minutes, I felt she was distracted and out of range, and it was safe enough to move slowly back to the bottom of the hill. I climbed up to the path and there was Hal.

"Rudy, I was watching you and the moose. That was the funniest thing I've ever seen." He laughed.

"Yeah?" I said, "I'll bet." What would he have said if that tree hadn't been there and I had had to shoot it? Or if it had run me over?

Hal checked his watch and thought it would be best to return to the motel and get an early start the next morning. Henry was glad to see us and brought out a fifth of Jack Daniels and a plate of bologna sandwiches. We had a few drinks, Hal told him about the moose, we had a few more drinks, then we sacked out and slept through the night.

23: Leda's Trailer

September 30 to October 6, 1961

On the ride back to Fairbanks on the Paxton Cutoff, blue-white glaciers edged the highway. We passed a herd of bison on federal lands near Fort Greeley. Hal told me they were off-limits for hunters except for once a year when the state issued two hundred hunting tags, which sold out in hours.

After a while, we both got quiet, thinking about what tomorrow might bring. For Hal, it was the start of a short break from the demands of hunters. As for me and my future, I had absolutely no idea what I would do.

As we neared Fairbanks, Hal looked over. "Rudy, I have a hunt scheduled in October in Juneau. I'm teaming up with Karl Lane who owns a charter boat. We have two duck hunters from Michigan signed up. You can come on as a dishwasher and general helper. We'll be out about seven days. Does that interest you? Can you get away?"

I didn't hesitate. "Yes."

"I can't pay you a salary," Hal said.

"How about help with plane fare?" I asked. He still owed me for the last two weeks at Post Lake. Maybe this was his way of negotiating. Offer nothing then work up to a minimum.

He stared out the front window. I think he expected me to jump at the chance even if I had to pay my own way.

"Okay. I can do that," he said after a brief hesitation. Then he relaxed a little. At least he had cheap labor. Not free but cheap.

This was what Alaska was all about. Adventure, doing new things. How lucky I was to be in driving around with this famous outfitter. People from all over the country wanted to book a hunt with him. He had helped clients get into the Boone and Crockett Record Book. It was word-of-mouth. Jerry and Phyllis Sherman had contracted with him from Minnesota. Erwin, Leo, and Howard booked him from Michigan, world traveler millionaire Floyd DeAngelo from California.

"What are the details?" I asked.

The dates of the Juneau hunt were October 10th through the 20th. But, like before, he wanted me there a few days early to help get ready and get familiar with the boat, and meet Karl, the captain-owner, and a sourdough cook coming up from Seattle, Ted Childers. I'd be helping Ted and he wanted Ted to teach me what I needed to know.

The duck hunt was less than two weeks away and Hal said he'd be in touch. Chuck Keim would be my phone link since I was homeless at the time. Hal reached down next to his seat and pulled out a business card and handed it to me. It didn't have a street address, but it did have his phone number.

I asked Hal to drop me off at the university. I figured I'd buy supper in the Union cafeteria, hang out for a while someplace, sack out on a lobby sofa in one of the dorms, and worry about tomorrow tomorrow. I was excited about the Juneau trip, but it was almost two weeks away.

I bought some fried chicken and a Coke in the food line. This was the first I had eaten since our breakfast of coffee and cookies. When I was done, I went down to the bookstore in the Student Union basement. Leda Juul was there, a girl I had met when I was a graduate student. I told her about the Lake Louise moose incident that morning. Then she told me that she had moved out of the Northward Building and was renting a mobile home in the trailer park on College Road.

"Why did you leave the apartment?" I asked. Her efficiency apartment was six floors up by elevator with a great view of the city. She had made it open, uncluttered, and comfortable. She said she liked her apartment, and she could afford the rent, but it was no longer private. It was no longer safe.

"It was the soldiers from Fort Wainwright," she said with sadness. "There was a constant line of them knocking on my door all hours of the night. I couldn't take it anymore."

I understood. I had visited Leda a couple times after she had gotten home from work. Just about every time, some G.I. would knock on her door and try to get in to see her. She would be polite and send him away, but minutes later another would show up. My being there in the room in plain sight in civilian clothes was a good excuse to turn them away. For that reason, she liked my company. I was her protector.

They say that beauty is a curse. That was painfully true in Leda's case. She was a telephone operator at Fort Wainwright. She was tall, thin, and statuesque, with beautiful, flawless skin and big, pale blue eyes. She could have been a New York model. When she spoke, it was with a soft high gentle voice. Leda was raised Jewish in Albuquerque, New Mexico, and had come to Alaska to find interesting work. She liked her job, but the cascade of young, sex-obsessed soldiers and their unwanted attention had taken their toll. She was a rare shining beauty caught in the mud of a dirty world. Leaving the Northward Building was a way out, at least a partial way out.

119

Leda said that she was rooming with Mary Donahue. When Leda found out I had no place to sleep that night, she asked if I would like to stay with them.

I had met Mary Donahue. Last April, three weeks before final exams, she had flown from New Haven, Connecticut, to Fairbanks thinking she could show up and get a job as a graduate teaching assistant in the English Department. I was sitting at my office desk grading papers when she appeared in the door.

"Hello," she said. "I'm looking for the department chair. I'm Mary Donahue."

"Hi, I'm Joel," I replied. "I think Dr. Magee is gone for the day. Is there anything I can help you with?"

"No. I need to talk to the department chair." She lurched in awkwardly through the doorway and leaned heavily against Marie Munsen's desk. "I'm looking for a job."

"What kind of job?" I asked. She said she wanted to get a graduate teaching assistantship and start work right away. Now I was curious. "Did you get an acceptance?" I asked.

"No," she said. She looked confused. She had no advance correspondence and had made no formal application. She didn't know Dr. Magee's name until I mentioned it. She had never heard of Dean Voldseth. She knew nothing of the university, its enrollment, its facilities, or its campus layout. The ratio of men to women was high in Alaska, but I don't think she was looking for a man. Something wasn't clicking. It was clear to me that she didn't think things through. Maybe she couldn't. She said she had MS, multiple sclerosis. She walked with two metal crutches strapped around her forearms and she could hardly climb a step. But somehow she had gotten from the East Coast up to Alaska, and to Fairbanks and the campus, and into the Bunnell building through two sets of heavy glass doors.

I told her about the department, what kind of courses we offered, the mix of students, and the teaching load for teaching assistants.

"Nice to meet you," she said suddenly and then left me to my grading.

A week later, Marie Munsen mentioned to me that someone named Mary had stopped by the office. That started me thinking about her and why she had come up here into the freezing rough wilderness with all her debilitating physical handicaps. And then I thought, "There are a lot of crazy people up here from all over the world. Maybe she's no different, looking for something different in life." Wasn't that my story? I liked Mary's spirit. My heart went out to her.

"Yes," I said to Leda. "Thank you." Any port in a storm, and Leda was a friendly port. I told her how I knew Mary.

I carried my gear to Leda's rental car, and she drove to her place in the trailer park on College Road I had walked past many times.

When we got there, she gave me a two-minute tour while Mary sat in silence on a couch. She was not welcoming.

The trailer was small, only about forty feet long and ten feet wide, but it had a 10x20 foot built-on room with an entrance door facing the parking lot. The mobile home had one bedroom with one double bed which Leda and Mary shared, a small bathroom with a toilet, a sink, a medicine cabinet, and a shower. The front third of the mobile home was the kitchen with a two-burner gas stove, a food storage cabinet, a small refrigerator, and a single-basin sink. If there were three feet of usable counter space that would be stretching it. I wondered what kind of crazy midget had designed this kitchen. A small kitchen table and two wooden chairs separated the kitchen from the living area, but at least it was a place to eat. Sandwiched between the kitchen table and the far wall in the small living room was a sagging three-pillow couch where Mary was sitting.

"I guess I'll be sleeping on the couch," I said. I didn't see any other alternative.

"No," Leda said. "You'll have to sleep in the cellar. We wouldn't feel safe with you sleeping up here."

This trailer had a cellar? Why would Leda invite me to stay with them if I made her feel unsafe? I didn't understand. Did she feel she owed me something for being her excuse to turn away all those horny G.I.s when she lived in her old apartment? I, myself, had never made a pass at her and only once did she ask for me to lay down with her. But we didn't have sex. She just wanted me to hold her and lay my body on top of hers. Which I did. When I started to move to take off my boots—we were both fully clothed—her need suddenly passed and she asked me to get off. It was a strange moment of innocent physical intimacy I would never forget. Her long bones under me, not moving. Her soft closed eyes. Needy and afraid of that need.

I felt surprise and disappointment because of Leda's distrust. Maybe the curse of her dark beauty had poisoned her. Maybe it was something deeper.

"How can this tiny trailer have a cellar?" I asked. I looked at her with doubt.

Leda pointed to a wooden trap door set into the floor next to the couch.

"The park owner built a concrete block basement under the trailer," she said. "That's where he put the furnace and water pipes." Leda pointed to a metal ring built into the top of the trap door. She reached down and pulled it open. I looked down at a wooden ladder that descended into a pitch-black hole.

"You want me to sleep down there?" I looked at her in disbelief.

"Yes. You'll have to."

I could tell she was uncomfortable about it, but the discomfort was more than her fear of having a man sleeping in her home. I had a bad feeling that maybe she had lost her mind, had gone off the deep end after she moved out of the Northward Building. But, I asked myself, what's the worst that could happen? She would never let me die.

"I'll need to lock you in," she said almost apologetically. I looked at the trap door. I didn't see a lock on it. "But there's a light switch behind the ladder so you can have light, and I have an extra blanket and a pillow you can use."

"Well, let me use your bathroom and then I'll go down," I said.

Okay, I thought. She's just haunted and scared. It'll be fine. So I got my shaving kit from my backpack and squeezed into the little bathroom to wash my face and brush my teeth.

Mary was out of sight when I came out. She had gone into the bedroom. But Leda was sitting on the couch. She got up and stood next to the open trap door. I got my backpack and started to climb down.

"Wait for me to turn on the light before you shut the door," I said. I got to the bottom rung, reached behind the ladder and found the wall switch. I turned on the light as Leda lowered the door over my head. I heard her above me pushing the couch over the trapdoor. I was certainly trapped for the night. "Well," I thought, "it is what it is."

I looked around. There was nothing in the concrete room but a humming oil furnace, a water heater, half an empty whiskey barrel with odd pieces of lead pipe and rods, a toolbox, a wooden chair, and the ladder I had climbed down. I checked for an empty tin can in case I had to pee in the night, but I saw none—the toolbox would do if neces-sary. I spread the quilt on the cement floor near the light switch, pulled off my boots, took off my coat, pants and shirt and draped them over the chair, and lay down. Despite my obscenely weird predicament, I slept well. The constant soft rumbling from the furnace was soothing and I felt safe and warm.

When I opened my eyes, I remembered I was locked in a cellar. I flipped on the light to look at my watch. It was 9:00 a.m. I put on my clothes and used a metal rod to knock on the ceiling. As soon as I did, I heard the couch slide away from the trap door and Leda pulled it open. I climbed out into the daylight, smiled, and made a beeline for the bathroom.

When I came out, Leda and Mary were sitting on the couch. Leda had made some instant coffee and we all had a cup. Nothing was said about my sleeping arrangement, no stupid questions. I think it was enough for Leda that she had given me a place out of the cold, regardless of what kind of place it was. She was still safe, I was safe, and I didn't make a big deal out of it. I understood the complexity of the situation; her fear was tempered by compassion. She liked me, but I was a man and men were to be feared. It was complicated. Anyway, that's the way I explained it to myself.

The calendar on the wall said it was the first of October. Hal wanted me to fly to Juneau on the 6th to join him on Karl Lane's boat, the *Ranger*, before the Michigan clients arrived. That was just five days away.

Since I had returned from Post Lake, things had changed. Leda had quit her job at Fort Wainwright and was now just biding time. She wasn't looking for work.

I offered to help her and Mary buy groceries and cook their meals in exchange for my bomb shelter in the basement. Leda didn't want a handout. She shared the cost of the food and helped make out grocery lists. But she didn't want to physically go to the store because she feared she would be harassed.

The thought of shopping in the wild city of Fairbanks brought terror to her eyes. Too many aggressive horny men. Too many G.I.s. At first, I didn't believe her when she told me of her fear, but I discovered that she wasn't paranoid. The one time we went together to a local grocery store, two soldiers followed her down every aisle and out to her car. I had to physically stand in their way to stop their pursuit. I heard them propositioning her, offering her money and a good time. It was beyond my understanding how they could be so dirty, wicked, mean and bad and nasty. Did they really think she was a prostitute? Why else would she go shopping and look like she was walking down a New York high-fashion runway?

Ironically, Leda wouldn't go anywhere unless her makeup was perfect and she was dressed in fashionable clean and freshly ironed clothes. It was part of her upbringing. It was who she was.

It taught me a hard lesson. Now I understood her fear and I didn't blame her for transferring that fear onto me, despite our innocent history. The only places she felt safe was in her trailer and on the University of Alaska campus. People there left her alone. She fit in.

While I was staying with the girls, Mary stayed in the trailer reading or listening to the radio. I never saw her go out. I watched as she got dirtier and sicker day by day. She never took a shower and I rarely saw her wash her hands and face. I had no idea when she did a laundry unless Leda did it for her in the kitchen sink.

October 6th came, and I had my plane ticket to Juneau. Leda wanted to drive me to the airport. "I'll see you when I get back," I said. I gave her a hug. She did not pull away.

Leda hung her head. "We'll miss you, Joel," she said. She got into her car drove off.

24: On the *Ranger*

We were sitting in the kitchen of Karl Lane's fifty-foot cruiser, the *Ranger*, moored in the Juneau boat harbor. Hal's two clients were Fred and Granger from Port Huron, Michigan. Hal Waugh and Karl were the guides, and Ted Childers, a young seventy-year-old, was the cook Karl brought up from Seattle specifically for this job. It seemed like a close and interesting group. But the day before, I wasn't sure our duck hunting trip was going to happen, what with the near blowup between Hal and the Michiganders and a near cancellation of the hunt.

Hal and I flew into Juneau from Anchorage Friday morning and checked into the Thunderbird Motel operated by another one of Hal's friends. It was sunny and bright and a warm 57 degrees. We took a cab down to the waterfront where the *Ranger* was docked, and after Karl showed me where to stow my backpack, Hal and I went into downtown Juneau to buy waterfowl tags. We stopped for a drink at the Red Dog Saloon, then at the Elks Club, Hal's favorite Juneau hangout.

Later, we met up with the two men from Michigan. We took their hunting gear to the boat, then Fred and Granger returned to their hotel while Hal and I went to the Department of Wildlife to buy more hunting tags and permits. Later in the afternoon, Hal and I went to the Baranof Hotel to rendezvous again.

Hal had a few drinks under his belt when the four of us sat down. Everyone seemed to be feeling good, but Hal had been worrying about getting paid. After Fred made a series of good-humored suggestions about how the hunt should go, Hal curtly asked for the rest of his money, "before the hunt begins, according to the brochure," he said. Granger said he had no brochure that said payment had to be made in full before departure. Hal said that he did, that it was common practice, and he wanted the conditions filled. When Granger leaned sullenly back in his chair, Hal stood up, slammed the table with his fist, and stormed away angry. The hunters got up from the table and went to their room. The good humor was over.

Hal called Karl from the pay phone in the lobby to complain and a few minutes later Karl walked in. After a couple more drinks, Karl drove Hal and me to the boat and left for his last night home. Hal took off on foot and didn't came back.

October 7, 1961. Day 1 on the *Ranger*.

In the morning, Karl came over to my bunk and woke me. It was raining hard and Hal was missing. Ted Childers made a pot of coffee and we waited

After an hour, the Michigan guys came down to the boat in a cab and Karl sent me to look for Hal.

"Rudy," he said. "Here's the keys to my car. Go into town and find Hal and bring him back. We need to get going or we're going to lose these guys." He pointed to his yellow Volkswagen Beetle at the back of the lot.

I had never driven a Volkswagen. It was a throwback to my first car, a 1950 Chevy, which had a clutch peddle to the left of the brake. I opened the door and got in, pushed the clutch pedal down to the floor, turned the key in the ignition, and started the engine. I put the car into reverse, took my foot off the clutch, and backed up. I braked, pressed the clutch down again, and shifted into first gear. The car jerked forward and stalled. I had been spoiled by automatic transmissions. I pressed my foot back down on the clutch again, restarted it, eased up on the pedal, and the car snapped into first gear and lurched forward.

When I turned the corner out of the parking lot to head back to the center of the city, I was on a narrow cobblestone street that climbed up a steep slope. The street rose up at forty-five degrees past dozens of tiny cliff-side houses painted pink and green and yellow and blue, colors, I found out later, which meant to add life and vitality to this city with its continual low hanging clouds and an annual rainfall of over sixty inches. I drove to the end of the street, turned right into the city center and onto flatter ground. By this time, I was getting the hang of the clutch and the continual acceleration it took to keep from rolling backwards on the steep roadway. Driving this VW was fun.

I drove up and down the streets of Juneau. They were nearly empty this early on Saturday morning. This time of day all the bars were closed. Where could Hal be?

Around 10:30, I returned to the *Ranger*. Hal came back in a taxi half an hour later. The hunters wrote Hal two checks for 1,200 bucks apiece, everyone shook hands, and the *Ranger* took on life. The engine began to throb, Hal and I undid the lines from the dock, and we cruised out of the harbor. No one asked Hal where he had gone and he never said.

The *Ranger* steered into Limestone Inlet at 5:00 p.m. Everyone but Ted Childers left the ship to go duck hunting. We climbed into a gas-powered canoe and landed in a marshy area. The idea was to make this a scouting trip, to get the clients familiar with the coastal terrain. Hal went with Granger and I went with Karl and Fred. We saw hundreds of ducks and two brown bears. When it started to get dark, we met back at the canoe. On the *Ranger*, Ted cooked supper, and we all were in bed by 10:30 p.m.

October 8, 1961. Day 2.

We woke to steady rain and heavy winds. After breakfast, Fred and Hal took the canoe to land. After a while, we heard gunshots and an hour later the canoe returned. Fred was happy. He had shot four ducks.

The boat left Limestone Inlet as soon as Hal and Fred were back on board. The wind picked up and the *Ranger* rolled and bucked. It was like riding a rodeo bull, but you couldn't get off. I almost puked over the side. I wasn't the only one. Karl maneuvered the boat into calmer water in an inlet at Admiralty Island and after lunch everyone took a nap.

All differences seemed to be ironed out between Hal and Fred. It looked like we'd have a good hunt.

October 9, 1961. Day 3

I began to get a cold in the night and woke up sniffling. Karl checked the weather report on the ship-to-shore radio and the *Ranger* got underway. I helped Ted clean the ducks. Mid-morning, we spotted a school of five humpback whales. We followed them for an hour. The hunters were as happy and excited as kids on Christmas morning. When we finally turned away from the whales, Karl asked me if I would run the boat. It was another first for me. First a ride in Hal's new jet boat, and now I was steering a fifty-foot cruiser. Two hours later, Karl took over the wheel and we anchored in our harbor destination.

Ted roasted the ducks for lunch. The fresh meat was fatty and sweet. It was fantastic. Afterwards, Hal and Karl took the Michiganders onto Admiralty Island to hunt for bear. Hal had gotten two bear tags in Juneau. Hal put me in charge of the power canoe. On the way to shore, five or six grey seal heads bobbed up around us to see what we were. The water was calm, and we all laughed and pointed at their curious little eyes. I left the guys on the beach with instructions to pick them up at dark.

October 13, 1961. Day 7

On Friday the 13th, our seventh day out I had a hacking cough. Hal said he could hear me everywhere on the boat. I weathered through the day, but Granger was less fortunate. He told me he had fallen six times when he was on shore. He stepped on his fishing pole and snapped it in half, dropped his new shotgun in the saltwater, and broke his binoculars apart jumping out of the power canoe in rain so thick he couldn't see fifty yards off the bow. At dinner, he dropped a dish of food on the floor and went to bed screaming and coughing, wheezing and sneezing. Our boat was caught in forty to sixty mile-per-hour winds, what we called a "southeaster" but what others would call a hurricane. Talk about bad luck. It was a Friday the 13 to remember.

October 14, 1961. Day 8

The winds didn't let up all night and we woke up to continual forty-six mph winds and twelve-foot seas. Karl moved our boat into a different cove on the east side of Admiralty Island and somehow we all were able to eat breakfast and keep it down. I washed the dishes afterwards as usual. Ted got started with a lecture on the ruination of Alaska through fishing mismanagement and Japanese pulp mills. The storm kept everyone inside for the morning and Fred, Hal, and Granger played gin rummy for three dollars a game.

That night I dreamt that I was flying a two-man jet with a beautiful girl with whiskers on her chin who wanted to climb into my sleeping bag with me. We were in the bottom of a double bunk and a younger girl with glowing skin kept climbing up over us to the top. I have no idea what any of that dream meant. I'm sure Sigmund Freud would have had a ball with it.

My mind wandered back to Leda and Mary. I wondered what they were doing. When I returned to Fairbanks, Wally Poland, the trailer park owner, had said I could rent the two-room attic apartment above their house for $25 a month until spring. They were planning a trip to Florida.

And what about Uncle Sam? My Army draft status was 1-A.

25: Deer Kill in the Rainbow

Nine days out of Juneau we anchored in Eliza Harbor at Admiralty Island. At low tide, Hal, Karl, and the hunters went onshore to look for game. On the *Ranger,* we were totally out of meat. Ted and I stayed on board. When I finished my chores, I felt a need to explore, to get on solid ground.

"Ted, I'm going to use the raft for a while. I'll stay near the boat."

"Okay, Rudy. If you see a whale, bring it back."

I grabbed a .35 caliber Remington pump action rifle from Karl's gun rack and jumped into the rubber raft we had on board. I took the rifle in case I came across a bear or a bear came across me. I was ready for the weather in full rain gear, hip boots, and my wide brimmed hat. I also took my camera.

My main interest was taking pictures of the scenery and, if I was lucky, get a photo of more gray seals with their cute bobbing heads. Whenever I saw them, they stared at me with curiosity. They made me laugh. I was too big to be their food.

I rowed over to a narrow strip of gravelly sand about four hundred yards from the boat. As I stepped out of the raft, for the first time in a week the sun broke through the deep heavy overcast. Suddenly a brilliant rainbow appeared, its far end arcing over the *Ranger.* The other end came to rest on a pile of glistening yellow rocks on the island's shore. My first happy thought was, "Where's the leprechaun with my pot of gold?" I took a couple of pictures, then stopped to look at the bright sunlit beauty shimmering around me.

Then I saw movement at the shoreline end of the rainbow. A young three-point buck was stepping down onto the beach out of the trees to be in the sun. "Meat," I thought.

Lying on my stomach on the wet sand, my rifle aimed and steadied, I held and waited. The deer stopped. I was about to shoot when he raised his head, looked around and then took a few steps closer. I held off. Now he was right across from me on the mainland, less than eighty yards away, but he didn't stop. He was a moving target, a difficult shot with open sights.

The rifle had no scope. I exhaled the air from my lungs to still my body and pulled the trigger. The buck lurched and dropped. I jumped back in my raft. When I got to it, the deer was dead. My shot was a good clean shot, broadside through the lungs. Its death was immediate and painless. In Alaska native tradition, I thanked the deer for his sacrifice. Now we had meat for dinner.

Ted heard the shot and popped up on deck. I waved and he motioned for me to row back to the boat. I did, leaving the deer at the edge of the water. I was worried about bears stealing the carcass and I kept one eye on shore as I rowed the raft up to the side of the *Ranger*. Ted had scurried down to the galley and was back on deck with some rope, a burlap sack, and his cutting knife. As I got to the side, he climbed down into the raft and we rowed back to the deer. I beached the raft and Ted jumped out. He moved fast for an old guy.

"Watch this," he said. "I'll show you how to gut a deer the proper way." He unbuttoned his denim shirt and dropped it on the ground exposing the white arm-length sleeves of his cotton undershirt. He rolled both sleeves up above his elbows and knelt by the buck's rear end. He looked up at me and grinned. I felt like I was about to watch an artist at work. Ted took a black-handled folding jackknife out of his bag and opened it up. The blade was only four inches long.

"This knife is sharper than a son-of-a-bitch scalpel," he said as he pushed it in and sliced easily into the flesh of the deer. He cut through the dense matted fur circling the buck's anus, then he hooked his forefinger in the loosened anus and yanked. It slid out like a floppy brown flower at the end of a thick slimy stem.

"Watch this," he said again with the pride of a master, and took his opened knife, gripped it blade end down in his right hand so that the flat side of the blade pressed downward against his wrist. He slid his arm into the deer's widened rear-end hole, inching his hand and arm inside, sliding it careful and slow up the colon, past the organs and the stomach, until his fingers touched the diaphragm. His arm up to his shoulder was completely inside the carcass.

Somehow, he turned the open knife around inside the deer and, with the razor-sharp blade, severed the esophagus below the diaphragm. Then he slowly pulled all the organs, connected and intact, out of the body and onto the sand. He didn't puncture the kidneys, gall bladder, liver, or stomach. He didn't cut or puncture the colon. All the organs lay outside the animal in one long neat surgical pile. No bile, feces or urine escaped to pollute the meat. I stood there in disbelief and admiration.

"Rudy, grab the two front legs and lift," Ted said.

We rolled the carcass onto its back. He grabbed the rear legs just below the hooves and we dragged it to the raft and lifted it in. It was heavy but manageable without the weight of the organs, which we left on the shore for bears, ravens, or any other scavenger that might appear out of the forest, sea, or sky. ·

Ted rinsed the blood and mucus off his hands and arms in the water — his undershirt was a red slimy mess — and I rowed us back to the boat. He climbed out first, tossed down a loop of the rope which I tied around the deer's hind legs. I secured the raft, climbed up on deck, and the two of us hoisted the carcass up and laid it out. Ted tied the deer's head to a low beam on the foredeck and we raised its hind quarters up to hang on a hook and bleed out. Ted told me to cut its throat and sever its head so it could bleed freely. I had seen Clark Engle do that at Post Lake. Ted secured a bucket under the carcass to catch the blood, and the rest of the day I spent cleaning the rack and mopping blood off the deck since, with the rolling of the boat in the wind and waves, the catch bucket would continually tip and slide off to the side.

Late in the afternoon, the sun came out again for a brief minute and shined through the rain. In front of us was a beautiful double rainbow. Far out I spotted a doe on the shoreline standing legs apart like a statue, staring out at our boat. A deer at one end of a rainbow and me on the other for a second time. I wondered if the doe had come looking for her stag, her lover. Could she see him hanging above the deck? I didn't want to overthink it and get sad, so I went back to work. Nature is wild and beautiful, but also harsh and deadly. We are all part of Darwin's survival of the fittest.

When Hal and Karl returned with Granger and Fred several hours a later, Ted had ready a gourmet deer steak dinner with sides of green beans and boiled potatoes.

"A toast to Rudy," said Karl, and everyone popped a beer.

The next morning, we had more cold rain with high winds and Karl moved the *Ranger* to another cove. It took three hours. I stayed up on deck and continued scraping clean the dear hide — its cape — until evening. The open air felt good even if it was raining. After dinner, Hal and Fred each gave me a dollar to play poker. Ted did the dinner dishes. Everyone was full and happy.

October 17, 1961. Day 11

After breakfast, Hal, Fred, Granger, and I went duck hunting. We were out till early afternoon, but no one brought anything back. I worked on the deer cape cape while we moved to Whitewater Bay about forty-five minutes away. After lunch, I boiled the buck's skull plate to get the fragments of meat out of hard-to-reach places.

The sun was out almost all day and it rained very little. This was the best weather we'd had since we'd left Juneau. Karl moored the boat under Table Mountain and told everyone that he planned to arrive back in Juneau in three days, on Friday.

October 18, 1961. Day 12

More heavy rain. When it finally stopped, Hal took me up on deck to show me the proper use of a .35 caliber Remington. At 9:00 a.m., I dressed in full rain gear, took the rifle, and climbed into the power canoe. I was supposed to look for another deer. Hal dropped me off on shore and continued down the peninsula. I was alone. It felt good.

I walked into the tree line and wandered into a small meadow. Its lush canopy over me cast a green iridescent glow that seemed to pulsate with life. I stood still and slowly turned around, listening for the movement of animals. The soft splatter of rain on the leaves above me was the only sound I heard.

It was a magical place, a place of peace. I was away from the others on the boat and their constant presence. I thought about leaving the meadow to hunt, but I knew we had meat on board and we'd be back in Juneau soon so I found a fallen tree and sat down, the Remington across my lap. I sat in silence listening only to dripping rain and my own breath.

I heard the power canoe in the distance coming back to pick me up and looked at my watch. I had been sitting in the meadow for over two hours. I stood. The rain was starting to come down heavy again. I walked back out of the tree line into the open as Hal came around the bend.

The Michigan guys went back out after bear in the afternoon rain. No luck again. Maybe the bears were in hibernation.

October 19, 1961. Day 13

Amazingly, the sun came out today and I wrote a letter home.

October 19, 1961

Dear folks,

Here I am after a morning of deer hunting, aboard ship at high tide, being buffeted by fifty mph winds, in a pair of blood-soaked jeans and tennis shoes split at the seams. I am laying on an air mattress on a wooden bunk bed, a rope wrapped around my wrist and tied to a pipe above my head to keep me from rolling out and crashing to the floor. The *Ranger*, a fifty-foot cruiser, rolls from side to side all night in the ocean tides off Admiralty Island. Every night so far there has been a deluge of rain, and the shifting winds swirling around us keep snapping the anchor chain under my bunk.

The meals on the boat are good although I've cut down on breakfast. The main meals consist of salmon which we catch, Dungeness crab which we catch, and venison. So far, I'm the only one to have shot a deer.

Right now, we're in a temperate rain forest. Imagine such a thing here in the Far North. At the same time, there is freezing weather in Fairbanks. When I left two weeks ago, there was snow on the ground. It is hard to realize how big Alaska is. You could put the land mass of Texas in it twice with space left over.

Love to all,

Joel, aka Rudy

October 20, 1961. Day 14

A northerly wind set in last night while we were anchored in Whitewater Bay. Winds were gale strength and I again slept with a safety rope wrapped around my wrist. Then winds blew the clouds away and, for the first time, we saw the moon over Table Mountain.

When we looked out at daybreak, the sky was cloudless, but because of the winds and rough seas, we dared not go out into open water. On the radio this morning, we heard news of a southeaster which might flatten the northern end of Ketchikan. When that passes, perhaps we can leave for Juneau. We were hoping to get there by Friday night because the Pan-Am flights leave for Anchorage only Saturday and Wednesday.

Good news. The radio just announced that a southeast wind knocked out the northerly wind. The seas are temporarily calm. Karl says we should get to Juneau by 8 o'clock tonight.

26: Danny Boy

It was dark when we got into Juneau. Fred and Granger had packed their gear and were standing on deck as we swung into position. We shook hands goodbye and they left for their hotel in a taxi. There was a sense of relief after the clients left. Karl got out some cold beers. I saw Hal hand Ted a check.

"Here's to the end of the trip," Karl said. And we all clicked bottles and drank. "What's next for everybody?" he asked.

"I'm headed back to Seattle," said Ted. "Got some business to attend to."

"Hal?"

"I'm going to stay here a day or two," Hal said. "I have nothing booked for a while." I looked at him. I thought he was flying back to Anchorage with me. It never occurred to me that he wasn't.

"Rudy?" Karl asked.

"I have to get back to Fairbanks. I need to find a job, money for food, and a place to live." I finished my beer and put the empty bottle in the trash.

"Rudy, if you want to stay a few days to learn more about Juneau, you're welcome to stay on the boat. I come down here every day anyway to make sure everything is working. There's a Chinese restaurant near the Gastineau Hotel. Good food and cheap."

I thanked Karl and told him about the cheap rental I might get when I got back to Fairbanks, but I said I would like to stay on board the *Ranger* that night since he had offered.

Hal had gotten moody and wasn't paying attention. There had been more words between him and the Michiganders. I had heard loud talk between them earlier when I was down in the galley. They were complaining that for all their money all they got was a few ducks and a seal. No bears, nothing exciting. And the weather was lousy. I had no idea how much money Hal had cleared on this trip after Karl's share and the cost of food, duck and bear tags, ammunition, and fuel. And Ted Childers had gotten a paycheck. A car horn beeped in the parking lot at the end of the pier and Hal got up and left. I looked out and saw him climb into a taxi. I knew he was going to a bar.

Karl, Ted, and I stayed on board to make sure everything was secure. Ted was going to sleep on the boat tonight, too. Karl wanted to do some paperwork before he left for home, "Because," he said, "I don't like to mix work and family time."

I kept thinking about Hal's comment that he didn't want to pay me for my time, even though I paid my own train and plane fare from Fairbanks to here. He said he would help with the plane ticket to Juneau, but I was still waiting for that. As he emphasized, the job and experience were worth it. He was right, I knew it, but it still bothered me. I asked Karl if I could borrow his car.

"Sure," he said, "but be back before nine. My wife is expecting me at home tonight." He handed me the keys to his VW.

I remembered the Red Dog saloon and drove there first. Hal wasn't there. The hotel bar was close by where we had met with Fred and Granger. Hal wasn't there either. After a few wrong turns, I found the Elks Club. When I went to the door to get in, it was locked. I pressed a buzzer and a man opened a little peephole in the door and asked me what I wanted.

"I need to come in," I said. "I'm looking for somebody."

"Sorry, buddy," he said. "The Elks is a private club. Members only." He slid the peephole shut. I pushed the buzzer again and held it down. He came back annoyed. "I said this is a private club and you can't come in."

"I'm looking for Hal Waugh," I said. "We just got back from a hunt."

"Oh, Hal. Why didn't you say so?" he said, and he unlocked the door and pulled it open. "Bar's first door to the right."

When I walked into the bar, Hal was sitting by himself at a table. He didn't look over as I came in, but the bartender saw me.

"What'll you have?" he called from behind the bar.

"Just a tomato juice," I said. I walked over to the bar as he poured it, paid with a dollar I had in my pocket, and went over to Hal's table.

The large room was empty but for three older gray-haired men sitting together at a card table, and two younger guys in fishing gear at the bar, their winter coats hanging over the low backs of their bar stools. The lights in the room were dim and the stale smell of cigarettes rose from everywhere. Between Hal and the bar, off to the left, a guy in a green corduroy jacket was playing an upright piano. Hal was bent over a whiskey, lost in the music. The tune was familiar.

I sat down at Hal's table. He still didn't look over. When I looked at him, I saw tears in his eyes. Sure, the cigarette smell in the room was strong but not that strong. Then the piano player began to sing:

Oh Danny Boy, the pipes, the pipes are callin'
From glen to glen, and down the mountainside.
The summer's gone and all the flowers are dyin.'
'Tis you, 'tis you, must go and I must bide'

134

A tear streaked down Hal's cheek.

> But come you back when summer's in the meadow
> Or when the valley's hushed and white with snow
> 'Tis I'll be there in sunshine or in shadow
> Oh Danny Boy, Oh Danny Boy,
> I love you so, I love you so!

When the song was over, Hal stood and applauded, went over to the pianist and gave him a ten dollar bill. "Play it again," he said and came back to his seat. The pianist played it through again, and again Hal applauded, went over, and gave him a ten dollar bill. "Play it again," he said. And the pianist played it again, and Hal went over and gave him a third ten dollar bill. The pianist knew he had a good thing going and kept it up. Finally, I had to say something.

"Hal, I just watched you give that guy thirty bucks for playing 'Danny Boy' for ten minutes and I get nothing for two week's work. Do you think that's fair?" Hal seemed to see me for the first time. For a moment, he stared at me like I had materialized out of thin air.

"I guess not, Rudy." And he reached into his back pocket, pulled out his wallet, and laid a hundred dollars on the table.

"Thanks," I said.

Hal didn't hear me and turned back to "Danny Boy." The tune and lyrics surrounded him in a mystical cloud. He was Irish to the core. And passionate about life. I admired that. He was a good man.

I put the money in my pocket, finished my tomato juice, and drove Karl's car back to the boat. At least now I had money for a cab and airfare to Anchorage.

27: BACK IN FAIRBANKS: LEDA REVISITED

With money in my pocket, the next day I flew into Anchorage. I got a taxi at the airport and went directly to the railroad station for a ticket to Fairbanks. The next train out wouldn't leave until the following morning, so I walked over the bridge to the Hofbrauhaus on Third Street for a beer and a sandwich. After my lunch, I went over to the piano and noodled around with my "Moonlight Sonata." Like the first time I was there, someone sent over a beer. I waved at a guy at the bar and wondered what he would have sent over if I had played "Danny Boy."

To walk to and from the terminal from town, you had to cross over the Ship Creek bridge, a narrow wooden walkway. A dozen fishermen lined the banks on both sides of Ship Creek trying to catch a salmon or a trout. I stood on the bridge, leaning on the railing to see if there was any action. After half an hour, a native man in a flannel cap and a parka snagged a fish and reeled it in. It was at least a foot long and enough of a catch to keep everyone else casting and reeling. I stayed to watch for half an hour, but no one else snagged anything so I went to the station to hang out and take a nap. The train was scheduled to leave Anchorage around 8:30 and I didn't want to miss it. It would be a long day. The train ride could take as much as ten hours if there were a lot of off-the-grid commuters or transit riders waiting along the tracks, and at this time of year there usually were.

When I got back to Fairbanks, I found out the deal I thought I had for the room was off the table. The Polands, the trailer park owners, had had a change of plans while I was gone and were not going to travel south. So, just back from Juneau, I had no place to stay. But I didn't dwell on it. Something would happen. The moving hands of the clock bring constant change.

I got a coffee and a slice of hot apple pie at the café across from the Fairbanks post office and, carrying my duffle and backpack, caught a ride with a student to the university. I went to the Bunnell building to see if Chuck Keim was in his office, but he was out. I peeked into my old office. It was empty. My next stop was the bookstore. As luck would have it, Leda was there. I told her about the Juneau trip and that the Polands had backed out of their offer. What she heard was that I was homeless. Again.

"Would you like to come back and stay with us till you find out what you're going to do?" she asked.

I thought about sleeping in her cellar again, but I also thought she wouldn't ask me if she didn't feel safe. "Sure," I said. "Thanks." Maybe things would be different this time.

Then Leda told me she had plans to leave town soon herself to visit her family in New Mexico. "And Mary," she said, "isn't doing well. She's going back to her family in Connecticut. She hasn't been able to find a job in town and the university has no handicap facilities. Hardly any place here has handicap facilities."

Leda finished her purchase in the bookstore, and we drove back to her trailer. When I walked in, there was a different feel to the place. It looked like it hadn't been cleaned since I'd left the month before. The kitchen sink was piled high with food-caked dishes and there was a sour foul, smell to everything. It was as if the place had been abandoned except that Leda and Mary were still living there. A muted sunlight shone in through dirty windows and half-closed curtains.

I was having second thoughts about moving back in, except I felt Leda was having a rough time and needed help. She was beautiful but lost. She had quit as a telephone operator at Fort Wainwright and still hadn't gotten another job. She was tired of being stared at and propositioned everywhere she went. She was too beautiful to ignore. Living in Fairbanks proved it to be oppressively obvious.

Mary made a noise from inside the bathroom and opened the door. She was dressed in a robe that hung on her like a bedsheet. Her medium length usually brushed brown hair was a mess of tangles. It looked like she hadn't washed it in weeks. Mary stood leaning against the bathroom door jamb expressionless. Not a word, not even a hello. Did she even see me?

"It's plugged again," she said with deep tiredness in her voice. I looked at Leda.

"It's the toilet," Leda said. "I bought a plunger, but I can't get it to work."

I offered to help, and she led me to the bathroom as Mary stepped awkwardly aside. The tiny room stunk with poop and urine mixed with Leda's perfumed shampoo. The floor of the tiny shower stall was covered with a film of dried soap scum and clots of hair. The sink in the vanity wasn't any better. I could not believe two adult women could be so filthy. Leda's old apartment back in the Northward Building had been spotless. I knew Mary couldn't do much to help, but I didn't understand how Leda could let things get so out of control.

Leda handed me the plunger and backed out of the tiny room. I leaned over the toilet and stared into an eight-inch mound of feces, wadded toilet paper, and bloody Kotex. "Well," I thought to myself, "except for the perfume, it's no worse than scraping the mangled guts

137

out of a dead moose." So I went to work. The crap was so thick in the bowl that I knew the plunger wasn't enough, so I went to the kitchen and found a wooden spatula and spooned poop into a paper bag which I handed to Leda to stick outside in the fresh air. With most of the thick stuff out of the toilet, the plunger worked and when I flushed it, clean water started to flow back into the bowl.

My deal with Leda was I would stay on with them until they left Fairbanks. I would sleep in the cellar again, but they could not lock me in. They said yes — anyone who had cleaned up their poop certainly could be trusted.

It was near lunchtime and I checked the fridge. It was nearly empty. Half a bottle of milk, a pitcher of cherry Kool-Aid, a few soft apples, a half carton of eggs, two sticks of butter, and a lemon.

"What do you guys do for food?" I asked.

"Oh, we drink a lot of tea. We eat a lot of crackers and cereal and Minute Rice."

"How about we clean up the kitchen and then I'll take your car to the grocery and pick up a few things?" I said. "I'll cook supper."

"Thank you, Joel. That would be wonderful," she said. I saw her body relax.

I found a quarter-full box of soap powder and hand scrubbed the dirty silverware, dishes, pots, and pans while Leda dried and put things away. Mary sat on the couch and watched. She looked lost and confused.

When the dishes were clean, I set the little table in the kitchen to give the room a sense of order. Leda handed me five dollars and the keys to her car. I drove over to Ray's Supermarket.

For supper, I cooked up hamburger patties with sliced beets and a big slice of sweet watermelon for dessert. As Mary ate her food, I watched life come back into her face. She smiled for the first time.

28: Looking for Work

In the morning, I got up, washed up in the slop sink by the furnace, dressed in clean jeans and a flannel shirt, and climbed out of the cellar. The trap door pushed opened easily and I held onto the metal handle attached to its underside so it wouldn't drop and make a noise. There was no sound from the locked bedroom, so I wrote Leda a note, put it on the kitchen table, and left to look for work.

It was a busy day. I went from place to place in Fairbanks applying for jobs, had lunch at my apple pie café, and headed back to the trailer to cook the girls supper. Afterwards I offered to buy them both a beer at Tommy's Elbow Room, but they declined. Mary didn't want to leave the trailer and Leda didn't want to leave her alone, or so she said. They stayed home and listened to the radio, but I went out. This was our routine for a week. Then I got lucky. On the fifth of November, I wrote a letter home to share my good luck.

November 5, 1961
Box 238 College, Alaska

Dear Homesteaders,

I should define the word Homesteaders. Homesteaders are people who would rather stay home instead of coming to Alaska.

Since I returned from Juneau, I have been doing the hardest thing a man can do in Fairbanks in the winter: find a job. I applied for work at the fire station, the police department, the post office, the university, three hotels, the employment bureau, a new grocery store, an old grocery store, and the university's experimental farm.

I did the impossible. Not only did I manage to get one job, I got two. A friend is going to Quebec for two weeks to visit his family. I'm going to take his nightshift janitorial job at the university while he's away. The job pays $2.40 an hour and I will work eight hours a night, from 5:00 p.m. to 1:00 a.m. I begin on November 6th and will work six days a week until the 17th when he comes back. After taxes, my net pay will be about $92 a week.

In addition, I expect to be called by the Agricultural Experimental Station near the university any day for work. There I could work as many hours as I want at $2.50 hour. If I'm called for farming this week, I'll try to work sixteen hours a day until the 17th. I'll be able to buy some of the little things I have wanted, like pay my dental bill and buy a Smith Corona electric typewriter. Maybe I can finally get contact lenses or, down the road, save enough for a car.

For me, things are looking good. There are a lot of guys out of work here, unemployment is fourteen percent, but I'll be able to earn enough to be comfortable. I thought I'd let you know so you wouldn't worry about me, and if for any unforeseen reason that I don't get the farm job, with the two-week janitorial job, I'll at least break even for the month. By that time, something should have happened with my other applications. Smile at my good fortune. Now I'll be able to afford to buy a friend a beer.

Even though the cheap rental in town didn't materialize, I've been staying in a trailer park with a couple of friends, Leda and her roommate Mary. They've given me shelter and I 've been cooking for them to return the favor. I've just invented a new type of dessert for them: several pineapple rings, a slice of whole wheat bread torn up in small pieces, some condensed milk, mix in a pan and heat until boiling, serve hot, and eat. In fact, I am eating some now.

However, both Leda and Mary are leaving Fairbanks. I plan to stay in their trailer three more weeks, through November. I'll take over their rent payments.

More anon,

Joel

29: Agricultural Experimental Station

The Agricultural Experiment Station was about a mile and a half past the university, at the end of a two-lane dirt road that t-boned off the highway. Officially, it was called the Agricultural Experiment Station, though everyone knew it as the Experimental Farm.

The first building I saw as I walked up the dirt road was a long, wide-open barn with dozens of cows in stalls lined up in a row. I wondered why the cows were exposed to the cold. It was freezing. I was told later by a worker that that was the experiment, to see if domestic cows could survive winters like a muskox.

I thought it was cruel to put dairy cattle through subzero weather. My background in undergraduate biology had taught me the significance of an animal's natural genetic makeup and that it was linked to survival. But I wasn't an expert. The discovery of DNA was only a few years old and had just been introduced into biology courses in the last four years. It was still being explored. I thought about moose and elk and caribou, and I guessed that the idea of the experiment was to see if domestic cattle could physically alter and adjust. If they could, it would help local dairy farmers grow their herds. Creamer's Dairy on College Road would benefit by it if it worked.

The second structure I saw was a large, red, enclosed barn. This was the building I was assigned to. When the supervisor opened the barn door and motioned me in, I saw more cows lined up. Each cow had a large steel ring in her nose which was hooked by a chain to a long metal rail. Large sucking electric milking machines were loudly pulsating and humming. They were clamped to the teats on every bulging udder.

"What the hell?" I thought. I looked over at the supervisor next to me. Didn't he see the pain these poor cows were in? Did he not see their huge brown eyes rolling up white in their sockets? Didn't he hear the long groans aching from their throats? He didn't react. He was used to it. He did this every day, as did every cow on the farm.

All I knew about milking cows was what I had seen in the movies, happy farmers — men and women, boys and girls — milking cows with names like Daisy or Elsie, milking them by hand, pulling firmly on the finger-like fleshy tender teats, aiming squirts of warm fresh milk

141

into tin pails, their foreheads resting against the sides of their animals with love and affection. But, wow, it was nothing like this here. The difference was the milk cows in the movies weren't tethered by their noses or had screw clamps pinching their tender teats until they bled.

At the far end of the row, cows already milked were being un-hooked and led out a door as other cows with full udders were brought in to take their places. A couple of workers fastened the new cows' nose rings to the holding bar and clamped the electric milking nozzles onto their undersides and flipped on the electric switches. The cows jerked and flinched. *MooooOOOOO*. Their painful voices rose and fell. To me it was a cacophony of horror.

The supervisor tapped me on the arm and handed me a long-handled shovel. He saw my expression of horror and shrugged. "You'll get used to it," he said. He pointed at two 6x8 foot empty two-wheeled open carts by the barn door. "Your job is to shovel the manure into those two wagons. Fill 'em up and then I'll show you what to do." Then he walked away down the line of draining cows to the far end of the barn. The buzz and snap of electric milking machines filled the room.

No one had told me what my job would be at the Agricultural Experiment Station when I was hired. When I heard the word Agri-culture, I imagined growing corn or beans or tomatoes, or maybe harvesting chicken eggs. It never occurred to me that I would be asked to shovel warm steaming cow manure piled six inches high. Had I known that, I would have worn my rubber boots. I was wearing sweat socks and tennis shoes. But it was what it was. I had a job. I needed the mon-ey, and I started in with the shovel, trying not to slip and get more than my shoes filthy.

For two hours, I shoveled, walked each scoopful over to the wagons, dumped it, went back for more, and did it again. And again. And again. I had no idea that a shovelful of cow manure could be so heavy. It was the repetition in addition to the weight. Each shovelful weighed about eight pounds. If I scooped one shovelful each min-ute for one hour, that was eight pounds times sixty minutes, or 480 pounds, and that barely filled one wagon. I had to fill two. I took a short ten-minute break, half-an-hour for lunch at noon, and filled both carts by 3:30 p.m. I was so tired I could barely move my arms. My back was a reservoir of pain. Worse, the manure had been so sloppy that the legs of my jeans were caked with splatter.

The super came over and smiled at me. "Good job," he said. "What do you think of it?"

"It's hard," I said, "but this is only my first day. At least now I know what the job is all about."

"Good," he said. "I've been watching you. You're not afraid to work. You'll do fine here. Tomorrow after you fill the wagons, if it's not too cold, I'll show you how to dump them." Then he left.

I looked at my watch. It was 4:00 o'clock. I punched out, gathered my gear for my next job, which, as tired and dirty as I now was, I dreaded, and walked back to the highway. I wasn't the only one getting off and another worker stopped to give me a ride back to campus. I was embarrassed about the manure on my clothes, but the driver was as dirty as me, so we drove through the twenty degree air with the windows down.

"You're new at the farm?" he asked, glancing over. "I don't think I've seen you here before."

"Yes. This was my first day."

"You'll get used to it. It's a good day's work and the guys there are good guys."

I nodded. A minute later, we got to campus and he drove me up to the Bunnell building parking lot.

"Thanks a lot," I said. "Maybe I'll see you tomorrow."

I went into Bunnell to start another first day of work as a night janitor. I had a change of clothes but there was nothing I could do about my shoes. I went into the janitor's closet, found a roll of paper towels, and did my best to wipe them down. I did what I could, but it wasn't good enough. The good news was the work was easy. All I had to do that first night was empty wastebaskets, wash chalk boards in the classrooms, straighten up student chairs, and mop the halls and restrooms.

That night during a break, I wrote a poem about what I'd seen that day at the farm.

The Cow in Hell

A spike in my teat,
a hook in my nose
pulling me apart
through the noose
of my yoke—

God!—
This screeching pain.
My buckling knees
slip in my dung.
I bleed from the hip
into a jar
clamped against my groin.

The Pain, the Pain.
How my eyes roll.
And my tongue is cut

*   *   *

143

When I went back to the farm on my second day, the temperature outside had fallen to -10. It was a cold day for early November, but I didn't really think about it since the heat in the milking barn was controlled at a constant 60 degrees. When the cows left or came in, the doors behind them were quickly shut.

Today, I wore my rubber waders and waterproof rain pants so I could move a little faster. When I stopped to think about it, shoveling manure was no worse than digging the gravel out from under the railroad ties when I was a gandy dancer earlier that summer. The manure smelled worse, but the shoveling was about the same. At least there were no mosquitoes here. I knew I could do this. I had both wagons filled by 3 o'clock.

As soon as they were ready to go, the boss came over. "Good work," he said. "Now I'll show you where to dump them. Follow me." I pulled on my coat and he led me outside to a small tractor parked next to the barn. "What I want you to do is to chain the two manure wagons together, hook them up to the tractor, and drive the tractor to that open field." He pointed to the other side of College Road. "Dump the manure in any empty spot and bring the tractor back." He showed me where the release pin was to let the wagon beds tilt down so the manure would slide out. With the help of a shovel, of course.

Here was another new adventure. I had never driven a tractor. I guess it was expected that anyone working at this farm had experience in all facets of farming. When I applied for the job, it was never mentioned. I didn't say anything stupid or ask questions, and the boss walked away assuming I knew what I was doing.

The keys were in the ignition. Luckily, the weather-exposed seat was thickly padded. I climbed up to start the engine. I'd have to jockey the tractor around, back it up to the wagons and hook them to the steel hitch post in the rear. The tractor had a manual transmission like Karl Lane's VW in Juneau, clutch peddle on the left, brake in the middle, accelerator on the right. It had an arm-long metal gear shift sticking up out of the floor.

The supervisor stuck his head out of the barn door. "Hey, Joel," he called. "I forgot to tell you that the manure will freeze fast when it's below zero, so don't dally or you'll have a mess."

"Okay, thanks," I said. He disappeared back into the milking barn.

I pulled on my work gloves and started the engine. It sounded strong. I shifted it into first and the tractor lurched forward. Good flow of gas. I pulled ahead about ten yards to circle back to the barn. No problem. I put it in reverse. Good. With the tractor idling in neutral, I climbed off, pulled opened the barn doors, and within a minute I had the two wagons hooked together. I backed up the tractor, but I pressed down on the gas a little too firmly and it hit the front cart slightly off center with a crack. I didn't see any damage. With a little jockeying, I got the tractor hitch and the tongue of the front wagon lined up, connected them, and started up the dirt road to the highway and the dumping field. The load behind me was heavy but the tractor had power.

I had buried the blade of my scoop shovel deep into the manure pile on the front cart. It wasn't long, just a minute or two, when I saw a thin coat of ice form on the metal shovel blade and a white film begin to form on the manure. It had long ago stopped steaming.

I was driving the open tractor into a frigid breeze and wished I had worn a second layer of wool to trap a little more of my body heat. My hands were freezing on the metal steering wheel, but at least I was getting close to the end of the dirt path. Several cars and a pick-up truck passed by ahead on College Road. Beyond that, I saw the low embankment separating the dumping field from the highway. Thank goodness, I was almost there. I could dump the manure and get back to the warm barn.

The tractor came to the edge of the concrete highway and bumped up onto and over it. The eight seconds of smooth ride was a welcomed change, then I drove down a short dip towards the bottom of the embankment. A ridge two feet high ran the length of the field.

As I started to angle the tractor up the slope, one of the wheels on the front manure wagon fell off. The tractor jerked left and tipped over on its side. Since the two manure carts were attached, they both flipped over. It happened in an instant.

I jumped off to get out of the way. What I was faced with was a tractor still in gear on its side and two carts of freezing cow shit upside down in a ditch. If I hadn't been so damn cold, I might have thought it was funny. But I was cold, and it wasn't funny. Driving an open tractor at -10 degrees was crazy. It was absurd. Everything was absurd. And this was only my second day on the job.

I grabbed the shovel and trudged back to the barn. The Super was not happy when I told him what had happened, but he was businesslike and was more concerned about the tractor than me or the manure, so he and two other workers got in a front-loader truck, drove to the accident, and set things straight. They got the wheel back on the axel, pulled the tractor upright, and got the wagons up onto the field. But the manure was ice-coated and solid, so they had to leave the wagons there.

"Don't worry about it, Rudinger. It could happen to anybody," the super said. "We'll get at them in the morning with a blow torch."

I thanked him for not getting pissed off.

"Tomorrow is another day. You're new at the farm," he said. "You'll get used to it."

30: Leda and Mary Leave

When I got back to Leda's trailer after my third day of work, Mary was there alone. She looked awful. Her face was red and swollen. She had been crying.

"Leda's gone," she sobbed. "She turned in her rental car and got a flight to Anchorage."

Anchorage? Today? This was a total surprise. I knew she was leaving, but I thought it was weeks away. And she had told me she was going to visit her parents in Albuquerque. Leda had been Mary's only friend and supporter. How was I going to work two jobs and take care of Mary, too? Did she even want me to? She was a private person and never had much to talk to me about. We were barely friends.

After a few minutes, Mary calmed down. "I bought a ticket back to Connecticut," she said. "I need you to take me to the airport on Friday. Can you do that?" She looked at me, visibly shaking. I didn't know if it was her Multiple Sclerosis or her nerves or her sadness about losing Leda. She could have gotten a cab, but she needed more than that. She could hardly walk with her arm crutches, and how could she carry her suitcase or check in?

"Sure," I said. "I'll tell my supervisor at the farm I'll need to take the day off. I know he'll understand if I explain why." At least I hoped he would. I had no other choice.

Mary started to cry again and fell back onto the sofa. I looked at her and felt helpless as I watched her fall apart, a lost soul who had lost her only friend. Leda's leaving so abruptly was a shock to both of us, but to Mary especially. What did they talk about when I was away? Why had Leda left without saying goodbye? How could she abandon Mary without notice? Had she been in mental pain herself and kept it private? Was she in physical danger? Had someone attacked her again for being beautiful, for being Jewish? There was so much I didn't know. The next day at work I explained to my boss why I had to take Friday off. He had no problem with it.

When Friday morning came, I carried Mary's heavy suitcase out to a cab and we drove to the airport. Her flight was scheduled to leave around 2:00 p.m. I wanted to get there early so I could buy her a goodbye lunch and help her to her gate. She had had a shitty week, was still weak from a cold, and was flying back to the East Coast alone.

One of the Alaska Airlines agents in the boarding area noticed that Mary was handicapped and came over to us as we approached. "What flight are you on, sir?" she asked.

"I'm not traveling. I'm only here to help my friend," I said. "She has a ticket to Seattle and from there to Connecticut."

"She's traveling alone?" The agent looked concerned.

"Yes. She's booked on the 2 o'clock flight." Mary said nothing. She looked pale and blank.

"If you'd like, you're welcomed to wait in the Alaska Airlines lounge," the agent offered. "It's quieter in there." She pointed down the concourse to a double door marked AA lounge. I thanked her, led Mary over to the door, and we went in. We had already had our lunch, but I offered to get us each a bottle of Coke.

Mary looked up. Something was wrong. She gave a yelp, turned white, the blood drained from her face, and she shot back into the cushions of her chair, contorted and ridged. She was having an epileptic seizure. Her eyes got big as she rolled from the chair onto floor of the lounge grabbing at the air, out of control. I remembered reading how people having seizures can bite off their tongues, so my first reaction was to get something between her teeth to keep her jaws open. She was already foaming at the mouth. I saw one of Mary's leather gloves sticking out of her coat pocket and wedged it into her mouth between her teeth. It worked. Another traveler waiting in the lounge saw what was happening and ran out into the lobby. Seconds later, the Alaska Airlines agent came running in.

"What's going on?" she said in panic. She stared at Mary in horror. "Is she okay?"

By this time, the seizures had almost run their course. Mary was still doubled up on the floor, but the rigidity of her body was subsiding, and she lay there, body still jerking a little, eyes squeezed closed, breathing without a sound. I could sense her muscles untightening as tears leaked from her eyes onto the carpet. When she went limp, I took the saliva-soaked glove out of her mouth.

"That was fast thinking," the agent said. But then that worried look. "I think you should take her back home. It's probably not safe for her to fly."

"She has no home here," I said. "Her best friend and care-giver left Fairbanks two days ago. She has to fly out today. Her family is waiting for her in Connecticut. I think she'll be okay by boarding time." I had to hope for the best.

The agent frowned but didn't argue. "I'll come by in half an hour to check on her," she said and left the lounge. I lifted Mary up off the floor and settled her back into her chair. She was coming around and could respond to questions. The color was coming back into her face. I pulled a chair over and sat in front of her observing.

"How are you feeling?" I asked. "Do you know what happened?"

"I'm not sure," Mary whispered softly. "Everything's dizzy."

"You had a seizure," I said. Mary looked exhausted and confused. "The agent wants me to take you home. Do you think you can handle the flight?"

She didn't answer for a minute. "Yes," she said. "I can do it. I want to do it."

I was relieved. If the airline wouldn't let her board, I wasn't sure what I would do. But she said she could do it and I knew she was a fighter or she wouldn't have been up here in Fairbanks in the first place. If nothing else, Mary was determined. It was a tough life for her. She was brave.

The agent popped her head in to check on Mary just as I was leaving the lounge for the Cokes. "She's doing better," I said. "She wants to fly out."

The agent nodded grimly. "It's not a good idea," she said, "but I'll tell the stewardess to keep an eye on her." Then she left the lounge.

I came back with our Cokes and just when we were done, the announcement to board came over the loudspeaker. I walked Mary to the gate, gave her an awkward hug, and watched her lurch forward and disappear into the boarding tunnel. We had never connected, but I knew I would never forget her.

I watched through the concourse window as her plane took off, then got on a shuttle back to Fairbanks, stopped at Tommy's for a beer, and headed on foot for the trailer and peace and quiet. It was then that I discovered that Mary had plugged the toilet again. I was glad I hadn't thrown away that wooden spatula.

November 10, 1961
Box 238 College Alaska

Dear Family,

Since I began my work last Monday, I barely have enough time for the extras in life—like sleeping and eating. At 7:00 a.m. I crawl out of my sleeping bag. I get dressed, wash, make breakfast (moose burgers), make myself a sandwich, get on my warmest clothes, pack a change of clothes, and run to the corner to catch my bus. At 8:00 a.m., I begin work, work straight on to 4:00 p.m. (lunch on the job), jog to campus one-and-a-half miles up the road, check for frostbite, eat, punch in at 5:00 p.m., work till 1:00 a.m., get a ride home to my trailer, grab a bite to eat, slap myself a couple of times, and slide into my mummy bag around 1:30 a.m. Such has it been since last Monday.

Last Wednesday, Leda Juul, who was letting me share her trailer, left town for good and yesterday, on Friday, her friend Mary flew back to the east coast. Now I have the trailer to myself, at least until the first of December when I have to leave.

On Saturday, I work only one job, noon to 8:00 p.m., then I will drink a pitcher of beer at the International Bar, my new haunt down by the Chena River, and then head home.

My night janitorial job lasts only one more week. My farm job is also temporary — not as I expected — but I never know when not to work. I'm on call. As far as I know, I'll just work on and off till spring. No forecasts dared now.

I'll write again soon.

Take care,
Joel

31: Frozen In

November 26, 1961

For several nights, I had trouble with sleeping. I was worried, wondering when I would find a full-time job or where next week I would be sleeping. The trailer park manager told me I had to be out of Leda's trailer by the first of December when her rent ran out.

On Thanksgiving Day, the temperatures dipped to a steady -30 degrees. That night, I slept restlessly, suffering (not that I'm complaining) from too much roasted turkey and dressing, cranberry sauce, and hot buttered rum (a lot of the latter) at my friends Penny Buck and Sally Erickson's trailer across the road. Finally dropping off to sleep around 3:00 a.m., I slept until 8:00, at which time I dressed, ate, and hurried to the main road to hitch a ride to campus to see about a new job which was opening up. Later that afternoon, I returned to my trailer. The temperature was dropping fast. I turned up the thermostat, cooked dinner, listened to the radio, drank a beer, and read part of C.P. Snow's novel, *The Search*. I went to bed at midnight and zipped myself into my mummy bag and snuggled down.

At three in the morning, I woke up and thought, "Damn, it's cold!" Then I realized that I hadn't heard the furnace go on for some time. Putting off getting out of the warmth of my sleeping bag for a half hour, I finally loosened the zipper under my chin and stumbled over to the thermostat. I turned it up with no results. I had tapped on the two oil drums outside the trailer that morning. One had a hollow sound and was empty, but one seemed to be partially full.

I was wrong. I must have tapped a thick spot or a weld on the metal. I was out of fuel and it was freezing. I smiled an unreal smile — is this really happening? — and crawled back into my sleeping bag. I wondered how cold it was, but I didn't feel like standing in front of the radio waiting for a weather report. I decided to stay in my mummy bag until morning when I could find a phone somewhere and use it at no one's inconvenience. There was no working telephone in the trailer.

The air above me was freezing. I could see my every breath. I did my best to keep warm but small surfaces inside my mummy bag which I didn't warm with my body heat were like ice. I loved the taste of the cold air, but that was as far as it went. I pulled the lip of the bag close around my mouth and rolled over. The only exposed part of my body were my lips. To breathe.

I stayed in my bag until 9 o'clock and when it was light enough to see. But I discovered that I was trapped. The moisture from my breath had coated the zipper's pull tab in a quarter-inch thick covering of ice. I had to suck and lick the ice off the zipper tab to get out of the sleeping bag.

My clothes were draped over the back of a chair next to my bed. My long johns were cold and stiff, and my boots, when I pulled them over my sweat socks, were frozen. I went outside and checked the fuel tanks. Sure enough, they were both empty. I returned to my kitchen and turned on the radio just in time to hear that during the night the temperatures had fallen to a negative 38. I chuckled. Then I groaned when I saw an icicle hanging from the water faucet. I was not only out of fuel but out of water as well. The warmest spot in my trailer was inside the refrigerator.

The Poland's house was nearby. I walked over and knocked on the door. No one came. Then I walked to the little grocery store on College Road across from the trailer park entrance. From there I telephoned Union Oil to schedule a quick delivery and for an hour I walked around the store trying to warm up. To kill time. I began a friendly chat with the storekeeper, but I got bored and went to the back of the store to sit next to a heat vent. Then I went to the front of the store and looked at a well-fingered *Playboy* magazine. I counted cans of soup. The storekeeper was patient with me and understanding. When the oil delivery truck drove past on the way to my trailer, I ran across the street to meet it.

I bought the minimum amount of fuel, twenty-five gallons. I wanted less since I had to move out in three days, but they had me over a barrel. It was twenty-five or none. I paid the driver the money and went to see about starting the furnace in the cellar. I was unsure of the location of the pilot light and went back to the Poland house to find out what to do. By this time, Mrs. Poland was up, but Wally was still asleep. She went into the bedroom and I heard him murmur some vague instructions. She related the instructions and I left to see what I could do.

Back at the trailer, the first thing I did was to look for my flashlight. Holding it carefully, I climbed down through the trapdoor into the cellar and tuned on the light. There were two large mechanical "things" down there, one of which had to be the furnace, and after following pipes around for a minute, I started to apply Mrs. Poland's instructions to a thick white tube where all the pipes seemed to converge. I turned screw nuts and pressed buttons and lit matches and dropped the flashlight. The pilot light went on, then my index finger froze on the button and when I pulled my finger away the pilot light went out. I lit another match.

I heard footsteps clomping on the floor above me. Then Wally, the landlord, climbed down into the cellar and asked me what I was doing by the hot water heater. He led me over to the furnace and showed me where the bleeder nut was, warning me not to unscrew it all the way because I could never get it back on to stop the flow of oil. He flipped the switch on a ceiling light over the furnace that I hadn't been aware of and began to unscrew the bleeder nut. He unscrewed it all the way and it fell into a can at his feet. Quickly he pressed his finger over the stream of leaking oil.

"Dog damn it!" he said. "Get that nut out of the can! Hurry!"

Wally was more annoyed than panicked. I took the can and reached into it with my bare hands and felt the nut at the bottom. Soon Wally had it back in place and, with a rag, we mopped up the floor. He pressed a button inside the furnace and heat began to rumble and roll out.

"Hooray," I said with relief, since now I knew I wouldn't freeze to death. Wally looked at me and smiled.

"All in a day's work," he said. He finished wiping his hands, brushed some ice off his pants, and invited me to his house for a cup of hot coffee while the trailer warmed up. Over at his house, we discussed things like cold weather, his trip to New York, and Alaska construction. I thanked him and, borrowing an extension cord to heat my water pipes under the sink, I left. At noon, the temperature announced on the radio was negative 34 degrees. That was the high for the day.

With the furnace generating heat, the ice had melted from my sleeping bag. With no water and no working toilet, I decided to see if my friends, Penny and Sally across the road, were at home so I could use their "facilities." They weren't in, but their front door was unlocked, so I went in and left a note that I has been there and was "going home to read and contemplate Rudy's future prospects."

At 5 o'clock, I heard a pounding on my front door. The girls had come to save me and to drag me to dinner at their place. I put on my boots, happily tossed my book aside and danced home with them arm in arm at 38 degrees below zero. We had more delicious hot turkey, sweet potatoes with brown sugar, and cider with rum. I relaxed with them and talked about my unreal day. When I returned home, I still had no running water. I just got in my mummy bag and went to sleep.

On Friday, I awoke at 11 o'clock and dressed in the warmth of my new bought heat. Still no water. I took a couple gallon containers over to Wally's home and filled them with their water and returned. That was when Wally told me he had another renter coming on December first and wanted to get the trailer cleaned and ready. I stayed in the trailer all day finishing food and reading my novel. In the early evening, I got most of my packing done for my exodus the next day. Late that evening, the water began to run out of the tap.

The next day, Wally was supposed to come over to drain the pipes and start his clean-up. Maybe I could shower before he arrived. This hadn't been a fancy place, but it had been a safe place. Who knew what tomorrow would bring?

32: CLEAR AIR FORCE STATION

November 28, 1961

The next morning, I put the key to the trailer on the kitchen table and left Wally a thank you note even though he had asked me to move out a couple days early. I had planned to leave on November 30th, but Leda and Mary had left the trailer a mess: a damaged outer door, a broken hinge on the bathroom vanity mirror, a cracked and leaking toilet reservoir, and a torn mattress on the bed. My two part-time temporary jobs had kept me away most of the time, leaving in the dark and coming home in the dark. The only daylight hours in November were between noon and four when I was working at the farm, so I never got around to do a good cleaning inside the trailer. If Wally needed to get the place shipshape quickly for a new renter, I understood. There was a lot that needed fixing.

Luckily, I didn't own much. I had shipped most of my stuff back to Ohio and I had sold my skis to buy food. All I had fit into my backpack and duffle. The university campus was only three miles up the road from the trailer court and that's where I headed. Maybe Bucky and Judy Wilson in Hess Hall would let me hang out while I looked for a fulltime job and let me store my gear there until I got settled.

Bucky was in class when I knocked on their door, but Judy was home. She was the perfect house mother, always smiling and friendly and welcoming. When I had been a graduate student, she and Bucky would invite me and other grad students over for tea and her living room became a stress-free haven. Their kindness kept us sane. Today, since it was almost lunchtime, she made us hot tea and tuna sandwiches. When I asked her about leaving my rifle, backpack, and duffle, she said "Yes, dear, of course. There's plenty of room in the janitor's closet."

Art Roy, for whom I had been subbing as night janitor, had returned from his two-weeks in Quebec and the on-call situation at the experimental farm was hard to continue. Leda had cancelled her phone service, and there had been no good way for anyone to get in touch with me, except face-to-face if I was on site. I needed a real full-time job with a predictable schedule if I was going to stay in Alaska. I put my bags in the janitor closet, thanked Judy, then got on a bus to Fairbanks to go back to the employment bureau to see if anything was available.

As I was approaching the bureau on First Street, Eugene Belland stepped out of the entrance. Gene was a young attorney who had set up a legal practice in Fairbanks. He had recently finished his tour of duty as an air force lawyer at Ladd Airforce Base before it became Fort Wainwright. A native Minnesotan, he loved Fairbanks weather and saw the city as a place of opportunity. I had met him before.

"Hi, Gene. Don't tell me you were looking for a job," I jokingly pointed at the city employment bureau office behind him.

"Hello, Joel." He came over. "No. I lease the apartment on the second floor of this building. The employment bureau and I share the same entrance. I haven't seen you in a while. How are you doing? Are you still at the university? You're in the English Department, right?"

I told him I had left the university and gave him a fast rundown of my railroad, Post Lake, and Juneau jobs, plus my recent temporary work as farmhand and janitor. Belland listened with interest.

"I like someone who's not afraid of hard work," he said. "The last couple of summers, I've been taking two weeks off to work on a cement barge for a client. The hard work makes me feel alive."

"Right now, I'm looking for a good full-time job," I said. "That's why I'm here at the employment bureau."

"Can you type?" he asked.

"Sure," I said. "What graduate student can't type?"

"I might have some good news for you," Belland said. "A client told me yesterday that RCA is looking for a teletype operator to work at Clear Air Force Station. Would you be interested in it?"

"Sure," I said, being positive. "I don't know anything about Clear or teletyping, but it sounds interesting."

"I'm going back to my office," Belland said. "Come with me and I'll give you the contact information."

His office was in a house on Fourth Street. On the way, he told me about a new client, Nuell Shofner, who had just started a business to build prefabricated housing for military families near Clear Air Force Station. When we got to his office, he copied a contact number off his phone pad and handed it to me. "You can call them from here if you want," he said. "I'm going to the kitchen to make coffee." I looked at the note. The top read "RCAS-BMEWS Project, Clear, Alaska" followed by a phone number.

"What does this mean?" I asked pointing at the letters.

"It stands for Radio Corporation of America Service—Ballistic Missile Early Warning Site."

I had heard of the DEW Line and the Distance Early Warning base near Point Barrow. It was part of the United States radar defense system to detect threatening incoming missiles and aircraft carrying atomic bombs from the Soviet Union. Students in the university's ROTC program had often talked with grave concern about the Cold

War with the Soviet Union. And I had had a beer with a DEW line worker at Tommy's.

Belland went into the kitchen and I called the number on the pad. It connected me to the Office of Employment at the Clear Air Force Station. I told the agent what I was applying for.

"Can you type?" he asked. When I told him I could and that I had a college degree, his response was immediate. "Can you take a physical exam tomorrow? Where are you calling from?"

"Fairbanks," I said.

"Good. We have a doctor in Fairbanks. How about tomorrow afternoon? We can get you in at 1300 hours."

"I can do that," I said, and the agent gave me an address. Belland came back in with two cups of coffee. I told him about the conversation with the Clear agent. Then his phone rang. It was a client. I said I'd let him know the outcome, thanked him, and left.

The next day, the doctor recorded my height and weight, took my blood pressure, made sure I had a heartbeat, peeked in my ears, stuck a thermometer under my tongue, aimed a pencil-sized flashlight down my throat, then ended up with the mandatory prostate finger probe. Luckily, he wasn't Dr. Funnybones who had done my exam for the railroad. This doctor wrote me a note to take to Clear to show them I had passed the exam, and I made a beeline to Tommy's for a cold beer.

I was hired at Clear Air Force Station. On the morning of the 29th, I got on the military transport bus which made daily runs to Fairbanks and arrived on base several hours later. The driver dropped me off at the employment office.

"Here we are," he said. "One-and-a-half klicks from the front gate."

"What's a klick?" I asked. I hadn't heard the term before.

"That's short for kilometer," the bus driver said.

"A kilometer?"

"Yeah, you know. A little over half a mile, .62 miles to be exact." I knew Canada and the rest of the world used the metric system, but I didn't know the U.S. military used it. I never heard the term when I was on Fort Wainwright.

I went in to process my paperwork, handed the agent my medical report, and got assigned a dorm room. The hiring agent explained my income and expenses. I was so glad to get the job I hadn't thought to ask before. My salary would be twenty-two dollars an hour for a fifty-four-hour week. First deductions: Teamsters Union ninety-nine bucks; school tax twenty-six bucks; federal income tax twenty-six bucks; and the social security tax of ten dollars. "However, every week after," the agent said, "you should net about a hundred dollars." I wasn't expecting a union fee. That was never something I had had to consider before.

The agent gave me directions to the dormitory and after I had stowed my pack and duffle, I went back to the employment office to get my base-ID card. A second clerk took me to the cafeteria for lunch and led me through the food line. All I had to do was flash my ID and the food was taken care of. I watched as he filled his tray.

After lunch, we went to my workstation located in a huge open room the size of two football fields. I was assigned to a small area bordered on two sides by a large L-shaped desk. On one wing of the desk was the teletype machine, a large gray-black box with a tangle of wires and metal buttons and a small rectangular screen attached by a cable to an electric typewriter-like keyboard.

The agent called over the floor supervisor who welcomed me into the RCAS crew and explained my job.

"First thing in the morning when you come to work, you'll be given a daily list of military and base supplies. Your job will be to order them from our main office in Paramus, New Jersey."

I had never worked much less even seen a teletype machine before and the thought of being able to type something and a minute later it would print out in New Jersey was exciting. The supervisor looked at me and saw my fascination. "You've never done this before?" he asked.

"No," I said. "This is fantastic. When I was a student at the university, I was writing poems and stories. What a great way to send stuff to publishers." The supervisor smiled and nodded.

"Okay," he said. "I'll see you here tomorrow at 0800." Then he walked off.

Nearby, a couple of other people on teletypes were sending messages. I saw that not all their communications were in English.

Two stocky men in wrinkled black business suits were walking in my direction. Everyone else in the area was wearing RCAS work shirts. These two men stood out. Maybe they were managers. But then the floor supervisor was a manager and he was dressed like the others. The shortest black suited guy had a folder in his hand.

"Are you Joel Rudinger?" he demanded. They stood two feet in front of me side-by-side like a wall. It was confrontational and intimidating.

"Yes," I said.

"We're from the Teamsters union. You need to sign these agreements. You have to belong to the union to work here." He pulled a fountain pen from his suit pocket and aimed it at my chest. I hesitated.

"I said you have to join the Teamsters to work here," he repeated.

I didn't like these union guys. I had read that the Teamsters union was run by Jimmy Hoffa and other crooks who never stood up for the workers whose dues paid their salaries. When I was in grade school, my childhood friend, Jerry Santee, lived across the street. His dad had worked at the Toledo Studebaker plant, and I remembered how the Teamsters union drove him out. No one knew why. Mr. Santee was a broken man after that. Jerry would never talk about it. For a year, I never saw his dad leave his house, not even to mow the lawn, and then they moved away.

The two dark men leaned toward me. I could smell their tobacco breath. I took a step back. "I'll have to think about it," I said and turned and walked towards the exit.

I put on my winter coat and went outside into the freezing cold and back to my dorm room. I didn't know what the next day had in store for me, but I unpacked my duffle and lay down on the bed to gather my thoughts. I needed the money. A hundred bucks every week could add up fast especially since here I had nothing to spend it on. My room was free. The food was free. The bus into Fairbanks was free. I just didn't want to join the Teamsters or be linked in any way to Hoffa, who made news even here in the Interior of Alaska.

I heard a soft knock on my door. "Housekeeping." I got up and opened the door. A pretty girl in her late twenties stood in the narrow hall. She was surprised to see me this time of day. "Housekeeping," she repeated. "I'm here to make your bed and clean the room."

"I just moved in," I said. "The room looks good."

"Okay," she said. "I'll come back tomorrow. I'm Lorna Lou," and she gave me a warming smile full of bright, little teeth. "Anything you need, sir?" It was quite a difference from the bully tactics of the union reps. I liked her.

The next morning after a big healthy breakfast, my first real breakfast in months, I showed up at the desk I had been assigned to. I was looking forward to learning how to use the teletype. The floor supervisor was there to get me started. Only he couldn't.

"Sorry, Joel," he said. "The Teamster reps talked to the site manager yesterday and they don't want you on the floor. I don't know what you said to them, but I can't let you start work on the teletype. My hands are tied. I'd like to have you. We need someone with typing skill, but there's nothing I can do."

"All I said was that I'd have to think about it."

Paying almost a hundred dollars a month in dues was part of my hesitation, but the memory of Jerry Santee's dad was what really made me hesitate. That hesitation had cost me this job. You're all in or you're all out. I told the floor supervisor my reason for not immediately jumping on the Teamster bandwagon. I told him about Mr. Santee.

"I understand. I don't agree with you if you need the money and the work, but I understand," the supervisor said. "Maybe if you go back to the employment office, they might find something else for you here on base. It's worth a try." He gave me a quick handshake, said "good luck," and walked away. I looked around. Not one person was paying attention to my being in the room. Yesterday I had felt welcomed. Today I didn't exist. I went back to the base employment office.

"Well," said the agent when I told him what happened, "We have an opening in the housing office, but it doesn't pay as much at the union job. We need a room clerk for the evening shift. It's from 2:00 to 10:00 p.m. Monday through Friday. It pays only two dollars an hour, but there's no change in room or benefits."

I had been lucky to find quick temporary jobs in Fairbanks and the university, but right now I felt I needed some security, even if only temporary. The shadow of being drafted into the Army at any time kept my life dangling. The Korean Conflict was over, but the Cold War with the Soviet Union was strong and ongoing and having read the ominous best seller *The Ugly American*, I felt anything could happen. Also, I had heard there was dangerous action starting up in a place called Viet Nam, but no one knew much about it. The Clear housing office job was what I needed right now, job security, a little money, a place to stay, and food.

"I'll take the job," I said. I would have been a fool not to.

The clerk nodded and telephoned the housing office, told them I would be coming over for instructions, had me sign new papers, cancelled my former agreement with RCAS, and gave me directions to my new workplace. It was, he said, "only half a klick down the road on the right."

I left with a feeling of ambiguity. Working here was nothing like tracking a Dall sheep or a moose, or teaching students at the university, leveling track or shoveling cow dung. Those were tangible pursuits. Now I felt like I was a wet sock dangling in the wind hung out to dry. As long as my psychological clothespin didn't let me down, I would be fine. For a while. The Book of Proverbs says "Pride goeth before a fall." There was no pride in being a room clerk on a secluded military base. But no pride meant no fall. There was nothing to fall from. I was safe. It was a comfortable twist of logic . . . for the time being.

Inside the housing office, a man in his forties looked up from his newspaper when I walked in. He was wearing a white long-sleeved dress shirt under an olive-colored wool vest. On his forehead above his eyes he wore a green plastic visor to shield his eyes from the harsh overhead lighting.

"Hi," he said. "I'm Ken. So you're the new evening guy." He stood up behind his metal desk. "You can sit over there." He pointed to an armless chair against a wall. I sat down. "So here's what you'll need to know. You'll sit at this desk." He sat back down. "Every morning, base command sends over a list of expected guests and new employees. Also, they send a complete list of rooms, occupied and unoccupied. The rooms marked with a star are for guests. Some might be high-ranking officers from the government or other bases, politicians from Juneau or Washington, DC, or RCA officials. Rooms not starred are for workers and non-classified visitors.

"When they come in, check their base identification, assign them a room, and give them their room key. You don't handle any money. That's taken care of by another office. You can also give them one of these." He opened a desk drawer and handed me a map of the base with each building marked and numbered. "I'm the one who starts the day," he continued, "and I usually start it with a copy of the *Fairbanks Dailey News Miner*. I'll put it on that table by the door for you. But when you're done with it, put it in the trash for housekeeping. Also, there's a radio you can listen to and, of course, the telephone. No incoming personal calls allowed. AT&T keeps track of all calls as this is a high security site, but you can call out if you reverse the charges. Any questions?"

I had no questions and said I would see him at 1600 hours, 4:00 p.m. At the moment, it was only 10:30 a.m. I had half a day to kill. I wandered back to the cafeteria for coffee and a slice of apple pie, then back to my room to think about my life.

My thoughts were broken by a knock. "Housekeeping," said a voice. I opened the door. There stood bright-eyed, smiling Lorna Lou.

33: Eighty Below

December 24, 1961

Working in the Clear housing office in the middle of winter was comfortable but boring. Every weekend, I took the shuttle bus to Fairbanks.

In mid-December, recorded temperatures got as low as 78 degrees below zero at Clear and 67 degrees below in Fairbanks. It was a record shattering historic cold. Strangely enough though, according to the *Fairbanks Daily News Miner*, few people died because of it. Most everyone had the sense to stay inside. Almost everyone. Not me.

This Saturday was Christmas Eve, but I didn't give it much thought. Stores back in Ohio usually stayed open for one last sale so I thought there'd still be a few places open, the grocery, the liquor store, my favorite Army Surplus, Tommy's Elbow Room. But between Clear and Fairbanks, the ice fog got so thick that it was coating the shuttle bus's windshield despite the heat blasting up against it from the inside. The driver was afraid of driving off the side of the road into a blind ditch and slowed to twenty miles an hour along the night-black, icy gravel road. We got into Fairbanks three hours late. By the time we pulled in, it was past five in the evening and all the stores I liked had closed. Nobody in their right mind would be out walking or driving unless they had to.

December 21st was the Winter Solstice, the shortest day of the year. The gray twilight-level daylight around Fairbanks lasted less than two hours, between 1 and 3 o'clock in the afternoon. This was only three days later, and total darkness was upon us.

Only the lounge in the Northward Hotel and the native hangout, the Chena Bar on Second Street, had lights on. The temperature showing on the First National Bank time and temperature clock was blinking - 67. And there I was standing in the empty street alone in the black of night, coated with a layer of white numbing frost from the ice fog. The only other light in the downtown area was the hazy glow of streetlamps along the curbs.

I was stuck. The university was five miles away, but there wouldn't be anyone there anyway. Besides, there were no cars on the road even if

I'd wanted to hitchhike. The city bus station was open twenty-four hours a day, but it was six blocks in the wrong direction and there was nothing to do there anyway except to sit on a bench and watch the locals stagger in out of the cold. There were always jobless people in there, sitting or squatting in the corners or along the dirty walls. To go there now would cripple my soul, so I walked down the freezing street to the Northward Hotel, thought of Leda, and ordered a rum and coke in the bar.

This Fairbanks trip was a bust. I decided to head back to Clear that evening. I knew that buses returning to Clear made a scheduled stop in front of the grocery store by the trailer park on College Road to pick up passengers. The revised schedule the driver had posted on the bus I had come in on said that its return trip would be eight o'clock that evening, so I finished my drink and stared out the windows at the ice fog floating and shifting back and forth in baffles of moving air. At 7:15, I paid my bill, pulled on my arctic parka, scarf, face glove, fur-lined cap, and leather hand gloves and left.

The only part of me exposed was my eyes. The problem was that ice fog was filming over my glasses. I took them off and stuck them in a coat pocket and trudged back up Second Street to Cushman and across the Chena bridge. Lights were on in the Catholic church, where they were having Christmas Eve mass. I could hear singing as I passed. The International Bar and Grill on the other side of the road was lit up as well, but its parking lot was empty. I lowered my head and kept going to get to the shuttle pick-up area in time.

Once I was out of town and away from the protection of the buildings and into the area of open fields, the wind picked up and I guessed the wind chill was at least eighty below. I walked along the side of the road the half mile to the grocery store bus stop, got there, and waited. It was Christmas Eve, the store was locked and closed. There was no protection from the air.

But my timing was good. Coming slowly up the road toward me was the bus. I could tell what it was through the ice fog by its wide headlights. "Thank god," I thought. "I'm freezing. I'm crazy to be out here flagging down a stupid bus."

I couldn't wait to get into the warmth inside it. I stood at the edge of the road. The bus came toward me and slowed. But it continued on about thirty yards past me.

"Hey! Wait!" I called out. "Wait up! I'm coming!"

I ran slipping and sliding towards the rear of the bus, but it never came to a complete stop. Instead, it slowed to a crawl then picked up speed and drove on into the ice fog and disappeared. I was wearing a dark khaki army jacket and dark brown wool pants. I could see the bus driver, but the bus driver never saw me through the ice fog.

I was left out on the empty highway. My hands, feet, face, and my legs were freezing, and my clothes covered in a thickening film of bone-chilling frost. My eyes were aching from the cold. I stared after the bus in disbelief. I looked back towards Fairbanks in the distance and thought, "This is the day I die."

Then the icy fog shifted slightly in an updraft of wind and I saw a tiny light at the end of a rutted driveway behind me cut back into a field. I staggered towards the light. It was a little table lamp in the window of a small log cabin. The light from the lamp was refracted by the ice fog and cast a ghostly yellow-white glow. I stumbled towards the light, up to a wooden door, and pounded on it with my fist. *Bang, Bang, Bang, Bang*. Moments later the door opened, and I fell forward into the room face down on the floor. Thank god, the room was warm. I felt a hand grasp my shoulder and roll me onto my back. I looked up. It was Art Roy, the maintenance man I had substituted for in Bunnell Hall.

"Hi, Art," I said. "Mind if I rest here awhile? I missed the bus to Clear." I just lay there on my back, arms at my side.

"Joel? Is that you?" I nodded. Art stared down at me. I pulled my face mask off and tried to smile. "How about some hot tea?"

I rolled over onto my hands and knees and pushed myself up. There was a chair next to a warm, wood-burning Franklin stove and Art led me over to it and went to his kitchen sink for a couple of coffee mugs. He brought over the tea and set it down on a table while I pulled off my hat, gloves, and coat. He shook his head and laughed. "What the hell you doin' out in weather like this?"

"Just came to visit," I said with a weak smile. My face was warming. "And, by the way, Art, thanks for saving my life." I meant it.

Art had an extra blanket and pillow, and I stretched out in front of the stove where I spent the rest of the night. The next morning was Christmas and Art made us coffee, hot oatmeal, and toast. Later, he called the bus station to see when the next bus to Clear was scheduled. He got his car started and drove me to the bus station where I caught the next bus back.

The weather report on Art's radio that evening confirmed the record cold, sixty-seven degrees below zero. The wind chill outside Fairbanks that evening was officially eighty degrees below zero, an historic low.

Around the end of January, there was a big personnel cut at Clear and being low on the seniority list I could be let go at a moment's notice. In addition to that, I got notice from my draft board in Toledo, Ohio, that I had to appear at Fort Richardson in Anchorage for a physical exam the first week in February. I believed I would soon be leaving Clear to be drafted into the Army. Two weeks later, I handed in my resignation.

34: Leaving Clear

February 19-21, 1962

I left Clear Air Force Station and jumped on a jet to Anchorage at government expense.

At Fort Richardson, I had my Army physical. It was no big deal. Just the usual, recording my height (72 inches), weight (145 pounds, a ten pound gain since I started at Clear), temperature, blood pressure, heart rate, and the inevitable finger up the butt along with an endless line of other young naked male pre-inductees waiting to bend over to touch their toes. I passed the physical along with ninety-five percent of the other guys who also had gotten their call from Uncle Sam.

After we all got dressed, everyone was herded into a large hall by a couple of MPs in full uniform. The room was filled with tables, four seats to a table, two on either side.

"Okay, you men, listen up," a middle aged solider with a row of combat ribbons on his chest yelled out. "You're all going to take a test. There are a hundred questions. This is to see if you are officer material."

At twenty-three, I was probably the oldest recruit in the room. A couple of bored-looking soldiers walked around the room handing out answer sheets and pencils as others came with a pamphlet with the test questions.

"Okay, listen up!" the middle aged solider called out. "No cheating. Cheaters will be disqualified and if you're caught, you do a hundred push-ups. Got it?" He looked around the room trying to look tough. "When I say Go, open your pamphlet and get started." Everyone grabbed his pencil and test sheet. "GO!" he said.

I opened my test booklet. It had fifty multiple choice and true-false, and fifty matching questions. The multiple choice and true-false questions were easy, but the matching section of the test didn't speak at all to my life experience. There were pictures of farm and construction tools which we had to identify. I didn't grow up on a farm. I had never built a barn or a house. My father was not a blacksmith or a barrel maker. I didn't know the difference between a backhoe and post hole digger. What term matched the picture? One or two tools I knew since we used them on the railroad or the experimental farm, but most of the others I had to guess.

I did the best I could, but what was curious to me was why there'd be questions like this if the army was looking for officer material, unless it was an officer's job to dig a foxhole or string a barbed wire fence. I looked around at the other recruits taking the test. A lot of them were openly peeking at their tablemates' answers. The middle aged solider with the ribbons was sitting in the corner reading a magazine. I thought this whole thing was a joke. The officers at Fort Wainwright had impressed me when I first arrived. But then, I was a wide-eyed newbie impressed by almost everything. If something was new to me, it was important. Who was I, a stranger in a strange land, to question tradition? But this was different.

When the test was over, we lined up and took our answer sheets to a grading table. I liked the idea of immediate results. I handed my answer sheet to the soldier at the table. He placed it next to a master answer list and started to check things off. Check. Check. Check. Lots of checks. When he finished, he penciled my score at the top, handed me a form with the score, and looked up without a smile.

"You got eighty-six percent. You need a ninety to be officer material." He looked away. "Next." The boy in line behind me stepped up. I took my results and left the room.

Outside the test building, a shuttle bus was waiting to take us back to the Fort Richardson housing units. I put thoughts of the stupid test behind me, but as some of the others got on, I heard them cheering and laughing about the exam.

"Wow," one said with excitement. "I got a ninety."

"Me, too," said another.

"I got a ninety-three, but that's still damn good," said a third.

I knew the guy who had gotten the ninety-three. He was a grocery clerk in Fairbanks. I looked away and shook my head. If my father had been a carpenter, I could have been a general.

35: Fur Rendezvous

Most of the recruits returned to their hometowns or villages to jobs and family, but as I had no job or girlfriend waiting for me, I decided to stay in Anchorage for a few days. There was nothing in Fairbanks calling me back. Besides, as luck would have it, the annual Fur Rendezvous was kicking off this Saturday.

Bob Larsen was on duty at the front desk of the Anchorage Westward when I walked in and, again, he rented me a room for five days at only five dollars a night. It was small but clean, and the price was right. I walked over to the Hofbrauhaus for a beer and a roast beef sandwich. As I opened the door, Jinksy, the cute blonde bartender, saw me. "Hey," she called out, "Mr. Beethoven is back." She waved, I waved back and went over to the piano and sat down. Hello, "Moonlight Sonata." She sent over a beer.

Even though it was February, the streets of Anchorage were alive with Alaska natives and tourists with cameras. The Fur Rendezvous was Alaska's first main winter event and the feeling of party was everywhere. It wasn't the Fairbanks dry cold, but it was cold enough that everyone was bundled up in heavy coats or parkas.

A circle of Inuit and Yup'ik Eskimos was gathered on the lawn in front of the City Hall building. Suddenly a young Eskimo girl dressed in a beautiful fur parka, leggings, and mukluks shot up into the air above the crowd. There were about a hundred people crowded around watching. When I got into the mix, I saw a line of men shoulder to shoulder in caribou parkas griping the edges of a large round stretched-out walrus skin. It was an Eskimo blanket toss.

The girl shot up twenty feet into the air again. A native man dressed in a fur parka trimmed in fox pelts jumped up on a small stage set up nearby.

"Ladies and gentlemen," he said, "welcome to the Fur Rendezvous. Thank you for watching our blanket toss. You should know that while it looks like a sport, it's more than that. It is a survival technique. We who live on the tundra use the blanket toss to spot game. We choose someone light weight and toss him or her high in the air. At the peak of the jump," he explained, "a jumper can scan the landscape for bears or caribou or other game. Our jumper here, Julia," he pointed to the girl who had been tossed, "can turn completely around in a single jump. If there's an animal within half a mile, she will see it."

The girl in the air came down and then shot up again, making two jerky ninety-degree turns at the top of her jump. The audience applauded.

"Why do they do that?" a woman tourist asked a man next to me wearing an Anchorage cap. She had just walked up. "Is this a sport?"

"Well," the man said, "it is competitive sport when they have the Eskimo Olympics up in Fairbanks, where athletes from different villages compete. But it's really a hunting thing. It's how they spot game."

The girl landed in the middle of the skin blanket with a big smile, walked to the edge and hopped off. She posed for pictures with the men who had been the blanket-tossers and then with some tourists. The crowd applauded. Some dropped money into a basket.

A corner lot at the end of the block was the site for an ice sculpture competition. Ice artists from Canada, Alaska, even the Lower 48, came up every year to chip away at large blocks of ice to form beautiful, sometimes powerful, glistening statues of pure flowing beauty. Two pieces caught my eye; one was a six-foot dragon spouting flames of ice. It had six thick muscular legs, two widespread wings, large piercing eyes, and every scale on its twisting body was etched with delicate lines. The other piece I liked was a ten-foot-high, open-armed polar bear which towered over the other sculptures surrounding it. One artist had created a huge bucket of twisting fish. Another from Sitka had carved a totem pole, which, according to a sign, told the history of his Haida village.

On Saturday morning, I awoke to a convoy of City of Anchorage dump trucks bringing in tons of snow for that afternoon's Fur Rendezvous dog sled run. After a hot breakfast, I went out to watch the city workers get the street ready for the dogs. They shoveled and spread the snow into a mile-long trail extending from curb to curb six inches deep, deep enough for the sleds to pull out without damaging their runners and deep enough for the dogs to get a good footing as they raced off through the cheering crowd lining the street.

The dog teams began to line up around 2 o'clock in the afternoon. When they came out, so did the children, dressed in their warm snowsuits and waving little blue and yellow Alaskan flags. The teams were lined up by a lottery pick so no team was given special treatment.

This was my first time seeing a line of professional mushers and their teams and I was excited by the excited energy of the dogs as they strained at their harnesses to get going, to be on the move. They yelped and jumped and leaped and pulled and looked back around at the crowd and their owners. I could almost hear them yelling in their secret Husky language, "Let's go, let's go, let's go!" I knew mushers called their dogs fine-tuned athletes and looking at this line of super energized dogs convinced me it was so.

There was no starting gun. That would have spooked the dogs. The festival starter stood next to the first team and looked at this watch. At 3 o'clock, he raised his hand and barked out, "GO!" The dog team jerked forward in their harnesses and the sled shot forward on the snowy street. The second dog team inched into position and sixty seconds later the festival starter signaled a go and they were off. Each team followed in this way.

Musher with dog team on University of Alaska campus.

I noticed the snow for the sleds at the end of the line was getting rutted and thin. By the time the final team was off, I could hear runners skimming over the dark slippery asphalt. The whole show was over by 4 o'clock and the people on the street wandered happily away until the worn-down snowpack was the only proof the Rendezvous run had happened at all.

Back up the street, the blanket toss had started again, but I thought it time I get back to the Hofbrauhaus. Jinksy, the cute bartender, was on duty. "Hey," she called out, "Mr. Beethoven is back." She waved and smiled. "How about a brew for the Rendezvous?"

I waved back and went over to the piano. Hello, "Anthem to Chopsticks! "

*   *   *

The next day I got on the train to Fairbanks. The Army had told me at Fort Richardson that I had twenty-one days before I had to go into the service. So now I had a firm timeline to think about. I wanted to tell Gene Belland the news because he had asked me about buying some property and I would have to say no. But when I got back to town and picked up my mail at the College post office, there was a letter from the Toledo draft board telling me that the March quota was filled and there were already volunteers for April, so I couldn't be inducted until May or June. The Korean Conflict was over (Walter Cronkite said on the radio it really wasn't a war since America never declared it a war.), and volunteers were replacing draftees, since they thought the Army was a safe place with free food, free housing, and a salary to boot. So again, I had no timeline for military service.

In that same batch of mail was a letter from the United States Post Service telling me I had passed the United States Postal Service civil service exam and could report for work at the Fairbanks P.O. Monday, March 28th. I also got a note telling me that I had a poem accepted by *Scimitar and Song*, a North Carolina literary magazine with national circulation. No money, of course, just the honor of publication. So here I was again, back in Fairbanks with a job if I wanted it.

In the same batch of mail was a second note from the Toledo draft board verifying that if I were to be drafted, it wouldn't be until June. This time they informed me that my name was number one on the A-1 draft list, but that if I were to return to graduate school, or teach, I could qualify for a 2-S deferment. A new conflict in Viet Nam was starting to heat up. I had heard on the radio that President John Kennedy had instituted the 2-S deferment to protect young post-Korean war families and potential students from the draft. I considered returning to graduate school. But I had a few months to decide.

On April second, I started my job at the Fairbanks Post office, working with a friendly old man named Walter who had been happily sorting mail for fifteen years. He knew every little native tundra and seaside village in Alaska, some with Eskimo names I couldn't pronounce, like Nuiqsut and Kwigillingok. Every day we got sacks of letters and packages addressed to these tiny native villages. My job was to put each piece of mail in the right cubbyhole, then pack them up for bush pilots to drop off across the state. The work was robotic, routine, and boring, but I knew this, too, was temporary, and so each day I went to work and worked until I could leave. My hours were from 1:00 p.m. until the mail went out at 9:00 p.m.

I was living in one of the dorms and walked back to the university every night after work. Since it was April, the days were getting longer. It was starting to get warmer, too. The walk was a pleasure when I was not too tired to enjoy it.

I did have one work-related problem though. Sometimes when I lifted heavy boxes, I got a sharp pain in my groin. It could have been a carryover from when I got hurt at Post Lake. I had it checked out by a local doctor. He said he thought it was a hernia and that I might need surgery.

A week after I started at the post office, Gene Belland asked me if I'd like to move into his apartment over the Employment Bureau on First Street. I would be rooming with two other young men in a four-bedroom unit that overlooked the Chena River. Now that I had an income, I said yes and moved into the apartment the next day.

36: Enter Bobbi

I had come home from work early since the post office mail transport truck had flipped over on the highway and there was nothing to sort that night. My roommates were having one of their Friday night parties. About twenty young people were in the living room drinking and dancing. I was in the kitchen making a pot of spaghetti for my supper when I saw this girl walk into the room. I sensed a powerful energy, something electric in the air. I didn't know who she was, who she came with, or who she was meeting. She just stood in the doorway looking around with a confident soft smile.

Bobbi Carter, a good companion

She was pretty with medium length dark brown hair, tan skin, and smiling eyes that had a slight look of oriental mystery. She was five-foot-four with an athletic body and was wearing jeans, a long-sleeved flannel shirt, and red tennis shoes. There was something comfortable and natural about her.

The living room was in full party mode. Big band music was playing loudly on a phonograph and four or five couples were slow dancing cheek to cheek. The counter that separated the kitchen from the party area was lined with bottles of Jack Daniels, rum, gin, beer, Coke, and Verners.

I turned off the flame under my boiling spaghetti and took the pot over to the sink to drain it in a colander. I poured it into a mixing bowl and stirred in a little tomato sauce and grated cheese. When I turned to get a beer out of the fridge, I looked down and saw the red tennis shoes. The cute girl in the red shoes had wriggled through the crowd and was standing next to me smiling into my bowl of food.

"Hi," she said looking up. "Do you live here?"

"Yes," I said. "I moved in a few weeks ago." She turned around to look at the party scene. I guessed she had been to parties up here before.

"I'm Bobbi. Who's your date here?"

"I don't have a date," I said. "I just got off work. Would you like a beer?"

"Sure," she said. I pried the cap off a bottle and handed it to her. "Would you like a glass for that?"

"Are you using one?" she asked.

"No."

"A bottle is fine," she said looking up at me as she took a tiny sip.

"Would you like some spaghetti?" I asked.

"Sure. But only a little."

I got two bowls from the cupboard, dished out some pasta for each of us and we carried our plates over to a small table in the back corner of the kitchen. Someone put on a Dave Brubeck record. My favorite jazz piece, "Take Five," filled the room, and Bobbi and I stood there eating and watched the partiers doing the popular new dance called the Twist.

Bobbi told me her mother was native Yup'ik Eskimo and her father was a white man from Canada. He had been killed on a moose hunt when she was ten. Now she was eighteen and had just graduated from the high school in Fairbanks. She had a brother Mike, two years her junior. The two of them loved adventures.

"Once we hitchhiked together down to Tok and Valdez and then over to Anchorage," she told me. "Last year we took a train from Fairbanks to Seward at the end of the line." She said because she had Eskimo blood, she could go to the University of Alaska tuition free un-

172

der the State's Bureau of Indian Affairs, or BIA, program. "But I'm not sure I want to go to college yet," she said. "I want to travel more first."

After that night, Bobbi came over to the apartment on a regular basis when I got off work. Sometimes I'd make us supper. Sometimes we just walked the streets and stop off at Tommy's. She was a natural, easy, effortless friend. I told her about my own adventures working for Hal Waugh, working on the railroad, my frustrations at Clear, and my situation at the post office, about possibly needing hernia surgery. She put her arms around me.

"I could be your private nurse," she said.

I put my arms around her. "I would love you to be my private nurse," I said.

"I would be a good nurse," Bobbi said leaning deeply into me. "Let me show you."

She took my hand and we turned toward the door of my bedroom and went in. I sat on the edge of my bed as she sat next to me and untied her tennis shoes. She pulled off her wool socks, unbuttoned the front of her shirt, took it off and dropped it on the floor. Then her jeans and bra. Finally, she stepped out of her panties and dropped them on the pile. She didn't dance around or try to be sexy or cute. Her undressing and nakedness were as natural as breathing. Then I did likewise with equal deliberation, leaving my clothes in a pile next to hers and we lay back on my narrow bed, naked, side by side. I felt her warm skin sliding down my body, slow and soft, sweet and tan. She put one leg across my thighs and turned her lips to mine for a kiss. She closed her eyes. We made love in silence with heart-deep joy into the night. And Bobbi was right. She would be a good nurse.

We lay sleeping together until early in the morning and woke to the scrubby sounds of one of my roommates showering in the bathroom. Bobbi turned into me and we held each other in silence. Soon both roommates had left for their jobs. Then nature called, as she always does, and I got out of bed to go to the bathroom. When I came back, Bobbi was dressed.

"I have to go," she said. "My mother will be worried if I don't come home."

I got dressed and we walked down to the street. We hugged, and I watched her walk up the block to Cushman, then turn left and out of sight. I stood on the sidewalk for a minute and then crossed the grassy lawn between the employment bureau and the river. It was a beautiful morning, the sun already high in the sky since it was just weeks before summer solstice. As I watched the river flowing slowly past in front of me, I thought how last night Bobbi had become more than just a friend. She had become a companion and a lover. I sat there for a while thinking, . . . no, . . . feeling, how suddenly my life had changed. And how little it took to change it.

The next day, the post office transport truck came back from the airport full of mail. It was my job to help unload it. Lifting the heavy cartons and duffle bags packed with packages and letters continued to cause sharp shooting pains in my groin. I talked to the office manager about it. The Fairbanks postmaster called me into his office. He wanted me to have surgery and assured me my U.S. government employment benefits would cover the medical expenses. Only with surgical repair, he said, could I safely lift the mail and be a longtime useful worker. I had been with the post office for four uncomfortable months. I saw no future doing what I was doing. Living day-to-day for a paycheck for the rest of my life was not what I wanted my life to be about.

I made the decision to return to graduate school at the University of Alaska with the student deferment 2-S classification. President Kennedy would approve. I had no idea what I would focus on for a thesis, but just getting back into the degree program would be a good first step, and it did have the promise of an interesting future. What would come afterwards would come out of opportunity and luck, hopefully good luck.

The next day I called in sick. I telephoned Bobbi and she came over. We took a bus to campus to enroll me for fall classes. While we walked hand in hand to the registration area in the student union, Bobbi was looking around with a look of wonder on her face. She said she had never been on the campus, that for most native kids growing up around Fairbanks, College, Alaska and the university was foreign territory. Even with BIA benefits, few Alaska natives were interested in going to college. Getting a job was more important.

When we got to the registration table, I looked down the list of course offerings and noticed that Dr. Bolgone, the professor who had been my nemesis, wasn't listed.

"What happened to Dr. Bolgone, the English professor?" I asked a woman at the registration table.

"I don't know," she said. "Hey, Bucky," she called over to the next table. "Do you know a Dr. Bolgone? In English?"

"Hey, Joel." It was Bucky Wilson. "Glad to see you back. Judy's asked about you. I think you left a pair of snowshoes in our closet. What's your question about Bolgone?"

"Hi, Bucky. I didn't see her name in the course listings."

"The university didn't renew her contract after you left. Your office partner, Marie Munson, had trouble with her, too, as did a few others who complained about her. They said she thought she was teaching Oxford-level students. Although I think she really quit because too many people knew the story of her having to pee in her wool socks when she was stuck flying in from Canada in a Cessna. No pilot is going to land a bush plane on the tundra because you have to pee. She hated that everyone knew about that. I guess she got teased about it too many times." He laughed. "Joel, when you have a chance, come on over to Hess for tea and cookies. Judy would love to see you."

"That sounds great. Mind if I bring Bobbi, my girlfriend?" I put my hand on Bobbi's shoulder. She smiled and walked over to Bucky to shake his hand.

"Glad to meet you, Bobbi," said Bucky with his welcoming smile. "Joel, just let us know." And he turned back to the students waiting to sign up for classes.

As I looked at the course schedule, two courses caught my eye: a graduate course in the classics being offered by Dr. Lewis Knapp, a visiting professor from Harvard, and a course in Shakespeare. I only signed up for those two classes. I already had twelve hours of graduate credit; these two courses would bring my total credit hours to eighteen. And I had to independently study French to pass the graduate degree foreign language requirement.

When we left the registration area, I gave Bobbi a tour of the campus. I took her upstairs to the student union cafeteria and she saw students sitting around the room at long tables drinking coffee together or studying. I took her down to the bottom floor where the bookstore and pool tables were. Then we walked across the center of campus to the Bunnell building. I took her into my old office. Her eyes got big when she saw Dr. Minnie Wells' wall of books, and she inched along the shelves mouthing titles as she passed. To her, this was a different world. How different I didn't know.

We climbed up the stairs to the library on the third floor. There was nobody in there, so we left and went back outside. We walked across campus to the outdoor hockey rink, and Bobbi laughed when I told her of the time after our basketball game with Fort Wainwright when I'd gotten drunk on wine and beer and puked up chunks of liver and onions on the rink's ice in the middle of the night where they froze solid into unidentifiable lumps. She loved the story.

"Maybe," I thought, "maybe she'll change her mind and use the BIA program to come here in September."

The next week, I got a letter from Bob Friedman, a high school friend in Toledo. He was getting married on the second of September and wanted me to be his best man. I showed Bobbi the letter. She looked up at me and grinned. What was this beautiful silent sexy girlfriend thinking? She only talked when she had something important to say.

"You should do it," she said. She looked up at me, her two hands pressing against my heart.

"But classes here begin September 17th," I said. I was expressing doubt, but, yes, it would be great to see my family again. It had been two years.

175

A friend of Gene Belland had recently told me he knew someone in Portland, Oregon, who sold cars. He said his friend would sell me a new 1962 Volkswagen Beetle for $1,600 if I bought it off the lot. Or he could ship it up to Fairbanks by rail for $300 more.

I had gone two years without a car and missed having the freedom. True, I had done okay without one and, true, I didn't have the expense of gas, oil, insurance, and repairs, but the idea of having a car to drive across country and see my family made me reconsider. The challenge was getting from Fairbanks to Portland without having to spend a lot of money. I had saved some money from my job at Clear and my four months at the post office, but it was just barely enough to buy the car without taking out a bank loan. A plane ticket to Oregon would be expensive and trains or buses didn't go directly there from here.

I told Bobbi about the VW for sale in Portland. She took my hand and smiled. We walked to the parking lot by the Bunnell building. In the distance, we could see the sun on the peaks of Denali rising above the horizon.

"I think we should hitchhike down the ALCAN and get that car," she said.

"We?" I was surprised. "Would you want to go with me?"

"Have you ever hitchhiked, Joel?"

"Well, I tried to hitch to Anchorage once but had to come back and take a train." I told her about my deadline to get to Post Lake.

"Well, you know I have, even though I'm a girl. I like it. I'd like to go with you." It was a crazy new idea.

According to the 1962 *Alaska Highway* travel guide I bought, the distance from Dawson Creek, British Columbia, at Milepost 0, to Fairbanks was 1,523 miles. And it was another 750 south to Sunburst, Montana at the U.S. border. That night we snuggled and talked about it. Bobbi was getting excited. I was getting excited. Why had I come to Alaska? To live a dream, to create memories, to have adventure. Bobbi was a part of all three.

In the morning, I woke up with Bobbi's arms around me. "Okay," I said, "We'll do it. We'll hitchhike the down ALCAN."

When I went to work at the post office that day, I handed in my notice.

37: Hitchhiking the ALCAN

We wanted to start hitchhiking down the ALCAN Highway on the first of August. With work no longer a concern, I had only few things to clear up. I let Gene Belland know I was going down to Portland, Oregon, to buy a car but that I would be back before the start of classes. Then I let my family and friends in Ohio know my plans. Bobbi told her mother and got her blessing. Not much surprised her mother.

All that was left to do was buy some hiking gear and go. I bought a two-man pup tent and a couple of rain ponchos. The tent and all our clothing and gear took up more room than our backpacks could handle so I took my duffle bag as well.

In the morning, I walked over to Bobbi's house. Her mother stood in the front window smoking a cigarette. I thought maybe she'd come out to say goodbye, but she didn't. We shouldered our gear and walked over to Cushman Street, then turned towards the south end of Fairbanks.

Bobbi knew how to show off her youthful beauty to the passing vehicles. To her, waving and smiling was as natural as breathing. A couple of large RVs came by and I saw people wave and smile back, but they didn't stop. Family recreational vehicles rarely stopped for hitchhikers. Several cars going our way drove past.

I thought about how we looked standing there at the edge of the road, Bobbi with her backpack on and me with my backpack on and duffle bag at my feet. I thought about stepping back off the road to let Bobbi do the thumbing, but just then a pick-up truck pulled over and stopped. It was a boy Bobbi knew from high school. We tossed our gear into the truck bed and got into the cab. But the driver was only going to North Pole, sixteen miles down the road. After he let us off, we stood at the side of the highway for over an hour.

A second motorist picked us up and took us as far as Eielson Airforce Base twenty-six miles further. Then an old man hunter in a rusty pick-up stopped — said he wanted company — and drove to us Delta Junction, another seventy-five miles. By then it was late in the afternoon. Bobbi and I walked and carried our packs down the road. A young soldier in uniform picked us up. He let us off after two miles where he was turning. Every ride was a crap shoot, but every mile was a mile closer to our goal.

The clouds above were dark and low but we got lucky. Two minutes before a downpour, a station wagon picked us up and took us all the way to Tok Junction. We were now over two hundred miles from Fairbanks and getting close to the Canadian border.

Outside of Tok, a heavy rain came down and Bobbie and I slept in our wet pup tent until eight the next morning. Within the hour, the rain stopped, the sky cleared, and we were back on the road, thumbs out. We ate some candy bars, drank some water from my canteen, and stood in the blazing sun until 3:00 p.m. We were tired, saw a small weather-beaten café, and went in.

"Where are you two headed?" the waitress asked. "Going north or south?"

"We're going south," I said. "We left Fairbanks yesterday, but traffic's been slow. We thought it would go faster."

"Yeah. That happens. Most of the tourists have started to leave," she said. "Not many RVs stop for hitchhikers. You might not catch a ride for a couple of days. You want to order something?"

Just then a large southbound moving van stopped across the road to gas up and I ran over to see if I could talk him into giving us a ride. The driver was hesitant but said he'd meet us in the café and discuss it. We waited, and he came in and ordered coffee and a doughnut. While he was telling us why picking up hitchhikers was against company policy, out of the blue, a young man came in for a coffee and asked if anyone here was going Stateside and wanted a ride.

"I don't believe it," the waitress said, and she pointed at Bobbi and me. Half an hour later we were on our way in a 1958 Chevy Corvair.

The young man who was driving introduced himself. His name was Mike. He was happy to have someone to talk to. He had just left his job on the DEW line after an eighteen-month tour of duty.

"The work was driving me nuts," he said. "It was either freezing daylight or black subzero night, at least for most of the year. There was nothing to do except watch the radar for Soviet aircraft, play ping-pong, poker or chess, drink, eat, and sleep. They did have nightly first-run movies in the mess hall, but there's only so much John Wayne or Marilyn Monroe you can watch," he said. He had plenty of money since there was nowhere to spend his paychecks and the pay was good. But he was anxious to get back to his girlfriend in Arizona. "If she is still my girlfriend," he said. "The last letter I got from her was month ago."

The ALCAN Highway's surface changed after Tok Junction. The Alaska portion of the road was concrete, but as soon as we crossed over into Canada, the road changed to packed down gravel. The Cold War had brought a lot of defense money into Alaska and the new state had to finance and maintain the upgrade. Not so for Canada.

As we were driving down the road, we hit a washout and a deep bone jarring pothole. I felt a jolt and heard a loud bang under the rear seat where I was riding. Mike pulled off to the side. When he got out, he got down on his knees to look under the car. Bobbi and I got out to see if we could help.

"Damn it! The oil line under the car is broken and we're losing fluid," he moaned.

Mike worked quickly. He pulled an old work shirt out of a suitcase and tore it into strips. Then with almost no clearance (he said he had lost the car jack), he wriggled under the edge of the chassis and tied the strips of shirt around the oil line. "I think I got it," he said. "I don't see any more leaking oil. At least we didn't get a flat tire." The pothole we had hit was six inches deep and a foot-and-a-half across.

I climbed back into the rear seat. Bobbie stayed up front with Mike to keep him company. But as I turned and glanced out the back window, I saw a young bull moose burst out from the tree line and stand wide legged in the middle of the road. His big eyes turned towards us and without hesitation he started to run at our car in a rack-down gallop.

"Mike," I yelled in panic. "A moose is coming at us! Get us the hell out of here fast!"

"Shit," he hissed. He saw it coming in his rearview mirror. "Shit!" It was scary stuff.

Bobbi turned around and saw it coming but said nothing.

Mike twisted the key hard in the ignition, shoved down on the clutch, and put the car in gear, but it was sluggish, maybe because of low oil pressure. I watched the moose closing fast. The car gave a loud clunk, kicked in, shifted, and lurched forward. The small Corvair's rear engine, two feet behind where I was sitting, could never withstand a 2,000-pound hit. If we got battered by that young bull, we'd be dead in the road. At least I would be.

"Holy Mackanoli," I gasped and then went silent waiting for the crunch of metal and the splintering of my bones. But the car somehow picked up speed, started to widen the gap, and the moose, without breaking stride, veered off and disappeared into the tree line. Mike saw him vanish in his rearview mirror, looked around wide-eyed at me and started to laugh. Bobbi grinned. This time, we were lucky.

Less than a mile down the highway, Mike pulled over. We all walked into the woods to pee, Bobbi going to a separate spot. Then he got down on his belly to check the oil line under the car. The strips of shirt were holding. He was satisfied and on we went. That night, Mike slept in the backseat while Bobbi and I put up our tent next to the road and slept in that.

Mike and I switched off and drove all day Friday and Saturday. At five in the morning on Sunday, August 5th, we crossed the border into Montana and an hour-and-a-half later, in Shelby, we found a diner and ordered a real breakfast of orange juice, coffee, bacon, toast, and eggs. So good!

"You guys look beat," the waitress said when she brought our food. Mike and I told her about the trip down the ALCAN. Bobbi smiled as the two of us told our stories.

"So, where to next?" the waitress asked. Mike said he was driving to Arizona to find his girlfriend.

"We're headed to Oregon," I said. "I have a new Volkswagen waiting for me. We want to get a bus to Portland. At least that's the plan. And then who knows?"

"Well. You're in the right place." She went to the front window and pointed. "The Greyhound station is just down the street. The cook says breakfast is on us. No charge. Good luck."

I waved at the cook who was grinning out the serving window. He had been listening to our story. He put his palms up to the side of his forehead and spread his fingers like a moose rack.

Bobbi and I said goodbye to Mike and walked down the block to the station. The bus to Portland was leaving at 10:15. When it was boarding time, we climbed on and settled back in luxurious comfort, knowing there was a working toilet behind us for ready use. Minutes later, the town of Shelby was miles behind us.

The bus ride was twenty hours long. We pulled into the midtown Portland station at 7:00 a.m., Monday. After breakfast, we found the Volkswagen dealership and waited until it opened. The sales manager said they hadn't been sure when I would be coming and that my car wouldn't be ready until the next morning. Bobbi and I checked into the Park Haviland Hotel down the street, showered, and went exploring.

Most of the Greyhound trip had been on narrow, two-lane, winding mountain roads. We had driven through the northern Rockies traversing Montana, crossing the Continental Divide into Idaho, and finally into Oregon. The two-lane road with its sparse traffic on this bus route wasn't much different from the traffic around Fairbanks, so when we saw the multilane highways and all the people in this modern large West Coast city, it was overwhelming. Being up north for two years, I had forgotten the pace and density of large cities. True, it wasn't as busy as Cleveland or Detroit, but it was still culture shock, at least at first. It was all totally new to Bobbi since this was her first time out of Alaska.

That afternoon we saw a live production of *My Fair Lady* then splurged and went to a Trader Vic's restaurant for dinner. Bobbi and I looked ragged in our flannel shirts, jeans, and boots, but that was all we had. Everyone else was dressed up. Back in the hotel, we climbed into bed and watched a black and white Motorola television set with a twenty-inch screen. I couldn't believe it. It had six channels. No one I knew in Fairbanks or at the university had television since it was too expensive to string power lines up through Canada. We still got our news by newspaper or radio.

The next morning, we checked out of the hotel and picked up my Volkswagen Beetle. It was a beautiful, shiny, white two-door.

White Tooth, my VW, ready to roll

"It needs a name," I said. "I'll call it 'White Tooth.' It looks like a big tooth. When I drive it, it'll chew up the road."

"That's a great name," laughed Bobbi and she walked over and patted the car.

White Tooth had a radio, an internal gas heater, an ivory colored cloth interior, four whitewall tires, and a standard floor-shift between the two front seats. It came to $1,886.

"Wait a minute. I was told the car was 1,600 bucks," I said.

"It is," said the salesman, "but that's before the tax and preparation." I had forgotten about a tax. There was no sales tax in Alaska.

I finished the paperwork, showed proof of insurance, wrote the dealer a check, made sure they had filled the gas tank, put our travel gear in the back seat, and drove it off the lot.

At the first corner out of the lot, I stopped for a traffic light. Suddenly, I felt a bump and heard a soft metallic bang. "What the hell!" I said and turned around to look back out my open driver's side window. Another Volkswagen Beetle, a red one, had hit the rear bumper of my brand-new car. I got out in anger and glared at the driver. She was a young woman with long, frizzy, blonde hair in a pale blue thin strapped tee-shirt. She put her suntanned arm out her driver's window and waved.

"I was just saying hello," she smiled. "Is that a new Volkswagen? Welcome to the club." I glanced down at my bumper. No damage. "Welcome to the club," she said again. "Sorry if I startled you. You must not be from around here." She showed a row of perfect white teeth between pink pale lips and leaned back and grinned. I had heard about west coast hippies. She must have been a hippy. They did weird things. It was impossible to stay angry.

"It's okay," I said. "I just drove this car off the lot two minutes ago." That was all I said. I got back in my car. The light turned green and we drove away.

We headed north up the coast to Seattle. The 1962 World's Fair had just opened there and we both wanted to see it. On the motel television, we had seen pictures of the new Seattle World's Fair Space Needle. The news on TV said it was the tallest building west of the Mississippi, over six hundred feet high with an outside elevator that went to a revolving restaurant at the top.

"Let's go to that restaurant in the sky for lunch, have a beer and a burger, sit back and watch the world turn below us," I said.

"It would be like flying," Bobbi grinned. "We could see the world with the eyes of Raven."

As we approached Seattle, we could see the silhouette of the Space Needle poking up into the sky like a giant steel mushroom. We didn't plan on so many cars headed in the same direction. White Tooth slowly inched forward in four lanes of northbound traffic. The closer we got, the slower we had to go, and I started to worry about parking. At an intersection two blocks from the fairgrounds, I saw a car pulling away from the curb and I made a hard right out of the traffic and beat another car to the spot. I pulled in, put our backpacks in the front-end luggage compartment, locked the car, and we started walking.

Inside the entrance, countries from all over the world, from every continent, had food and souvenir booths set up along the walkway: Germany, New Zealand, Australia, South Africa, India, Norway, Japan, Mexico, Italy, Scotland, France, Canada. But no Soviet Union or communist China. Given what Mike had told us about the DEW Line and the fear of a Soviet attack, I wasn't surprised. But our sights were set on the Space Needle. The problem was there were hundreds of other people with the same idea. The wait for the top-of-the-tower restaurant was hours long and we said, "to heck with it," and went to see other things. We were disappointed, but not for long.

We heard the mystic sound of a sitar and stopped to watch beautiful, body-flowing, bare-bellied dancers from India. On the next block, we heard the blare of bagpipes and the staccato roll of drums while a line of military-stiff blonde and redheaded Scottish girls in white shirts and short green plaid skirts wearing black tap shoes danced in perfect synchronicity, perfect rhythm. They were sexy and exciting.

Ten minutes later the sound of different deep drums led us to a Navaho rain dance with men and boys in full leather and feather costumes. On another street, Bobbi grabbed my arm and pointed at a line of men wearing loincloths and wielding ornately carved clubs. Their faces and bodies were covered in tattoos and streaks of white paint as they did what looked like a war dance chanting a loud strange language in unison, their long wide pink tongues defiantly stuck out. A sign by their stage said they were Maori warriors from New Zealand. A polka band from Poland, fiddlers from Appalachia, jazz trumpets from New Orleans, the familiar chanting and regular beat of wide skin drums from the Tlingit people of southwest Alaska. Walking the street was a feast of blended smells and sights and sounds as the whole world seem to come together.

At four in the afternoon, we bought hotdogs and Cokes and headed back to our car to get going on our road trip to Ohio. I had forgotten the name of the street we had parked on, but I recognized the entrance gate we had come through and we headed for that. Bobbi and I walked hand in hand so as not to get pushed apart in the flow of people pouring into the fairgrounds. It was a good thing my new Beetle was shiny white, because it stood out like a golf ball on a putting green from the dark cars parked along the street. It's sloping front hood seemed to smile, "Hello, hello." I felt it call, "Here I am. Time to go."

At 6 o'clock, we stopped at a laundromat to do a quick wash and headed north of Seattle to the Olympic National Park, a place we wanted to see. I don't know why we wanted to see it; we just did. Maybe it was the promise of pristine mountains and the silence of isolation.

We found a wooded campground and set up our tent just as a storm started to blow in from the Pacific. The rain came pouring down with a rumble of thunder and hammered our tent as Bobbi and I climbed into our sleeping bags which we zipped together. Together they were warm and soft and great for making love. Her strong bare body tight against mine melted as we held each other against the onslaughts of the storm. Joy and love, the relaxation of breathing deep, a soft long closing of the eyes and together a wonderful sleep of forgettable dreams. The next day we drove southeast to Denver.

Bobbi had a sister in Columbus, Ohio. Before we left Fairbanks, we planned for Bobbi to visit with her sister for a week then take a Greyhound bus to Toledo. We'd go to Bob Friedman's wedding, then get back on the road to Alaska. On Friday, August 17th, I dropped Bobbi off at her sister's house as planned and drove the last 150 miles north to Toledo.

Since I knew Bobbi would be in Columbus, I had made plans for the time while she was visiting her sister. I wanted to visit Uncle Charles, my father's older brother, in New York City. He had invited me to meet him at his office in the Empire State Building where he was a financial consultant. Uncle Charles had helped me pay for my undergraduate tuition and I wanted to thank him.

The following two days with my family were good. Dad took us to dinner, I went swimming at a swim club our family belonged to, sat on the back porch and drank beer with Mom, and drove into Cleveland to visit my grandfather to catch him up on my adventures.

The next day, the phone rang. Bobbi's visit with her sister wasn't going well and she was taking the next Greyhound to Toledo.

"Can you up pick me up at the bus station tonight?" she asked.

"Sure," I said. "What time does it get in?"

"Ten o'clock."

"Okay. I'll be there." I didn't ask questions. If she wanted to tell me why she cut her visit short, she would.

When her bus pulled in, she came over and threw her arms around me. She didn't want to let go. Neither did I.

"Bobbi, I'm so glad you're here," I said. 'But I didn't expect you so soon."

"I didn't expect to be here so soon," she said. She didn't say why she had left. If it was important, she would tell me. If it was painful, she wouldn't. In the few months I had known her, I had never heard her complain or criticize anyone or anything. To tell the truth, I rarely knew what she was thinking. I could see happiness in her eyes when we talked, but her private thoughts were her private thoughts.

Driving back to my folk's house, I told her of my plans to go to New York City and see my Uncle Charles.

"Now that you're here, you can come with me," I said. "Just think, when you get home, you can tell your mom you not only travelled the ALCAN, but you drove from sea to shining sea, from the Pacific Ocean to the Atlantic. From California to New York Island. You could even write a song about it," I joked, thinking of the popular song, "This Land is Your Land." By the time we pulled into our driveway, our plans were set.

Everyone at home was waiting to meet Bobbi, but it was almost eleven at night and past everyone's bedtime. Mom made a bed for her on the living room sofa and the family all went upstairs to bed. I was tired myself, so I showed Bobbi where the bathroom was, we kissed goodnight, and I went upstairs. Mom was not a believer in hanky-panky in her house before marriage and I honored her code, although she was savvy enough to know Bobbi and I were lovers.

Bobbi and my sister Susan were about the same age, but they were from totally different cultures. Susan was intrigued by Bobbi's open life and fearless personal freedom. To think of hitchhiking over a thousand miles down the ALCAN Highway, having adventures, going to strange unfamiliar places without knowing what awaited, driving across the country and camping out under the stars and in the rain, it opened her mind. Susan was about to leave home herself to move into a dorm at Ohio State University to begin her freshman year.

38: New York and Uncle Charles

After breakfast, Bobbi and I got in my car and left for New York. When we crossed over the New Jersey border, we stopped at the first motel.

We drove into downtown New York City around noon the next day and found a cheap hotel a couple of blocks from Central Park. It was the Hotel Ashley. Our room was three flights up, no elevator, with one window that opened onto a dismal interior courtyard that looked like an abandoned factory shaft. The double bed had a sagging mattress and squeaky springs, and the room smelled of stale cigarettes and bug spray. I wondered who else had been in this room. But it was only eight dollars a night. We had already paid for parking our car nearby. We wouldn't be spending much time in the hotel, so I booked it for two nights.

I could feel a sadness come over Bobbi as we lay our packs down on the bed. Even when we left the building for lunch and to explore the busy streets and walk through Central Park to the Museum of Natural History, her usual wide-eyed spirit of adventure seemed drained.

"Let's call my Uncle Charles," I said. I thought Bobbi meeting him would give her New York stay a focus. I was anxious to see his office in the Empire State Building. His secretary answered when I called from a payphone in Central Park.

"Hello" I said. "Is Mr. Charles Rudinger there? This is Joel, his nephew from Ohio.

"I'm sorry," said the woman's voice. "Mr. Rudinger is not in today. He called this morning and said he was ill. May I take a message?" I was disappointed.

"Yes, please tell him I'm in New York for two days and that I and my girlfriend from Alaska would like to see him. He knows we're coming. We're staying at the Hotel Ashley. Is there another number I can call to talk to him?"

"I'm sorry," said the voice. "I can't give out his personal number, but I'll let him know you're here. If you want to call back later, I'll pass on his message."

"Okay. Thanks," I said. "I'll call back by 5 o'clock."

"We close at four," she said.

"Okay, I'll call back before four."

Bobbi had gone over to a park bench nearby and was staring at pigeons perched on a windowsill of a tall building across the street. My Triple-A city map showed Times Square and the theatre district ten blocks away. I thought maybe walking down that way would make her feel better. We had spent a lot of time in the car and walking would get our blood moving again. She agreed.

The stop and go street traffic was thick with the sound of engines and the smell of gasoline exhaust. Yellow cabs, delivery vans, private cars, and commuter buses filled the street. The sidewalks flowed with tourists and businessmen. I saw hippies who reminded me of the girl in the Volkswagen in Portland.

People were everywhere, gawking or staring. On a street corner, a musician dressed all in red played a guitar. On the next block, a ten-year old girl danced while playing a trombone. Across the street, a Jamaican bongo player. I could hear his sharp heavy rhythm even over the sounds of traffic. They all had hats or little baskets laying on the sidewalk for money. We passed a group of Amish, the men with uncut beards and the women in clean gray bonnets and long gray shapeless dresses. Behind them were two orthodox Jewish men in black suits and hats, and white shirts with prayer shawls fringed with knots draped over their thin bent shoulders. Couples passed by speaking French or Spanish or Chinese. A few blue-suited mounted police sat high in the street on muscular horses, watching traffic and ready for anything.

A native American Indian dressed in torn jeans, worn cowboy boots, a sweat-stained floppy ten-gallon hat, and an open buttonless leather vest came over. "Any extra change?"

While I was taking all this in, Bobbi was slowing down. She had lost the bounce in her step. Something was wrong.

"Bobbi, are you okay?"

"No. I don't feel well," she said. Her voice was flat.

"Do you want to go back?"

"Yes."

We turned around and slowly walked back towards Central Park and headed for an open bench. We sat for a while watching people. Horse drawn carriages clopped past loudly on the street. At a quarter after three, I called my uncle's office.

"Your uncle said that he can meet you in his office tomorrow. Come around noon and you can join him for lunch," the secretary said. "Just call half an hour before you come." I told Bobbi the plan.

The next morning though, she was feeling worse. The air in that crappy hotel room was like spiritual poison, but she didn't want to go anywhere.

"I have to step out briefly to call my uncle." I couldn't stand the smell of the room and didn't understand why she didn't want to get out into the open air, even if it, too, was a little rancid.

"You go" she said. "I'll stay here and rest."

"Are you sure?"

"Yes."

"Okay," I said. "I'll only be gone a few minutes."

When I got back to the hotel lobby, Bobbi was coming out the elevator door. She looked better and she came over and gave me a hug. Maybe it was a hug of relief because I made her feel wanted. Which I did. She felt so good in my arms.

A girl in the lobby told us of a better, cheap, and clean hotel nearby. We needed a room just for that night. We checked it out and it was perfect. The hotel had a small, affordable, well-lit restaurant, in the room the mattress was firm, the linens were clean, the bathroom was spotless. Plus, it had a window that opened onto the street. Not at all like the claustrophobic Hotel Ashely rathole.

We walked to the Empire State Building seven blocks away. At 11:45, I called my uncle from a payphone on the ground floor, then we took the elevator to his office on the 69th floor. The elevator operator in a fully-pressed, immaculate uniform gave us a sideways look. It was the first time I had been in the Empire State Building. I had seen it only in magazines and movies. It was clear to me now why Uncle Charles was considered the patriarch of our family.

Bobbi and I walked into a large waiting room.

"Hello, Joel. I'm Mrs. Fisher,' said the woman sitting at her desk.

"Hi," I said. "Nice to meet you. This is my girlfriend Bobbi from Alaska."

"Hello, Bobbi," said Mrs. Fisher. "Is this your first time in New York?"

"Yes." Bobbi smiled.

"It's quite a city," said Mrs. Fisher. "Lots of good restaurants, great shows on Broadway, lots of good music. Joel, you've been here once before, Mr. Rudinger tells me."

"Yes. In 1956, I came in from Philadelphia on a train with a friend. We went to Birdland and saw Buddy Rich playing drums, then met up with Uncle Charles at the Carlyle Hotel. He took us to Frank Cerutti's, a restaurant on Madison Avenue."

"I've heard of it," she said. She pointed to a closed door across the room. "Your uncle is waiting for you in there, Joel. Please go on in."

The first thing I saw when I opened the door into Uncle Charles's personal office was a wall of windows overlooking the vast skyline of the city below. Uncle Charles came around from behind his large mahogany desk and we shook hands. I introduced Bobbi.

She told him a little about herself when he asked, her native heritage, how we met, what she thought, things even I didn't know. My uncle, in his rise to making his fortune, had met hundreds of people—businessmen, contractors, lawyers, chefs, university presidents, bankers, politicians — but no one like Bobbi: young, open, quiet, adventurous, living life in the moment, without a need or desire to impress. Uncle Charles put his hand tenderly on her shoulder and guided her over to the windows.

"Look at the view," he said. He pointed out the window. Beyond the dark brick and concrete, sharp-edged buildings, in the distance we could see the Statue of Liberty glowing green in the late morning sun. "There's the Statue of Liberty on Liberty Island," he said with pride. "And just in front of that is Ellis Island. My parents, Joel's grandparents, both came to America through Ellis Island in 1888 when they were just thirteen," he told Bobbi. "They came to America to escape the pogroms in Russia and Poland. They didn't meet each other until years later and got married here in New York City. I was born here. Joel's father was born here, too." He paused, looking out the window.

"What's a pogrom?" asked Bobbi. It was a mood changing question.

A heaviness fell upon my uncle's face. She had asked and now he felt a need to tell her. It was our history. "A pogrom was a savage movement to kill the Jews," he said. "In Russia and Poland, as well as other countries, Jews were slaughtered like animals as the governments looked the other way. Local farmers and soldiers would get drunk and ride their horses into Jewish ghettos and hang or hack up the men, and rape and stab the women and children. Every night, men in the ghettos took turns standing watch to warn the ones sleeping in case of an attack. Somehow my parents as children got passage and found their way to America," said Uncle Charles. "Their own parents and family were not so lucky." Another heavy pause. "Are you hungry? Ready for lunch?" When Bobbi turned away from the window, there were tears in her eyes.

I remembered hearing a little of the immigration history of grandparents from my father, but he never told me any details.

I got to thinking about how raw and brave my grandparents must have been, to leave everything behind, their worlds blowing up around them, their parents doomed to violent extinction. They came here penniless, not knowing what the future would or could bring. What would the land of America offer a poor Russian boy or Polish girl who didn't know a word of English? Neither had a sponsor, no one to care for them in time of trouble.

True, my grandfather had the rudiments of a trade. My father told me that he had worked as a furrier's apprentice in Russia, a tailor sewing animal skins into fur coats. Maybe he got a job in the New York garment district using his skill. Again, I never got answers when I asked. When I was old enough to ask him myself, Grandpa Rudinger had had a stroke that left him paralyzed and mute. In some ways, his leaving everything to come to America was a parallel in terms of my

189

going to Alaska, walking away from everything familiar. But I always had a fallback, people I could count on. He had none. For him, it was an adventure of necessity. He could either persevere or die.

My uncle took us to a little restaurant nearby where the maître d knew his name and favorite table. We ordered a gourmet lunch, taking Uncle Charles's recommendations. I thanked him for helping with my last two years of college. He smiled and ordered himself a vodka martini. When we finished dessert, he handed me an envelope with money in it. Then he said he had to leave us to meet with a client. He gave Bobbi a hug, and me a firm handshake and a pat on the back, then walked us out to the street.

"Good luck back in Alaska," he said. "Give my love to Ruth and Irv." And we said goodbye.

39: Ohio Wedding

By mid-afternoon, we were back in New Jersey headed home. Bobbi had recovered from her New York sadness. I understood. Yes, New York City was the famous cultural center of the western world. It had great music, art, and theatre, and an infinite variety of shops and restaurants. But we were surrounded by concrete buildings and skyscrapers that blocked the sun and the stars. Cars and buses and trucks filled the air with noise and rancid exhaust. For someone like Bobbi, who had grown up in the wide and open unpopulated land of Alaska, New York City was oppressive and artificial. In Alaska, she felt she had meaning. In NYC, she had none. It was as simple as that.

I had to stretch the money Uncle Charles had given me. It was almost 4,000 miles from Toledo to Fairbanks and gas was not cheap.

The few days we had in Toledo went quickly. I took my car in for its first 5,000-mile check, then Dad wanted to take everyone out to dinner and show Bobbi his store, which had been his life and had supported the family.

The next morning, I had an appointment to have a protective undercoating applied to my car so we could survive the gravel and potholes on the ALCAN. Bobbi stayed at home with my sister and brother. They were fascinated by her and sat on the back porch trading stories and drinking lemonade.

On Saturday, I bought a Smith-Corona portable electric typewriter and picked up a rented tuxedo for that evening's wedding rehearsal dinner. Bobbi wore one of my sister's party dresses and looked beautiful. My friend Bob Friedman was marrying a girl I had introduced him to the summer I left for Alaska.

The wedding was at 2:00 p.m. in the Toledo Collingwood Avenue Temple. A dinner and reception followed later at a downtown hotel. After dinner, the dance floor was bursting with loud music full of joy and celebration. A parade of beautiful colorful gowns and black tuxedos, the three-foot-high wedding cake, the six-piece orchestra, and the tables that lined the walls with wine and fancy hors d'oeuvres arranged like hearts in a banquet hall full of glowing candles. Then there was the ritual of the men paying the bride for a dance, and afterwards half the couples up on their feet doing the hora singing "Hava Nagila," their hands over their heads, fingers snapping, heads bobbing, arms high and waving side to side in ancient traditional Israeli jubilation — all this was new and eye-opening for Bobbi. She had never seen anything like it. She laughed and danced into the center of the happy chaos. I understood her joy. There was no such celebration of marriage in her native world. And the music went on.

PART TWO

40: BACK TO ALASKA

On the third of September, the day after the wedding, my car was packed and ready to go. My mother and father, my sister Susan and brother Jonathan gathered in front of my car to say goodbye. Bobbi had my camera and took a group photo of us. Even our dog, Pepper, got into the shot.

OCT • 62 C

My mother Ruth, me, brother Jonathan with Pepper, sister Susan, and my father Irv posed in front of White Tooth, my packed and loaded VW, the morning of our departure to drive back to Fairbanks.

By mid-afternoon, with a full tank of gas we were on our way and headed northwest.

"Look at the odometer." I pointed. Bobbi looked at it. "We've driven over 5,500 miles. That's a lot of miles. Portland, up to Seattle, down through the Rockies to Denver, east to St. Louis, Columbus, up to Toledo, then to New York City and back to Toledo. And all our little side trips. Wow!"

"Wow," Bobbi said.

As we crossed into Indiana, I looked over at Bobbi. We had only been driving for two hours but a wave of exhaustion hit both of us. "It's only 5 o'clock," I said, "but I'm tired. How about we stop for the night?" She leaned over and squeezed my hand. The unknown, the excitement and anticipation were behind us now. We had a better sense of what was coming. Our minds were quieter.

"Good," she said. "I'm tired, too." I was so happy she was with me.

A mile down the road, we saw a small motel next to a truck stop. We got a quick eat-in meal, checked into the motel, and fell asleep in each other's arms.

The next day we bypassed Chicago and only got as far as Eau Claire, Wisconsin. It was a slow drive. An accident blocked traffic going northwest and for hours we went nowhere. Bobbi slept with her head against her door as I patiently inched forward. We had lunch at a rest stop, got back on the highway and were stopped again by an overturned semi in a construction zone. A long day going nowhere. At 8 o'clock, I saw a blinking motel vacancy sign and we stopped. Over twelve hours on the road and little progress to show for it.

We left the Eau Claire motel in the morning, drove all day, and at 9:30 that night. stopped in Bismarck, North Dakota. We stayed in a motel the next night in Sunburst, Montana, eight miles from the Canadian border.

When we woke up in Sunburst, there was a driving snow. Holy cow. What was going on? It was suddenly freezing, and the world had turned white. The wind whipped the snow horizontally across the road and visibility for hours was down to fifty yards. That day, we only got as far as Edmonton, Alberta, about 360 miles north of the U.S. border. White Tooth now had 7,831 miles on its odometer.

We left Edmonton early in the morning and drove across Alberta to Dawson Creek at the border of British Columbia. Dawson Creek was Milepost 0 of the ALCAN Highway. It was like the beginning of coming home.

Only the first thirty miles of the ALCAN past Dawson Creek were blacktopped and smooth. Beyond that, we were back on tamped-down gravel and potholes. The speed limit on the ALCAN was fifty miles an hour, but, because of the lousy roads, we had to drive a lot slower. We had learned when we came down the ALCAN that trucks paid little attention to speed limits and come barreling past, spraying up loose stone and gravel that cracked the windshields and headlights of on-coming cars. It was illegal to cover your headlights with cardboard to protect them, so driving slowly was a necessary defense. That night when we got to Fort Nelson, the odometer read 8,490.

September 9, 1962

We left Fort Nelson at early morning, heading for Whitehorse in Yukon Territory. This was now our seventh day on the road.

We were in constant awe of the beauty that appeared at almost every turn. Around one curve lined by trees, three wild black stallions appeared on the side of the road. They reared and lunged back into the tree line as we came near. An hour later, a mountain goat with curl-and-a-half horns loped across the road in front of us. The day before, we saw a bull moose coming up an embankment.

But the best treat was a small hand-painted wooden sign off the highway that read "Hot Springs" and an arrow pointing up a narrow dirt road. We needed a break, any kind of break. I stopped, backed up, and took the road. It ended in a small dirt parking lot. On one side was a side-by-side men's and women's outhouse built out of peeled logs for changing. Bobbi and I dug into our packs for our bathing suits. There was no one around so we just stripped next to the car, suited up, and slowly lowered ourselves into the gurgling, luxurious, steaming, hot pool of water. It was heaven. What a gift, after all that driving and dodging potholes to find this hidden secret of perfection. We just leaned back and let the hot water steam up around us. The air was chilly, but the hot water made all the cold disappear. Bobbi and I said nothing. We just closed our eyes and soaked in silence.

After about an hour, we heard another car coming up the road. A khaki-colored Jeep pulled in and a fat bald man and a 300-pound, middle-aged woman with long gray hair tied up in a bun the size of a football waddled out talking and talking. Blah blah blah blah. Something about a chicken, dead flowers, her grandmother's piano, farting in the car, a dead raccoon, potholes . . . blah blah blah nonstop. Each carried a cloth sack in their hands and went into the separate changing rooms. I looked at Bobbi and she looked at me. She rolled her eyes and we sat up. For us, the bliss was over. The couple came out, still talking. We nodded hello. They ignored us. We climbed out of the water and went into the outhouses to dry off and change.

That evening, we stayed in a Whitehorse motel and ate supper in a Chinese restaurant, a delicious happy meal of hot won-ton soup, chop suey over fried rice, and hot green tea. When the bill came, we got our fortune cookies. My little white strip of paper read, "Okay to look at past and future. Just don't stare." We went back to the motel and lay down on the bed, Bobbi breathing softly in my arms.

We left Whitehorse early on the 10th of September. Driving off the Canadian gravel onto smooth Alaska concrete signaled the beginning of the end of our journey. Thirteen hours and 610 miles later, we drove in darkness past Indiantown and into the middle of Fairbanks.

When I took Bobbi to her house, her mother was away. We unloaded her gear, hugged goodnight, and I drove to my apartment. I carried my backpack and duffle upstairs. Neither of my roommates were in. I was drained and tired. I got a cold beer out of the fridge and sat down to think. Now I had a car. I was going to finish my degree. What else would change?

41: *Purity in Distress*

It was strange starting a new semester as an ordinary graduate student. Teaching had been so much of my routine. Instead, I focused on studying for my French exam. Dr. Michael Krause, the new professor of linguistics, had told me the exam would be a written one. He would give me an article written in French and I would have one hour to translate it into English. French, it seemed, was the foreign language most used in literary criticism. That first semester back, I took several graduate English courses and studied French. I did well in the litera-ture courses, but at the last minute, Dr. Krause decided to give me an oral exam instead of a written one. I wasn't prepared for that and had to postpone my language exam a month. He changed it back to a writ-ten exam and I passed it.

In the meantime, since I wasn't earning money as a teaching assistant, I got a job in the university bookstore as a fulltime clerk. It made enough to pay for my tuition, rent, gas, and food.

The spring semester was a chance for me to sink my teeth into a creative project. The professor of the Contemporary Drama course I had signed up for was Dr. Arthur Wills. We had just finished Samuel Beckett's *Waiting for Godot,* a major play in the Theatre of the Absurd. It opened my mind to the freshness of the theatre in a new way. The more I studied Becket's scripts, the more I started to think of creating a walking, talking character of my own.

When Dr. Wills announced the deadline date for the course term paper, the students groaned. They knew it was required, but they groaned anyway. With Beckett in mind, I had an idea that could be a win-win for me and others in the course. After class, I went to Dr. Wills' office.

"Hello, Joel. Come on in," he said. "That was a good paper you wrote on *Waiting for Godot.* With a little touching up, you might get it published. The *Evergreen Review* might be interested in it. Have a seat."

"Thanks," I said. "Beckett is my favorite playwright so far in the course. There's something about that play that speaks to me."

"Why is that?" he asked.

"Well, maybe because I'm kind of waiting for Godot myself."

He laughed. Godot was a metaphor for god, a savior, someone who would appear out of nowhere and save the day.

"A lot of people are," Dr. Wills said. He leaned back in his swivel chair. "Only a lot of them don't know it. And sometimes Godot never comes. Like in Beckett's play."

"But maybe sometimes he does," I said. "What if he did?" Dr. Wills smiled. "I came to see you because I have an idea," I said. "I've been thinking it would be fun to have our class write and perform an original play. I think they would welcome the chance to do something creative and make it come to life."

"What kind of play would it be?" he asked.

"A two or three-act play. Something with drama. Not a musical."

"We're already well into February," he said. "Class is over the middle of May. Is that enough time?"

"I think we can do it," I said. "It's a strong group, but it will take work and, as you said, time for the writing and rehearsals. What I would like to propose is, for the students who take part in this project, that you grade the finished play after our performance and that grade would be their term paper grade."

Dr. Wills cocked his head, looked at me for a few seconds, then grinned.

"It's different, but I like it. I agree. Yes. Give it a try."

The deal was sealed. Now, how would the students react?

When the class met two days later, I looked around the room. It was an impressive group, at least to me. I saw talent and potential in everyone there. Dr. Wills walked in, went to the front, wrote the words TERM PAPER on the chalkboard, and turned to face the class. A dramatic silence in the room.

"Joel came to see me a couple days ago," he said. "He has an idea he wants to share. Joel?" He motioned me up to the front.

I looked around. Everyone was staring at me. I was anxious to tell them about my idea.

"We all enjoy talking about the plays we read every day, right?"

No response.

"I thought it would fun if we, as a class, together, wrote, and produced an original play for the course and performed it for the campus."

Silence. No applause. Some glanced nervously at Dr. Wills, but he stayed quiet. This was my baby.

"I see it as three-act play with most of you, if not everyone, acting in it or taking some part in the production."

"What is it about?" one student asked. There was doubt in his voice.

"I don't know yet," I said. "We'll know after we write it."

"When will you write it?" a girl asked. She must not have heard the word "we."

"It's supposed to be a group effort. We have to get together a few times to talk about it."

"Dr. Wills," said a whiny voice from the back of the room. "This sounds like a lot of work."

The professor smiled. "Well," he said, "Joel and I talked about that. He had a suggestion which I agreed to. And that is, if you are a part of the production, I will excuse you from writing a term paper." He went over to the board and put a big question mark after the words TERM PAPER. "If you choose not to be a part of it or drop out of the project, you will need to write a paper." He looked around the room. "I'll evaluate and grade the play and its production and that will be your grade."

The students were looking around at each other. Some nodded. Some grinned. Some looked confused.

"So, how would we be part of the play?" They all looked at me.

"You could be an actor or a scene designer, or help write the script, something like that. Okay?" I said. "How about a vote? Who wants to participate?"

Eighty percent of the class raised their hands. Success!

"Okay, good," I said. "The class has voted yes. But just to be sure, think about it and next Monday I'll bring a sign-up sheet. Then I'll have a better idea of possible characters and behind-the-scene helpers. And for those who didn't vote for it today, the weekend will give you a chance to talk to the others who did."

When the class met on Monday, everyone signed on. No surprise. None of them wanted to write a term paper. So now it was up to me. This was going to be a creative challenge. I couldn't wait to start.

My apartment above the employment bureau was the perfect place to have rehearsals. It had a large living room and, since my roommates were rarely home except at night to sleep or to party on weekends, it would be a good place to meet and rehearse.

A few of us met at Tommy's Elbow Room to brainstorm plots and characters. I suggested doing a melodrama. That would give us the type of play that could have lots of minor roles which could involve most of the students. Everyone urged me to write the first draft. I agreed since I planned to do most of it anyway. Most of them knew that and were more than happy to let me do the work.

Because our country was involved in a Cold War standoff with the Soviet Union, I called the melodrama *Purity in Distress, or Better Dead than Wed*, a take-off on the anti-Soviet slogan "Better Dead than Red."

I worked on the script for weeks, getting ideas and comments from classmates if they showed up at meetings at Tommy's. When the first draft was finished, I invited everyone with an acting part up to my apartment for rehearsals.

Professor Wills lent me a book entitled *The History of the Theatre*. In it was a reference to a French director of melodramas named Delsarte.

201

On a whim, I checked the university's library card catalog, and, by a miracle, I found an old, ragged, leather-bound copy of *The Delsarte System of Expression* published in 1902. I couldn't believe my luck. How did such a rare and classic book wind up in this obscure library and what were the odds that I would need it?

The book had photographs of actors demonstrating postures and facial expressions popular in the days of silent films. I remembered seeing silent films with Buster Keaton, Charlie Chaplin, and Boris Karloff, with their exaggerated actions and facial expressions. As I read, I discovered that each pose or gesture had a specific meaning. It was a physical body language for a film-going audience that they could understand. Perhaps a knowing theatre audience might respond the same way.

As we got into rehearsals, everyone in the class came to know what each pose meant, but people not in our class, our future audiences, wouldn't.

"Why don't we start our play with a short introduction and demonstrate some of the postures with a short explanation," I suggested.

"Great idea," said the villain of the play. The group agreed and I went into a deep study of the Delsarte method.

When the full script was finished, the department secretary ran off mimeographed copies for the actors. We met at my place for rehearsals over a dozen times. They memorized their lines and practiced their gestures. We went over how they would interact, how gesture preceded dialog, and how they would deliver their lines. No two rehearsals ever went the same. A final dress rehearsal on the auditorium stage with our make-shift scenery was scheduled for the morning of May 11th.

Our first public performance was scheduled for the next day, a Sunday. When I peeked through the curtains to see if anyone was in the audience, I saw that the auditorium was packed. Somehow the word had gotten out. The theatre was filled with faculty, students, and visitors from Fairbanks and Fort Wainwright.

At 1:30, I walked on stage and over to a podium. The audience applauded. The weeks of planning and rehearsals and revising were about to come together. I was too excited to be nervous.

On cue, the actor playing Jedred Stone, the stepfather, appeared from stage right and stood center stage in a spotlight. He was dressed in ragged jeans and a rumpled flannel shirt. The audience applauded again. The moment was right. I began the introduction.

"Ladies and gentlemen, the students of Dr. Wills' Contemporary Drama Class are pleased to present an original melodrama *Purity in Distress or Better Dead Than Wed*. Before we begin, we would like to say a word about the melodramatic technique so that you can better appreciate the meaning of old-time drama and the actors' movements therein.

"As we today are trained to appreciate the theatre of realism, so the early Twentieth century audiences were trained to follow melodrama. Every gesture had a meaning, every nod or wink had a special significance. Melodrama was complex. With the help of this old book, *The Delsarte System of Expression*, we will attempt to demonstrate a few melodramatic stage techniques.

"Dave Gilbert, who plays Jedred Stone in our play, will demonstrate some of the Delsarte hand poses used many years ago. I will instruct Dave what to do, then I will read a sentence which explains what the gesture means.

"One of the laws of the melodrama is the Law of Sequence, which states expression of face precedes gesture and gesture precedes speech."

With eyes looking up, Dave placed his right hand on his forehead, the mental zone. I interpreted its meaning: "There's a fearful thought."

Then with the tips of the fingers, he threw a kiss outward from the mouth. "This gesture means, 'A thousand times goodnight.'"

The audience watched Dave demonstrate more hand gestures and applauded when he stepped back.

Then victim-heroine Mary Heartthrob walked on stage dressed in a loose-fitting white dress and ballet slippers, looking sweet and innocent. We demonstrated arm and torso movements. She was followed by the play's villain, Clutchclaw Grimsbuck, totally dressed in black — black trousers, black shirt, a long black cape, and a black top hat. He demonstrated sitting and standing positions as I called them out. When Clutchclaw Grimsbuck was done, all three actors stepped forward and bowed. The audience applauded.

I turned to the audience with a final comment: "We invite you to return with us to the days of yore, to hiss our villain and cheer our heroes, but we ask that you please don't throw any rotten tomatoes. Keep them for your salads." They laughed.

Everyone in the audience had a program listing the characters with a brief descriptor to prepare them for what was to come and for whom they should boo or cheer.

Purity in Distress, or Better Dead Than Wed

The cast of characters were:
Clutchclaw Grimsbuck: a fiend if there ever was one
Rex Handsome: our hero, What a man!
Mary Heartthrob: ah, sweet bird of youth
Granny Heartthrob: a heart as big as her umbrella
Jezebel: a wicked woman, but oh boy!
Jedred Stone: the depraved stepfather

Nosey Nipper: a sneaky spy, with technique
Flower Girl: a poor urchin of the gutters
Reverend Humble: "Be ye therefore perfect"
Belinda Humble: a shoulder to cry on
Salesman Charlie: a man of the world
Vagabond: a soul of poetry and treachery
Porter: an honest simpleton
Sherriff: a devoted servant of justice
Travesty: a maid

===============

The play opens with Jedred Stone sitting alone in a train station cursing his weakness for gambling and booze. Enter the villain, Clutchclaw Grimsbuck, and his sidekick Jezebel, holding a bottle of whiskey. Jedred and Clutchclaw sit down at a table to gamble at poker. Jezebel pours Jed a whiskey which he drinks. Jed wins the first hand and feels his luck has returned. Clutchclaw eggs him on, knowing he will ultimately win.

Jed feels confident and bets everything he has. Grimsbuck raises the stakes: the cancellation of a pile of IOU's plus the mortgage on Jedred's house which Clutchclaw owns. If Jedred loses, he must agree to give his daughter, Mary Heartthrob, in marriage to Clutchclaw. Clutchclaw then throws down four aces to beat Jedred's queen-high flush and makes Jedred sign a contract of agreement. Enter Rex Handsome who has just gotten off the train. He comes to Mary's aid.

Mary lives with Granny Heartthrob. When Clutchclaw discovers his plot has failed, he plans to set Granny's house on fire.

Grimsbuck says: "That dastardly Jedred Stone was so drunk when he signed my contract that he misspelled his name, with three M's. Only I know it's not legal. Well, if I can't have her, neither will that rural churl, Rex Handsome. I will fix her and him both. (He dashes behind the house and back on stage again.) There! It is done! In a minute there will be a flash, and then, ha ha ha, a pile of ash. I'll make a lamp stand of her maiden bones."

Grimsbuck sets the house on fire with Mary and Granny in it. Enter Rex who runs in to save them. As the house burns, the sound of falling metal is heard. Granny runs into the house and discovers gold coins falling out of the walls. Now the Heartthrobs are rich and Rex can marry Mary. A sheriff chases Grimsbuck off the stage to arrest him for arson. End of play. Stage goes dark.

Granny Heartthrob bashes Clutchclaw Grimsbuck on his head with her umbrella as Mary lies unconscious on the floor. "Take that, you evil villain!"

===============

Chuck Keim and his wife, in the front row, led a standing ovation. It was a fantastic moment for everyone in the class. For me, it was the first time I felt genuine validation as a writer. Each actor came on stage to take a bow. It was a moment of success. We had done it.

I asked Dr. Wills to stand. "Ladies and gentlemen," I said, "our play *Purity in Distress, or Better Dead than Wed* wouldn't have been possible without Dr. Arthur Wills. As professor of our Contemporary Drama course, he embraced the idea of our class writing and producing this original play. This is an experience none of us will ever forget. Thank you again, Dr. Wills, for believing we could do it." Dr. Wills stood. The audience applauded.

Purity in Distress, or Better Dead than Wed got great reviews in the *Fairbanks Daily News Miner*. Every student in Dr. Wills' Contemporary Drama class who was part of it got a grade of A. No term paper required!

205

Rex Handsome (myself) declares his love for Mary Heartthrob. "Will you marry me?"

42: The Move

Dear family,

Well, it's the second of June and classes are over. Work at the university bookstore is going well. I get regular hours and a regular paycheck. I can sit down without interruption and write.

Last week I moved all my things across town. Gene Belland bought a house and cancelled his lease over the employment bureau. My new address is 708 Sixth Avenue. I will live in his basement for only $50 a month.

When I was moving in, I saw a horse in the backyard on our side of a picket fence. Yes, a horse in the backyard. In the middle of town! A stinky, skinny, blotchy, mangy horse. When I tried to lead it back into its own yard next door, I saw it was infested with thousands of stinging black flies all over its back and rear. The miserable horse was stamping its feet and scraping its butt raw against the now pushed-out fence. It whinnied in agony.

The next day I gave a set of Cuban maracas a student had given me to a little girl next door whose family owned the horse. She started to beat on the horse's rear with the rattles. I thought I'd die laughing when the horse farted and she ran away screaming with the maracas rattling into her house. Two minutes later, she came back out and started to hammer on the horse's butt again. The horse didn't seem to mind. The maracas were keeping away the flies.

Last night, the horse came back into our yard and started to rub up and scratch itself against the wood siding of Gene's house. I ran out and grabbed it by its halter and tried to drag it back off our lawn, but it bucked sideways and pinned me against the side of the house. After I squeezed out, I turned a garden hose on it and it went back into its own yard.

Gene's new house is a single story. The main floor consists of a small living room; a bedroom which is now Gene's law office; a kitchen; and a bathroom accessible only from the bedroom/office. A flight of stairs from the back door and the kitchen leads down to the basement. The main portion of the basement is a large room divided in half by a gas furnace. On the far side of the furnace is a washing machine, a slop sink, and an open area for storage.

The rest of the basement is my living quarters with a desk, a goose-neck desk lamp, a typewriter, and an office chair. It is the perfect place to write. At the foot of the stairs leading up to the kitchen and back door, we put one of Gene's leather armchairs and a floor lamp. The rest of the furniture from Gene's previous apartment he is using upstairs.

On the other side of the wall behind my writing desk is a narrow room just big enough for a twin-size bed, a folding chair, and a wooden orange crate that I stand on end to use as a nightstand. The top of it has just enough room for an alarm clock and a candlestick lamp. At the end of the bedroom is a tiny built-in closet. All-in-all, my basement apartment is all I need. It's small, warm, and comfortable. I also have access and full use of the kitchen. It looks like this will be my home until I graduate or something unexpected happens.

Gene does a lot of pro bono work for people who can't afford to pay for legal help. In addition to the clients he is helping to incorporate new businesses, some of his clients are local prostitutes. Sometimes when I walk into the living room/waiting room, a bedraggled young woman is sitting on the couch waiting for her appointment. Our house is a fascinating place to live. You never know who might come through the front door. Eugene Belland has a heart of gold. He is a good friend.

Love to all,
Joel

Joel (left) and co-worker in the university bookstore.

43: Solar Eclipse

July 20, 1963

I saw Dave Gilbert, who had played Jedred Stone in my play, outside the Student Union after my shift in the bookstore. Students had been coming in and out all day talking about a full eclipse of the sun that was supposed to happen the next Saturday. The timing was great. I didn't work on Saturday.

"Yes," Dave said. "The *News Minor* had a feature article on it."

I had seen the headline in the newspaper rack outside the bookstore, but I hadn't read the details. I had seen lunar eclipses in Ohio. The moving shadow of the Earth as it passed between the sun and the moon was impressive, but a full solar eclipse I had never seen. Now one would appear right over us and I had a car to take me to the best place to view it.

"Are you interested in seeing it?" I asked.

"You bet," Dave said. "Julie and I were just talking about it." Dave and his wife Julie lived off campus in the university trailer court.

When I got back to my apartment, I called Bobbi to ask her to join me. Ten minutes later, I heard her boots coming down my basement steps.

"My mom told me about it," she said. "It's all her euchre club's been talking about. She and her friends are going to walk out to the field at Creamer's Dairy and watch it from there."

"It's a big topic at the university, too," I said.

"Do you have goggles?" Bobbi asked.

"Goggles?"

"Yes, can you get some welder's goggles? They're the best for looking at the sun. That's what Mom said."

I told Bobbi I would check with Dave Gilbert who was coming with us. He had friends in the engineering department.

Dave came into the bookstore the next day. He already knew about the goggles and had arranged to borrow four sets. "Anything else you'd like us to bring?" he asked.

"Sure. Can Julie make some sandwiches, maybe bring some grapes? I'll pay for the gas and I can bring Cokes and candy bars. And,

210

oh," I added, "and don't forget a hat, gloves, and mosquito repellent. Just in case."

Dave took a piece of paper out of his shirt pocket and jotted down a few other things as well, like long-sleeved shirts, water, bandanas, dry matches, and, of course, his hunting knife and rifle. Just in case.

I had something special for this spectacular once-in-a-lifetime event: a yellow Wham-o Frisbee I had bought the week before. It was called a Flying Saucer and had the planets imprinted around its circular edge: "Pluto, Uranus, Mercury, Mars, Venus, Earth, Saturn, Jupiter, Neptune, Sun." What better universe-centered toy to play with under a full solar eclipse? Dave laughed when I told him I was bringing it.

"What time do you want to leave?" he asked.

"The newspaper says the eclipse will start around 8:30 in the morning and will become a full total eclipse exactly at 10:00 a.m. The complete blackout will last only a minute or two. According to the paper, it will all be over by 11:20. So we need to leave here early," I said. "I was thinking of driving down to Delta Junction. It's about a hundred miles. Does that sound good?"

"Yes," Dave said. "Delta Junction is perfect. Miles of open tundra."

"Okay. I'll pick you and Julie up at your trailer at 6 o'clock, and then pick Bobbi up. That should get us to a good spot before the action starts."

"All right. Good plan," said Dave. "I'll tell Julie. I can't wait to see it! See you in the morning."

After work, I called Bobbi. Twenty minutes later, she was clunking down my basement steps with her backpack. Seeing an eclipse was her kind of adventure. She wanted to sleep over that night to save time in the morning.

"A good adventure is worth a warm cuddle," she said. I fully agreed. I whipped up a light supper in the kitchen. Then we walked downtown to get the sodas for the trip.

We got to the Gilberts' trailer exactly at 6:00 a.m. and we were on the way. Bobbi rode shotgun in the front. We drove down the Richardson Highway towards Delta Junction. Everyone settled in to enjoy the ride.

Being mid-July in Alaska, there was still about twenty hours of daylight. The sky this morning was bright and cloudless, the temperature in the mid-60s, a perfect day to buzz down the highway. White Tooth, freshly washed and fueled-up, felt like an uncaged beast under me, chewing up the road, hungry for action as we drove, windows down, over the winding miles of concrete.

The Richardson Highway was beautiful. The long road followed the contours of the land. The miles of open tundra on either side was an endless garden of purple and yellow and white. Julie wanted to take a picture, so we stopped and got out to feel the beauty.

In the distance, on both sides, the horizons were jagged lines of mountains. In two months, their peaks would be deep in snow, but for now, in July, their slopes were gray shale and granite with only a few white patches where the snow never melted, where cold shadows ruled. Mile after mile of tundra, summer colors blending into the rising foothills, the air clear and fresh, we all gazed open-eyed happily out the open windows as we drove. It was like sitting in the cabin of a tiny rocket traveling through a dream.

Of course, we have all seen this kind of scenery before, but it is scenery that changes from minute to minute. The sun moves, the shadows shift, the colors deepen. The flowers bow and whisper in the wind. If there is no wind, they raise their little heads in still and silent smiles with glowing petals that follow the sun as it inches across the sky. The flowers move or they do not move. The flowers glow or they do not glow. They may be yellow in the morning and deep gold in the afternoon. The land is alive. It changes. It is never the same.

"It's almost 8:00 o'clock," I say. "I see a good place to park."

Ahead, on the left is a flat gravel area where we can pull off. We get out, slip on our backpacks, and head across the road and down a rolling slope onto the open tundra. It is the perfect place to wait and watch. The world around us is silent and alive.

The sun is high above. As I look west out over the unbroken miles of knee-high grass, off in the distance, I see movement. I take my binoculars out of my backpack. I see a cow moose and her calf, their tall bodies grazing slowly in the morning light.

"Look," I whisper. I hand the binoculars to Bobbi.

She grins. "They're beautiful."

Dave has his own binoculars focused on the moose and then hands them to Julie. After she watches them for a minute, she scans the land to see if there are bears or other animals around.

"Eagles!" I point up. Circling above us are two bald eagles on the hunt. Their widespread wings soar over us in the updrafts of air rising from the earth below. I know they see us but know we are no threat.

I look at my watch. It is almost 8:30. The eclipse will start any minute.

"Frisbee time," I announce and pull my new toy out of my pack. Bobbi, Julie, Dave, and I form a loose circle and stand about ten yards apart and sail the little yellow disk through the air from one to another. I don't know why it's so much fun to play Frisbee under the beginning of a full eclipse, but it is. We all will remember it as a part of this cosmic experience.

Dave gets the welders goggles out of his backpack and hands them out. They are heavy and black with dark opaque lenses. We put them on and look at each other. We look like aliens.

212

"It's starting," Dave says. We look up at the sun. A tiny slice of it is missing. The moon is slowly beginning to move in front of the sun.

It was a slow process. The newspaper said absolute total eclipse wouldn't take place until 10 o'clock. That was almost an hour and a half away. Julie went to the car and came back with a sack of egg salad sandwiches and four cans of Coke, and we sat cross legged on the tundra to eat breakfast. The eagles circled high above us.

A subtle change of light became apparent around 9:15. The land around us lost its glow. The distant mountains began to fade. Then something like evening started to happen.

At 9:30, there was unusual movement from the moose. The mother and baby were no longer feeding. The cow moved erratically, as if she were confused. By this time, the moon was covering eighty percent of the sun. It was weird and exciting to watch a sunset taking place directly above us. It was a sunset without deep coloration.

The cow moose and her calf thought it was the coming of night. She reared up on her hind legs, her head jerking from side to side. Then she dropped to all fours, ran in several tight little circles, and abruptly stopped. Her calf just stood there. Then both mother and child stood still and started to bed down, ready to go to sleep. The two eagles also responded. They glided to the earth and disappeared into the tundra.

At 10 o'clock exactly, the moon passed fully in front of the sun. For the first time since the middle of May, the sky was black. I put my arms around Bobbi and held her. One minute and seventeen seconds later, a sliver of sun reappeared and slowly light returned. The eagles rose out of the grass flapping back into the sky. As the daylight increased, mother and baby moose stood, looked around, then trotted off and disappeared behind a hump in the tundra. By 11 o'clock, the sun was mostly exposed and normal daylight had returned.

We repacked whatever we had dropped, I put my Frisbee away, and we drove back to Fairbanks sharing our thoughts and feelings of this magical day.

44: Enter Ed Skellings

September 10, 1963

Two weeks before the start of the 1963 fall semester, Edmund Skellings appeared. Young Dr. Ed Skellings and his wife Louise got everyone's attention when they drove into the center of campus in their red, two-door, sporty, top-down convertible. Those of us who had lived through a couple Fairbanks sub-zero winters smiled. This was brutal territory. Maybe in Anchorage, which was warmed by the Japanese current coming in from the Pacific, but the University of Alaska in Fairbanks was smack-dab in the middle of the frigid Interior.

I flashed back to that time I was out just five miles down the road from here trying to catch that damn bus to Clear Air Force Station when the wind chill was -80. Here was this young professor and his wife in a sporty convertible. But I had to admit, he knew how to make an entrance. That was a classy looking car. I wondered what subjects he would be teaching. I assumed that was why he was here.

The next day, Skellings came into the university bookstore while I was working. As he looked around, he stopped at the bookshelves with the literature collection. I watched him checking out the titles. Then he came over to the cash register where I was standing.

"Who ordered the poetry books?" he asked. "It's a nice collection. A lot of contemporary writers. Not what I expected to find up here."

"I did," I said. "The bookstore manager asked me to upgrade the literature section since she knew I wrote poems." I had ordered collections of Robert Frost, Yeats, Dylan Thomas, William Carlos Williams, T. S. Eliot, and others. Skellings said he knew Robert Frost personally, had had his picture taken with him at a writers' conference in Vermont. He said that he was a published poet and was the first to earn a doctorate in creative writing from the University of Iowa's Writers' Workshop.

"What brought you up here?" I asked. I was curious.

"Alaska seemed like a good place to make a difference," he said. "It's a young state, a young school, and not a lot of poetry here. Yet." That's when I found out Ed Skellings had been hired as an associate professor in the English department.

After he left the bookstore, I looked at the fall course schedule on the bulletin board. Skellings was listed to teach Form and Technique of Modern Poetry, an upper level course. Skellings was a well-published poet. That was important to me. I was struggling with writing my own collection. I signed up for his class the next day.

When I had returned to the university to finish my degree, I had asked Dr. Magee, the chairman of the English Department, if I could write a creative thesis, a collection of poetry. The fact that I wanted to do something different, something other than jargon-laden traditional academic scholarship was a new idea. It also would allow Magee to use me as a statistic for the school's infant graduate program. He assigned Dr. Art Wills to be my advisor.

In November, I joined the staff of the university's student newspaper, *The Polar Star*, and started a poetry column called "Lifestreams." The first poem published in "Lifestreams" was my sonnet, "Adam and the Hummingbird." It was a metaphor for my new beginning.

ADAM AND THE HUMMINGBIRD

As Adam caught his breath from the wind
and reached his stretching eyes to the skies
like beacons in a dazzled night,
one star fell across his glare.
A hummingbird bolted from the air,
its path a flame arcing peak to peak,
and though there was a whirr of quick
wings hushed among the mists,
there was more shock within the blaze
that burned in silence afterward.

Adam followed with his brow
and watched the bird streak into a rose.
Glowing brightly with a sudden pulse,
they shook, the rose and he, with life.

Skellings read the poem when I turned it in for a class worksheet. "Good poem," he said. Rare words of praise from this guy. In class, he made it clear that when students submitted work, it wasn't automatic that it would appear on the worksheet. If a poem did make the worksheet, he let the students do the commenting. He himself rarely gave critical input. If no one raised a hand to comment, he would simply say, "Next poem!" And we moved on. It created a sense of competition if a poem appeared and someone had something good to say about it. Skellings' approach created a desire to turn in good work. It got results.

"Joel, read your poem," he said. It was standard procedure. He liked to have the students hear a poem in the writer's voice.

When I was asked to read my poem about Adam from the worksheet, no one had anything to say about it. Skellings waited. The class was silent.

"What kind of poem is this?" he asked. A roomful of silence. "How many lines is it?" he asked. The students looked back at the worksheet.

"Fourteen," said a girl in the back row.

"If it's fourteen lines, is it a sonnet?" someone else asked.

"What about the rhyme?" Skellings asked.

"Well, it doesn't have any rhyme."

"Then what kind of poem is it?"

One of the students, Ken Warfel, said, "An unrhymed sonnet, a sonnet in blank verse."

"Yes," said Skellings. "There is occasional rhyme. It doesn't overpower and it's deliberate. The strongest part of this poem is the visual imagery in the final four lines, the quatrain. Joel, very good."

"Next poem."

Skellings came to the following class without the usual worksheets. Instead he went to the blackboard and gave a chalk talk that changed my approach to writing and my life. It was about the power of language and the complexity of seemingly simple ideas.

He printed the word KNOW across the board in large capital letters.

"KNOW," Skellings said, "means to be aware of the world. We Know on a broad canvas. We listen, we see, we smell, we taste, we feel. The five senses flow around and through us as we read a poem or a story, see a painting or a figure frozen in marble or bronze, or when we hear a symphony or the whirr of an engine, the whisper of the wind through trees. These things touch us. We reach out, bring them in, become aware."

Skellings turned to the word KNOW on the board and with his chalk drew an arrow after it followed by the word NOW. "The power of KNOW is its impact on the NOW, the present," he said. "What we know affects our senses where we stand. What and who we are in the NOW depends on what we KNOW. The NOW is the present. It is in the NOW, for everyone, that both good and evil exist."

He drew another arrow after the word NOW and wrote NO.

"It is the NO in life that turns our journey inward," he said. "Sometimes we're disappointed, but NO is not always bad. Sometimes it means look deeper, look again. Never accept without question."

Another arrow followed by OW. "OW exposes the pain of life. It is the pain, the disappointment of failed expectations, the poet tries to express in words." He drew a fourth arrow pointing to an O. "But it is this awareness that leads us into unexpected understanding. The ordinary is no longer ordinary. When words combine, they lead to surprising ends. The darkness sometimes leads to surprising joy. That is the genius, the purpose, of the art."

Skellings turned to face the class. I saw the excitement and the passion in his eyes that we understand the power of a poem.

The room of students was silent. I was transfixed. There on the chalkboard in front of me was the secret of poetry: KNOW→NOW →NO→OW→O. There on the board was the pattern of my life.

My daily routine was predictable: Tuesday evening creative writing with Skellings and a Monday-Wednesday afternoon literature course on the Epic. I had my daily work schedule in the bookstore, then back home to make supper and write, often until four in the morning.

My life revolved around my writing, and I was struggling with it. I felt something was off, but I didn't know what. Dr. Wills, my thesis advisor, was not a poet. The person I needed feedback from was Ed Skellings.

We set a time to meet in the Student Union cafeteria when lunchtime was over. A few students remained doing homework. I thought my poems were technically good because I had been working hard on poetic forms, and I looked forward to Skellings' comments. Some of my poems had gone through twenty drafts. What I lay in front of him was a year-and-a-half's collection of work.

Ed pulled my stack of poems over in front of him and started to read. Twenty poems, twenty pages, it wasn't enough for a final collection. I knew that. I planned to double what he was looking at for my final submission. Writing a creative thesis wasn't supposed to be easy.

Skellings read and turned the pages. I looked for a reaction, a sparkle, a smile. But I felt a growing distance, an existential silent sigh. He stopped reading and looked over at me sitting across the table.

"Joel," he said, "there's no connecting theme tying these poems together. Some poems show promise, but some don't." I was disappointed but not surprised. I remembered the lecture on KNOW.

Ed had given me a copy of his book, *Duels and Duets and The Marriage Fire*. It had poems using rhymed couplets and strong rhythms, but it also displayed a conscious abandonment of form. Skellings' poems, like Robert Frost's, spoke with a strong personal voice. Did mine have a personal voice? Were they unique or were they trite? Did I have a unique style? If someone read one of my poems in a magazine, would they know it was by me by its sound and imagery or only because my name was printed under the title?

"Joel?" Skellings was waiting for me to respond. I looked at him, picked up the sheets of paper, tapped them on the table into a neat stack, and tore the entire collection in half. This was his professional feedback and I trusted him as an artist. I knew that he was right. He verified my doubt. I could do better. I would do better.

"Yes," I said. "Thank you. Tomorrow I'll start over."

I left the torn-up collection on the table.

When I got outside, I drove into Fairbanks, had a beer at Tommy's, and headed home to plan the resurrection of my thesis.

I still liked fixed poetic forms. They were an artistic challenge. They each had boundaries. I wanted to keep using them, but I understood how the individual poems I had shown Ed had not blended. They had rhyme but no reason. Then I remembered something he had said in class. One day he was talking about his own struggles and how Robert Frost had once told him, "Don't write poems, write books."

"That's how my *Duels and Duets* came to be," he said.

That evening as I sat at the kitchen table, I thought of my melodrama *Purity in Distress* and the dramatic interaction of the characters: the evil villain Clutchclaw Grimsbuck; the beautiful victim Mary Hearthrob: the hero Rex Handsome: and Granny, the protecting elder. The plot held together, at least on stage. Then my fork clinked against the edge of my plate of spaghetti and I had a breakthrough: I would write a series of interrelated poems using different fixed poetic forms which could create different dramatic voices, different characters.

In my Epic course, we had been reading Norse mythology with characters with foreign sounding names. I started drafting ideas for a series of interrelated poems which eventually I titled "Thea's Fall." The sequence had four characters: Thor, the villain; Thea, the innocent young sister; Alben, Thea's weak and helpless brother; and Valgard, the old distracted father. The storyline was Thor's incestuous rape of his sister, and Alben and Valgard's failure to protect her.

I started work on the sequence that night and throughout each day thereafter. I composed lines and refined ideas, even when I was working in the bookstore or shopping for food. When I went to sleep at night and when I got up in the morning, I was angry at Thor, in love with Thea, frustrated with Alben's impotent morality and Valgard's moral blindness. Draft after draft, waste basket after waste basket filled with crumpled paper. I bounced between tight forms and formless verse. I was obsessed with the project. I felt I was learning, that I was on the right track. It was hard work, but I was learning.

One poem I brought to Skellings' workshop was "The Cow in Hell," the crazy angry piece I had written when I worked at the experimental farm. The poem didn't fit any traditional fixed form, but I liked it. Its raw emotion, violence, and pain were clear. It stabbed at the heart. The one-syllable words fell like hammers. Skellings liked it. Later that semester, I entered it in a state-wide poetry contest and won first prize of $50 and got to read it to an audience. They applauded. I had finally tapped into the spirit of the art.

Ed Skellings said he wanted to introduce poetry to Alaskans. He began to organize public readings and contests. At the beginning of his second year, he got a grant from the university to fly well-known poets up from the Lower 48. One such poet was Karl Shapiro., who co-taught one session of Skellings' writing workshop. He liked one of my new poems "My House is Shiny Scattered Stones." Skellings smiled and gave me a thumbs up.

A week later, Skellings organized a public poetry reading featuring himself and his work. The auditorium was packed. He let me bring my reel-to-reel tape recorder and record his program. It was the first formal poetry reading I and most of the audience had ever heard. While such events were common back in Iowa City, San Francisco, or New York, they were new up here. Like the little vinyl record sandwiched into the covers of his first book, Ed Skellings was helping the voice of poetry escape from the silence of the page.

Earlier that month, we had all heard the tragic news that Ed Buckingham, a new instructor hired to teach French, had put the muzzle of his revolver into his mouth and had blown the back of his head off. The *Fairbanks Daily News Miner* reported that he had, the year before, been discharged from the army after fighting in Viet Nam. Buckingham had told Ed that he couldn't sleep and kept hearing explosions in his head. He had "shell shock." It just got to be too much. Suicide was his only way out. Skellings had served in the military as a paratrooper and Buckingham's death hit him hard. He wrote the poem, "To a Friend Who Died of his Own Hand" and read it at his performance. Everyone in the room was moved. The words of the poem were powerful and important at that time and place. They motivated me to reimagine the purpose of my own work.

Poetry for me had always been a private art form. I had written poems in grade school in the privacy of my bedroom. Collections in books were a good way to share the ideas and the music of the words, the ideas of the poet, but what was missing was the voice-sound of the poet by the poet himself. Hearing Skellings read his impassioned words to an audience, with his pauses, the rising and falling of his voice to control and direct our thoughts into his thoughts, made the poetry real in a new way.

I continued to write, but with a better integration of sound and sense. Still, I liked to play with forms, but they were now more a means to an end than an end in themselves. Free verse started to flow. It was freedom. The shape and breadth of my poems changed.

Ed Skellings liked what I was writing. When my poem "The Cow in Hell" won first place, my thesis collection was in its final stages.

"Congratulations, Joel," Skellings said. "How did you feel about reading your poem in public?"

"I was nervous," I said, "probably because I didn't know a lot of the people in the audience."

"A lot of them were poets who came in from around the state," Skellings said. "Most of them had submitted poems to the contest. While they didn't win, they liked your poem. I've already had people ask me about the contest for next year. But what I wanted to talk to you about was your future plans. After you get your degree in May, what are you going to do?"

The question caught me off-guard. I had been so focused on writing that I hadn't thought beyond that. What would I do?

I had applied to teach English, after I finished my graduate degree, at Sheldon Jackson Junior College in Sitka, Alaska. I thought that having a degree in American Lit with a creative thesis would make me a good choice to fill their vacancy. But I was soundly rejected. I was told that my non-Presbyterian background showed up glaringly clear in my application. The junior college's letter of rejection almost shouted that Sheldon Jackson was a Presbyterian college and they only hired Presbyterian faculty, and that my response description of a religious ritual surrounding the holy trinity was wrong.

I liked the idea of a future teaching in a college in Alaska. It was one way not to have to leave the state. Alaska Pacific University and Alaska Methodist University, both in Anchorage, were the only other in-state choices, but neither had openings in my area.

I had no interest in being a homesteader. I didn't want a job where I would have to pay dues to a union. I could enlist in the Army, but the Viet Nam War was still going on. The newspapers and radio broadcasts focused on kill rates and dead GIs. Ed Buckingham was a good example of why not to enlist.

"I'm not sure what I'll do," I said. "I've been so focused on my writing that I haven't thought about it. Nobody has ever asked me about my future plans. Not even my family."

"Would you be interested in going to the University of Iowa's Writers Workshop to work on a Master of Fine Arts degree in creative writing, in poetry?"

More graduate work was something I hadn't considered. I knew a little about the Iowa program since Ed talked about his own experiences, and I knew it was a fantastic pathway into meeting and learning from published writers. But how could I afford it with no immediate income to pay for tuition, books, rent, and food? Sure, I had done well at surviving in Alaska, but it had been a break-even four years. And a lot of luck.

"It sounds interesting," I said. "How would I apply to get in? And if I were accepted, I'd have to figure out how to pay for it."

"I can write you a letter of recommendation," Skellings said. "The way the workshop is set up, there are only a hundred writers from across the country accepted, two from each state. With my recommendation, Paul Engle, the workshop's founder and director, will give you serious consideration. And in terms of paying for it, while I can't get you an assistantship, I have a friend, Jerry Stevenson, who owns the Paper Place bookstore in downtown Iowa City. He modeled it after Lawrence Ferlinghetti's City Lights Book Store in San Francisco. Jerry would be happy to hire you as a Writers Workshop student. The choices of fiction and poetry books you ordered for the bookstore here is proof you'd do a good job as a buyer for him. I would let him know."

"Okay," I said. "It sounds promising. Let's go for it."

A week later in the mail I got an application from the University of Iowa's Writer's Workshop asking for sample poems. I mailed some the next day. Two weeks later, I received a letter of acceptance. Classes would begin in late August 1964. My assigned advisor was Dr. Donald Justice. I showed the letter to Ed. He grinned and shook my hand. Ed Skellings had transformed my future.

It was KNOW→NOW→NO→OW→O in action.

45: My Pet Ghost

December 28, 1963

The 28th of December 1963 was another sub-zero night. The concrete walls in my basement apartment were cold even though the furnace in the middle of the room pumped out heat in a constant low rumble.

I had spent a solid four hours working on my collection. I was so tired I was numb. I went over to the slop sink behind the furnace to wash up, slumped my way into the bedroom, undressed, and fell into bed. I pulled my sheet and blankets over my body, and, propped up on my right elbow, reached over to switch off my bedside lamp. The clock read 3:30 a.m.

A second after I clicked off the light, the warm air in the bedroom felt like it was being sucked out and replaced by a sudden chill. I stayed motionless, still propped up on my elbow, my arm unmoving, frozen in motion by the lamp. I sensed something extraordinary was happening.

Something invisible had entered my bedroom through the open door and hopped from the floor up onto the edge of my mattress. I felt a weightless gentle pressure. It was a sensation I will never forget. I wasn't afraid, just suddenly alert. What I felt was wonder.

I remained still. The weightless pressure hesitated, then slowly slid over the top of my bent legs, circled three times like a dog when it settles, and snuggled in silence into the back of my knees. It didn't move.

I held my breath waiting for something to happen. The pressure against my bent knees was familiar, but still and unmoving. Without thinking I whispered, "Pepper?" Pepper was my dog back in Toledo.

No response.

I didn't want to break the mystery of the moment, but I was still propped up on my elbow, my hand still outstretched by the turned-off bed lamp. I moved my hand ever so slightly to see if the strange pressure behind my knees would remain, but instantly as I moved, it uncurled and weightlessly slid back over my knees and off the edge of the mattress into the blackness of the room.

Seconds later the temperature in the bedroom returned to normal. I waited a few more moments but nothing more happened. I lay back with a smile, closed my eyes, and went into a deep sleep.

When I awoke, my alarm clock read 11 o'clock. I lay quietly for several minutes thinking and wondering about the mysterious visit. Why had I thought about our family dog back in Ohio? I felt an edginess as I lay there, and got up, dressed, and went upstairs to the kitchen to make breakfast.

I heard Gene leave for a courthouse hearing. We only had one telephone in the house, the one in his office. I went in and dialed our number in Toledo. It rang six times before Mom answered.

"Hi, Mom."

"Joel?"

My call was unexpected. We rarely talked on the phone because of the cost.

"Yes. How is everything?" I asked.

"Oh, we're fine," she said.

There wasn't the usual joy in her voice.

"Listen," I said. "I'm calling because I had a weird thing happen to me when I got into bed last night." I paused. "Did anything happen to Pepper?"

I heard her deep intake of breath.

"Pepper was hit and killed by a car around 7:30 this morning," she said with a tremble.

I told her what had happened, about the soft, silent, moving pressure over my legs, when it had happened. She listened in silence.

There was a four-hour time difference between Ohio and Alaska. Pepper had died the moment I'd had the unexplainable sensation. His loving spirit had transcended space and time to find me to say goodbye one last time as I lay in the basement of a frozen house in Fairbanks, Alaska, 4,000 miles away. It was a moment in time I would never forget.

223

46: Good Friday Earthquake

Mach 27, 1964

Cecelia Ulroan was an education major from a small Yup'ik Eskimo village near Hooper Bay on the Bering Sea. She had just started to work in the university bookstore. When I told her that I was writing poems, she agreed to translate a few of them into her native language. She liked that I wanted to record her on tape and then give her a copy to take back home.

On Good Friday, I invited her over to my house to do a recording session. Cecilia came over around 5 o'clock. She had the poems I had given her and her written translations in a large envelope.

"Hi, Cecelia" I said. "Come on in." I led her to the kitchen where I was getting ready to make us supper. My tape recorder was set up next to the kitchen table to record our session.

At 5:36 p.m., while we were setting up to record, a violent shudder shook the house and the hot iron skillet with the caribou chops I was frying for our supper slid off the stove and crashed to the floor. We looked at each other. Cecilia's eyes got big and we ran outside. People were running out of their houses in panic, yelling and shouting.

It was an earthquake and, though it lasted only a few minutes, it seemed to go on forever. Cars parked along the curb were rolling forward and back. Across the street, windows in the three-story city building were cracked from corner to corner. The ground rolled. The radio tower a block away swayed side to side. Store signs clattered against glass windows. Powerful tremors rocked the world. The whole universe seemed to throb. Then everything settled down as quickly as it started. The commotion in the streets stopped.

Cecelia and I agreed that this was not the time to record my poems. We went back inside to check for damage. Our supper was ruined, but luckily my tape recorder hadn't crashed to the floor. I drove her back to her dorm on campus.

I didn't fully know what happened until the next day when I saw the *Fairbanks Daily News Miner* headlines. An earthquake had devastated the Seward and Anchorage areas. It was powerful enough to shake up Fairbanks, hundreds of miles north. According to the article, the quake lasted four minutes and thirty-eight seconds and was the most powerful recorded earthquake in U.S. history. It had a magnitude of 9.2 on the Richter Scale. It came to be known as the Good Friday Earthquake.

The newspaper had pictures. Anchorage looked like a war zone. Buildings were caved in, streets sunk out of sight leaving cars in ten-foot deep sink holes. Houses crumbled to the earth, huge open gaps under them. Ground swells crushed them, thrust them off their foundations. Water and sewer mains, electrical systems were torn up. The new J. C. Penney department store's front end had collapsed, killing three people. The Hofbrauhaus, my favorite bar where I played the piano, was destroyed. Jinksy, the pretty blonde bartender I had joked with many times, had disappeared.

The town of Seward south of Anchorage was hit worse. It was almost completely leveled. Valdez, across the bay, was devastated as well.

Whole native fishing villages were wiped off the face of the earth along with their populations. Hundreds of fishing boats were gone, hundreds of people were missing or dead, harbors and breakwaters were gone. The paper didn't know how many had been killed. It was too soon to tell.

Many students at the university had families in Anchorage, Seward, and Valdez, as well as in smaller towns and villages nearby. They were all wandering around campus in a state of shock, dazed, empty, blank. One boy read in the paper that his father was swallowed up in a crevasse near Valdez. No one could comfort him. No one could stop his crying,

A bunch of us at the university wanted to drive down to Anchorage to volunteer to help. But unless you had immediate family in the area, Civil Defense warned everyone to stay away because of falling buildings. Anchorage, Seward, and Valdez were under martial law to hold down looting. "Besides," they said, "you can't drive there from Fairbanks anyway. All the roads are impassable." Many roads had been torn apart, buried under buckled concrete and landslides. Some students who could fly small planes wanted to get to Anchorage that way, but airport runways were in ruins, too. The best most of us could do was hope for a safe recovery. The pain and anguish around campus and Fairbanks was palpable.

The next week, the catastrophe behind us, I picked Cecelia up from her dorm. I made spaghetti and meatballs and then set up my tape recorder. I was interested in the sound of her native language. Dr. Michael Krause, the university's linguistic professor, had gotten a grant to preserve Alaska's native languages and he triggered my interest.

Cecelia opened her envelope and got out her notes.

225

"I read your whole collection," she said. "I liked 'The Dancer' and 'Hiroshima.'"

"Great,' I said. "Those are two of my favorites, too. How about you read each one in English and then say them again in Yup'ik?"

"Okay. I'll do 'The Dancer' first. Is that all right?" I said yes.

She read my poems perfectly with feeling. Then she switched to Yup'ik, her throat and tongue making sounds I couldn't reproduce. I tried, but I was terrible. She laughed at my attempt.

When Cecelia finished reading and translating "Hiroshima," she asked, "Would you like to hear a legend from my village?"

"Of course! Is it an Eskimo legend?"

"Yes. It's a village story my father told me."

"What is it called?"

"The Fiery Hand."

"I'd love to hear it," I said. I turned on the tape recorder and she began.

> "One day while the men were away hunting, one of the women took all the young children to the Oziyuk, the village celebration house, to keep them busy. The kids were very noisy in the Oziyuk and two little quiet boys, who were feeling ignored, went outside to play. When they were outside, they saw a red flaring thing out over the Bering Sea. They ran back into the Oziyuk and told the other children, but the noisy kids ignored them. The two little boys went back outside; they were afraid but curious.
>
> The fiery thing over the water looked like a big burning hand, and it was getting closer. The little boys ran back into the Oziyuk and told the other children again that something was coming, but the other kids were too busy having fun. When they saw that the fiery thing was real close, one of the little boys hid in a barrel and the other rolled himself in a seal skin.
>
> "The big fiery red hand came ashore and went through the tunnel into the middle of the Oziyuk and ate up all the noisy children except for the two little ones who had hidden themselves.
>
> "When the women came back, the two little boys told them what had happened, and the women told the men when they returned.
>
> "The men planned how to catch the fiery hand. They made a big ulu, a big round-bladed knife, and attached it above a window in the Oziyuk so it would fall when they wanted it to fall.

"They got little kids from another village and had them make lots of noise in the Oziyuk. When the fiery hand came back to eat the children, they let the ulu fall and killed it."

Cecelia leaned toward me with a smile. "That's a favorite story in my village," she said.

I opened a couple Cokes and rewound the tape recorder so we could listen to Cecilia 's translations and her story. She beamed with pleasure. She had never heard her own voice.

As I listened to the folktale, I knew it was teaching the village children an important lesson about survival. Loud noise attracts predators, animal or human or supernatural, and sometimes it's important to stay quiet. In a land teaming with hungry animals, it could be a matter of life or death.

Cecelia leaned toward me. "Would you like to hear a song about a snowball?"

I turned the recorder on again and her soft voice sang a little song in Yup'ik with a rhythmic melody that was simple and sweet. "It's about a man who tries to make a snowball," she said, "but he can't make it stick together, and then he gives it one more tight squeeze and it holds."

I spooned out some cherry Jell-O I had made for our dessert and then drove her back to her dorm, my mind immersed in the folklore of fiery hands and snowballs.

47: Goodbye Bobbi

One late night while working at my typewriter, I heard a click at the top of the stairs. The door to the outside opened and I felt a sudden downdraft of cold air. I recognized the clunk of Bobbi's boots coming down the steps.

"Joel, are you here? Are you alone?"

This was the first time in weeks I had seen Bobbi. We had drifted apart. She had enrolled in a few classes at the university, a serious move that changed her. I knew she had been dating her high school math teacher and also a faculty member at the university. We were friends but no longer lovers.

I had had dates, too. With Magdel, my former student and ac-tor in my play, and a few others. Hey, if a cute coed wanted a beer at Tommy's Elbow Room or to split a bottle of Jack Daniels at my place, who was I to say no? Even so, when I saw Bobbi standing there, I felt a rush of happiness.

"Bobbi! Sweetheart! Come in!" I got up from my desk. She took a few steps towards me as she unzipped her parka. We put our arms around each other and held each other tightly. It was wonderful hav-ing her in my arms again. All the memories of our ALCAN and coast-to-coast adventures came flooding back.

For a long minute, we were a part of each other's silence. I could feel her heart beating under her flannel shirt as she pressed her cheek against mine. I thought I felt a tear. I closed my eyes. Then I felt her grasp release.

We went over to the cushioned easy chair in the corner of the room and she fell back into it, her eyes on mine. I sat on the floor by her knees and lay an arm across her lap. "It's so good to see you," I said. She looked at me and her lips curled into a smile. But it wasn't a smile of happiness.

"I came to say goodbye," she said. It caught me off guard. I looked into Bobbi's brown eyes. There was no joy in them.

"What do you mean 'goodbye?' Are you dropping out of school? What are you going to do? Look for a job?"

"'I'm going to hitchhike down to Seattle." I sat back in surprise. "Are you going alone?"

"Yes."

"Does your mother know? What did she say about your leaving?"

"She didn't say anything."

"When are you leaving?" I asked.

"In the morning. I wanted to come by and let you know," she said.

"What are you going to do when you get there?"

"I don't know."

Bobbi shifted in the chair and stood. She zipped up her parka, gave me a long, sad kiss on the lips, and walked slowly up the steps. I heard the click of the handle, felt the sudden coldness of the air, and the door closed behind her.

48: Denali Camp Out: Moose on the Loose

June 22, 1964

As I leaned over the side of the billiard table outside the bookstore to take a shot, I felt a finger tug on my back pocket. I turned around to look into Magdel's smiling eyes.

"I got the job," she said. "I start on Monday."

I had seen her at Tommy's two nights before. She told me she had applied for a housekeeping job at the visitor's lodge at McKinley National Park. I had seen the lodge several times from trains traveling between Fairbanks and Anchorage. The lodge was a long, two-story, log building. The foothills of the mountains sloped steeply downward to the edge the property. It was an impressive peaceful place. Tourists were discovering it.

"That's fantastic. What a great place to work," I said. "I'm on lunch break now, but how about getting together for supper? And we can crack open a bottle of Dewars."

"Sure," she said. "I like scotch even though I'm from Germany." She laughed.

"Well, I have beer too. You can choose. I get off work at 5 o'clock. Can you meet me upstairs in the lobby? We can drive into town." Magdel touched me on the arm.

"Okay," she said. "I'll be there."

The next weekend I took the train to McKinley Park. After I got off, I lugged my duffle bag a couple hundred yards up the mountain's slope and pitched my pup tent above and behind the lodge. From my campsite, I could look over the rooftop of the building and see the trains stop at the station.

When my tent was tied down and secure, I hiked to nearby Horseshoe Lake and saw beavers building a dam, a cow moose eating along the shoreline, and parka squirrels getting ready for their spring mating, building their nests with dried grass they pulled up with their teeth.

Magdel said she worked until 8 o'clock. At 8:15, she came out a back entrance. I had told her where I would be. When she looked up and saw me, she started up the slope. She was young and tall and strong and beautiful as she climbed up the slope towards me. I remembered that first day at the university teaching my first class, how she had come up to introduce herself. So much had happened between then and now.

We hugged and went over to the pup tent and got busy building a little campfire out of the view of the lodge. I planned to cook up some corned beef hash for supper. I had an army field cooking pan. Magdel had brought her own backpack with half a loaf of bread, a bottle of water, and two pieces of cherry pie. Our supper on the mountain was delicious. She had also brought her sleeping bag and a roll of paper towels. Always thinking.

When it got chilly, we went into the tent. We both had mummy bags that could zip together. When we were sure the lodge below us was closed for the night, we slid into our warm cocoon and fell asleep in each other's arms.

"WHAT THE HELL?" I yelled and sat up. Something was crashing into our tent, crushing it around us. We heard the sudden loud ripping of canvas, then a heavy thumping. I could feel a quick tremble on the ground.

Magdel stiffened at the noise and I unzipped us as fast as I could and jumped out of our broken tent into the frigid air. Then I saw the moose, its huge dark rear loping away. It had run over the top of our tent, its huge deadly hooves trampling the ground inches from our heads.

Magdel peeked out from under a tent flap torn away and laying on the ground.

"It was a moose," I said. "It almost killed us."

"I love Alaska," she said.

The cold early morning sky began to brighten in the east. "Let's find our clothes in this mess and get dressed."

"Or we could get warm again in our mummy bags," she So said.

we did. I loved Alaska, too.

49: Last Days: Coming Full Circle

In late July, my fifteen-year-old brother Jon flew up from Ohio. Our plan was for him to drive down the ALCAN with me when it was time for me to leave Alaska.

When I told the bookstore manager I was leaving, she said that I had built up twenty-three days of vacation. That meant that I could have plenty of time to show my brother what made Alaska so important to me. He had read all the letters I had sent home over my four-year adventure. All 179 of them. When Jonathan stepped off the Alaska Airlines plane at Fairbanks International Airport, he was excited.

Classes at the Writers' Workshop at the University of Iowa began at the end of August. Jon's plane landed on July 26th and our plan was to leave Alaska around August 10th. That would give us almost three weeks to explore.

I showed up at the airport with Betty, a UA student from London, England. She was fluent in four languages. For fun, she thought she would speak only French when she met Jon.

"Hi, Jon," I called when he walked into the terminal. "Welcome to Alaska." Jon waved and came over. Betty was standing close beside me.

"*Bon jour,*" she said. Jon smiled and looked at me. He didn't know what she'd said but she was obviously with me. He gave me a brotherly hug, then Betty came over and gave him a long affectionate hug. "*Bienvenu a' Alaska.*"

This was new to him, being hugged by a stranger, a beautiful stranger at that. And a beautiful stranger who was with his brother. And who spoke a foreign language.

Two years before, Jon had met Bobbi Carter when we had driven to Ohio. Betty was not Bobbi. Betty was older, twenty-five, and spoke a foreign language. And she was tall with shoulder-length, sandy-brown hair, and affectionate. Definitely not the short, dark haired, silent, mysterious, tan-skinned Bobbi.

Jon got his suitcase from the baggage area, and we walked out to my car. As I put it in the VW's front storage area, Betty said, "Jonathan, *je t'adore.*" Jon was confused. The car door was already shut, but, wanting to please, he opened the passenger-side door and then shut it again. Betty laughed. That confused him even more. What was so funny? He didn't know that it was French for "I adore you."

Betty slid into the rear seat and I pointed out key sites as we drove back towards the city. I told him about Chena River on our left and the annual spring Ice Break-Up lottery, when people bet on the exact second the ice in the river would melt and start to shift downstream. Then I pointed out some of the taller buildings in town, like the silver Northward Building where Leda used to live. We crossed the bridge over the Chena and headed up College Road towards the university to drop Betty off. We passed Creamer's Dairy and the trailer park I used to live in, and the roadside kennel full of racing dogs sitting on their little pee-stained houses. We passed the small College, Alaska post office, and finally came to the hill that wound up and around until we arrived at the campus.

"*Au revoir, mon ami*," Betty said when Jon got out of the car to let her out. "*Je te verrai bien tôt*. I'll see you soon." Then she came around to my side of the car, gave me a kiss, and walked towards her dorm.

Jon and I drove back to Fairbanks to my basement apartment to get him settled and have lunch.

Over the next two weeks, Jon and I explored.

In the army surplus store in town, I bought some metal sluicing pans to pan for gold and took Jon to an old abandoned gold-mining dredge twenty miles east of Fairbanks. We spent six hours wading in a rocky stream with our pans looking for gold nuggets and flakes. I didn't think we would find anything valuable, but I was having fun just watching my brother's intensity as he dipped his pan into the water, filled it with bottom silt, and swirled it around and around looking for a find.

This was moose country. I had written about them in my letters, so Jon knew about my moose encounters while hunting with Hal Waugh, the crazy moose that chased our car on the ALCAN, and the one that ran over my tent in McKinley Park. He kept a nervous lookout for wild animals, especially moose. We did find moose tracks but no moose.

Suddenly clouds of Alaskan mosquitoes rose out of the tundra near the gold dredge. Some were as big as quarters. Their maddening whine engulfed us. Sourdoughs jokingly called them the Alaskan state bird. I hadn't brought my mosquito face nets or insect repellent, so with the swirling cloud of mosquitoes attacking and coating us with their hungry bodies, we ran to my car and drove back to town.

The day's *Fairbanks Daily News Miner* had an article about the World Eskimo Olympics to be held the next day in a circus tent in Fairbanks by the Chena River. The paper said it was designed to bring different native groups together to preserve cultural practices and traditional skills. Their games were based on ancient and current hunting and survival techniques used by the Inuit, Inupiat, Yup'ik, and other native cultures. This was only the third year of these Olympic games. They started in 1961. For some reason, no one on campus had talked about this event and it was the first time I had read about it. It would be an Alaskan adventure for both of us.

After breakfast the next morning, we got our tickets. The tent had seating for hundreds of people. Many of the spectators were the families of the native athletes in the competition. I saw a few students and faculty from the university scattered throughout the tent. I thought of Bobbi, how she would have loved this.

Most of the events were tests of physical strength and survival. In front of us we watched young men compete in an event called the knuckle hop. It was a timed race. The athlete to get to the finish line with the fastest time without disqualifying himself would win. The young man we were watching was about twenty. He got face-down in a push-up position with only his bare toes and bare knuckles touching the ground. When the starter yelled "Go," he started to hop forward on his knuckles as fast as he could, pushing himself forward with his toes until he reached the finish line one hundred yards away. If any other part of his body touched the ground, he would be disqualified.

"Why do they have a contest like this?" Jon asked a native sitting next us. He was the father of one of the contestants.

"The knuckle hop mimics the motion of a seal on the ice or land," he said. "When seals come out of the water to mate or rest, our hunters can openly approach them using the knuckle hop because that's the way seals move, slow, heads bobbing up and down, bodies low and flat out. The movement is familiar to them and they don't get alarmed. It's a pretty good hunting technique. It fools them," he said. "My son is up next, but this boy who just finished is good." Jon and I winced every time the young racer pressed his full weight on his knuckles on the dirt track. When he got to the finish line, everyone applauded.

"You want to try that when we get home?" I asked Jon. He looked at me with crinkly eyes.

"I will if you will," he said.

In another area of the tent, an announcer was introducing the Eskimo ear pull. This was something else I had never heard of. We saw two men in their thirties sitting across from each other knee to knee. At first, I thought it was going to be something like arm wrestling, but it wasn't.

"Ladies and gentlemen," said the announcer. "The ear pull is unique to the Eskimo culture above the Arctic Circle. It is a contest of pain. When hunters leave their villages in winter, they know they may suffer frostbite or other injuries. Their ability to withstand the pain of frozen skin or broken bones and get home safely is what the ear pull is about."

The announcer took a six-foot-long piece of twine and tied it into a large loop. With the two contestants facing each other, he looped the twine over the right ear of one contestant and over the left ear of his opponent. On the count of three, the two men leaned back and away from each other to try to pull the cord off each other's ear. It looked painful. By the grimacing on the men's faces it obviously was.

We watched three matches. In the first match, after a few seconds, the loser's ear just bent forward where it joined his head and the cord was pulled forward and off, but the other two contests were more aggressive. In each one, one of the challengers couldn't take the pain and, after a long three minutes, raised a hand to concede. I said to Jon half-jokingly, "The one whose ear doesn't pop off is the winner." That's what it looked like anyway.

Then came a second kind of ear pull contest more brutal than the man-to-man contest. The judge tied a heavy weight, maybe as much as five pounds, to a piece of twine, which he looped over the athlete's ear. The test was to see who could lift the weight from the ground without using his cheek or the side of his head and walk the farthest with the weight hanging from his ear. It was sometimes bloody. It was always brutal. It was painful to watch.

"Jeez!" Jon said in amazement, "Who would put himself through that on purpose?"

"Someone who has to prove to himself he could survive in the arctic winter," I said.

We watched three young native men try the walking ear pull. They each moved forward slowly to keep the swing of the dangling weight to a minimum. When the winner was named, at least half the people in the stands stood and applauded.

Following the ear pull torture contest, Jon and I watched a dozen young natives compete in the single-foot high kick. A leather bag was suspended by a rope about eight feet off the ground. The challenge was to leap, kick the bag with one foot, and land standing. For those who could kick the bag on their first try, it was raised another six inches, and then again until only one winner was left.

Back in the knuckle hop area, a circle of a dozen men in native costume were starting a blanket toss. Jon's eyes got big when he saw how high a teenage boy on the huge stretched-out walrus skin could fly into the air.

"All the events here," I said, "relate to what Eskimo hunters do for survival. When a person shoots up in the air like that, he can see things far away on the flat tundra and ice fields. If he sees a musk ox or a seal, or any food animal, a hunting party goes after it. If it's a polar bear, it doesn't."

The boy on the blanket came down and shot back up again, jerking himself around at the top of his arc. The heads in the audience followed him up and down each time he landed and then shot back up again higher and higher. I told Jon about the girl on the blanket toss I'd seen at the Fur Rendezvous in Anchorage two years before. "A woman can be a spotter, too."

It was fun watching these Olympic events with my brother, especially since some were new to me. I had been in Alaska four years, but these games showed me how complex and different the cultures within this state were. Other than Horace Smoke, my Athabaskan bunkmate on the railroad, and Yup'ik student Cecelia Ulroan, I hadn't talked in depth with many natives. The local natives I had as students in my classes tended to be shy and disappear when classes were over. But they all had their own unique cultural folklore; many practiced their village's or family's special customs and beliefs. There was so much more to learn about and experience in this new state.

The next day, Jon and I drove south towards Fort Greeley just to see scenery. At the top of a hill, we parked White Tooth and got out. Spread in front of us was a hundred square miles of golden tundra. In the distance, a band of dark clouds was slowly sweeping over the land, coming towards us. The billowing dark sky, the spits of lightning, the distant roll of thunder, all were wild beautiful nature. We were in no hurry. We watched it come, and when the rain began to wash over us, we got back in the car.

Driving past Fort Greeley on the way home, I pulled off the road. A herd of bison was grazing and standing around. I told Jon of the annual Fort Greeley buffalo hunt when the State issued two hundred bison hunting permits by lottery. When the date was advertised, hunters from all over the globe put in their bid. The permits were usually sold out within an hour.

We walked the railroad tracks between Fairbanks and the university. I told Jon how I had made this walk a hundred times. The hike down the tracks gave me a chance to tell him about my work on the Alaska Railroad. I pointed out the spikes and the heavy ties, the lengths of steel track we had to lay by crowbar, teamwork, and muscle; the tons of gravel we had to shovel and tamp in by hand to shore up the embankments. We saw plenty of small animal life along the way, chipmunks, ground squirrels, birds, and one fox, but nothing larger. Jon was always looking out for the larger animals, especially moose.

Once we got some bamboo poles and went fishing from the banks of the Chena. We didn't catch anything, but we could watch small power boats traveling downstream to the Tanana with food and homestead supplies, or to fish in deeper water.

When I took Jon to Tommy's Elbow Room to show him my go-to place throughout my four-year stay, we noticed a hand-printed sign taped to the window that advertised a go-cart race open to both men and women in a track near campus. The first-place prize was $50 and a trophy. The race was on Saturday, two days away.

"Can we go to that?" Jon asked. "I've never seen a go-cart race."

"Sure," I said. "I haven't seen one either."

I knew the field where the track was. I had snow-shoed on it many times. Someone had bought it, fenced it in, and built an oval dirt track a quarter of a mile around.

Since there were no bleachers to sit on, we found a good spot at the turning area to stand and watch. The starting gun went off and six go-carts roared forward. I knew the driver in the lead vehicle, an ROTC geology major who loved to buy PayDay candy bars in the bookstore. But the driver who caught my eye, and Jon's eye, was a tall blonde girl wearing a red jacket and white, tight pants. We watched her determination as she roared past and went from last place to third. On the final lap, she moved up and finished second. The look of focused determination on her face was worth the price of admission. The ROTC student, who had come in in first, went over and gave her a hug. A bunch of other racers walked over and they also gave her hugs. Her white pants weren't white anymore. They were as muddy as the track.

That night was our last night in Fairbanks. After we cleaned up, Gene Belland took us out to dinner at the restaurant in the Northward Building. As a parting gift, he gave me one of his prized books from his personal collection, *Old Yukon: Tales – Trails – Trials* by James Wickersham, published in 1938. I looked at the author's name: Wickersham. That was the name on the girl's dormitory where the moose cape had hung out the window. Talk about irony!

On the morning of August 10th, 1964, we loaded my VW and headed south. Jon became quiet as we drove. As we rolled down the highway, I thought about how my last four years had come about because I had seen a little photo in a magazine. The jobs, the life changing adventures, and the people were my Alaskan treasures, memories I would have for the rest of my life.

I looked over at my brother. He was peering out his window, probably searching for a moose. In a few hours, we would pass through Tok Junction and cross into Canada and leave Alaska behind.

Alaska. In the beginning I was lost. And now I'm found. I know I will be back.

About the Author

After earning his Master of Arts Degree from the University of Alaska in 1964, Joel Rudinger enrolled in the University of Iowa's Writers Workshop and, in 1966, finished a Master of Fine Arts degree in creative writing. That fall, he entered the doctoral program in English Literature at Bowling Green State University in Ohio. In 1967, BGSU began construction of a new satellite campus in Huron, Ohio. Joel was one of three people first hired in 1967 to teach fulltime at the new Firelands branch. He finished his Ph.D. in 1971 with a 658 page field-study in American folklore, *Folklore of Erie County, Ohio*, the home county of the new campus. In 1972, he incorporated the nonprofit Rudinger Foundation and initiated a long-standing creative arts scholarship program. In 1972, Joel started the *Firelands Arts Review* literary journal. He published it for ten years, his creative writing students acting as editors. In 1978, he started the Cambric Press which published the *Cambric Poetry Projects* series and other books.

During his years of teaching at the BGSU Firelands College, Joel taught creative writing, the short story, intro to poetry, children's literature, folklore and popular culture, and The Alaskan Experience, thirteen day summer field trips to Alaska to experience native culture and the wild beauty of the state. His illustrated children's book, *Sedna: Goddess of the Sea*, is a retelling of an ancient Eskimo creation myth of how the warm-blooded sea animals came to be. He retired after forty-five years of teaching in 2013 with the rank of Professor Emeritus.

In 1995, Joel became a Third Degree Reiki Master and an Ohio ordained minister in the Church of Radiant Lights. Awards from BGSU-Firelands include a Links to Progress Award (2003) and Distinguished Creative Scholar (2004). He was Huron's Poet Laureate for three years. Joel is also an artist and has illustrated several books, such as Harry Eiss's *The Mythology of Dance* and *Divine Madness*, using the medium of black cut paper. He is an active member of the Huron Rotary club, loves golf, backgammon, and sweet, warm apple pie.

He lives in Huron, Ohio with his wife Susan, near the shores of Lake Erie.